D1304543

A CUP OF COMFORT®
Women of the Bible
DEVOTIONAL

Daily Reflections Inspired by
Scripture's Most Beloved Heroines

Edited by James Stuart Bell
and Susan B. Townsend

Avon, Massachusetts

Copyright © 2009 by F+W Media, Inc.
All rights reserved. This book, or parts thereof, may not be
reproduced in any form without permission from the publisher;
exceptions are made for brief excerpts used in published reviews.

A *Cup of Comfort*® is a registered trademark of F+W Media, Inc.

Published by
Adams Media, a division of F+W Media, Inc.
57 Littlefield Street, Avon, MA 02322. U.S.A.
www.adamsmedia.com

ISBN 10: 1-59869-724-2
ISBN 13: 978-1-59869-724-7

Printed in the United States of America.

J I H G F E D C B A

Library of Congress Cataloging-in-Publication Data
available from the publisher.

This publication is designed to provide accurate and authoritative information
with regard to the subject matter covered. It is sold with the understanding that
the publisher is not engaged in rendering legal, accounting, or other professional
advice. If legal advice or other expert assistance is required, the services of a
competent professional person should be sought.

—From a *Declaration of Principles* jointly adopted by a Committee of the
American Bar Association and a Committee of Publishers and Associations

Many of the designations used by manufacturers and sellers to distinguish their
products are claimed as trademarks. Where those designations appear in this
book and Adams Media was aware of a trademark claim, the designations have
been printed with initial capital letters.

Unless otherwise noted, the Bible used as a source is *Holy Bible: New Living
Translation*, Tyndale House Publishers.

*This book is available at quantity discounts for bulk purchases.
For information, please call 1-800-289-0963.*

Contents

INTRODUCTION

Since childhood, I've been acquainted with women like Eve, Mary Magdalene, and Mary, Mother of Jesus but, like many people, I viewed the rest of the women in the Bible more as a cast of supporting characters than as having their own unique and significant stories to tell. I've discovered that nothing could be further from the truth. Not only is the Bible filled with fascinating women, but their stories also provide overwhelming proof that women played an indispensable role in biblical history.

As with their male counterparts, I hoped that studying the women of the Bible would help me draw closer to God and assist me in understanding the complexities of His relationship with His children. Apart from this, I confess, I wasn't sure how much these women from the distant past could teach me.

After all, they lived thousands of years ago in a patriarchal society vastly different from anything I've ever known. Many of them were treated more like property than human beings. Despite all this, however, I found myself marveling at the universal experience of all women, not just those from my culture and time. I realized that there's a great deal of truth in the saying, "The more things change, the more they remain the same."

Rahab was a prostitute, living in the walled city of Jericho, and yet, she taught me a profoundly moving lesson about family loyalty. Sarah lived in a tent in the middle of the desert, but she knew the heartbreak of infertility as intimately as the woman who has been treated by a clinic filled with fertility specialists. Then there was Deborah, who proved that a woman could be a wife, a mother, and a powerful force for good among her people.

Each day, this book gives you the opportunity to meet someone new or learn more about an old friend. Every devotional is accompanied by a relevant scriptural reference, making it possible for you to read further in your Bible about the woman featured that day. You will find out why a particular woman's story resonates with the writer of the day's devotional. Maybe you will discover a kindred spirit of your own. Most importantly, you will find yourself growing spiritually and strengthening your fellowship with our amazing Creator.

ACKNOWLEDGMENTS

To my sister Cathy, who has a lot in common with these women of God. —JSB

To my precious girl Emily, who has the wisdom of Deborah, the courage of Rahab, and the loving heart of Ruth. And to Jamie, whose friendship is a gift from God. —SBT

As always, our heartfelt thanks go to Paula Munier and Brendan O'Neill, whose wisdom, guidance, and encouragement made this book possible.

JANUARY

Clouds Overhead, Rainbows on the Horizon

When everything was ready, the Lord said to Noah, "Go into the boat with all your family, for among all the people of the earth, I can see that you alone are righteous."

GENESIS 7:1

*A*bout three days before we moved from Nebraska to Indiana, my son Michael asked, "Mom, where are my books?"

"Sorry," I said, putting the finishing touches on the cardboard box I'd just taped shut. "They're already packed."

Michael frowned. "But I finished this one, and there's nothing else to do. Can you just tell me what box they're in?"

"Forget it," I said. "You're not going to open up boxes and rummage through them for a book. I spent all morning packing up the toy room. I still have to pack the kitchen and bathrooms, and I need to clean the house again. Why don't you go play with your sister?"

He shook his head. "She's sitting in an empty box pretending it's a boat."

"That sounds like fun."

"Not to me. Can I watch a video instead?"

"Packed. Along with the video player. That means we can't rent a video either, so don't ask."

"Can I do a puzzle?"

"Packed."

"My action figures?"

"Packed! How about going outside—away from where I'm working—and climbing a tree?"

"I already did that," he complained. "For an hour. Then I read. Now I'm bored."

"Okay, fine," I huffed. I looked around the room for inspiration, but found only rolls of packaging tape and brown boxes, stacked like misshapen towers. Thinking fast, I fished a black marker out of my pocket. "You can draw on the boxes."

He gave a halfhearted shrug. "Okay."

At that point, I think poor Michael finally figured out what I already knew. Moving is an exciting event, no question about it, but it's also a big pain. You have to sell your house which means you have to keep it spotlessly clean, and pack everything, including reams of worthless paper notes and magazines you can't bring yourself to throw away.

You have to run a thousand tiresome errands, like collecting medical, dental, and school records, and getting one more decent haircut. Little by little, the pantry empties—and isn't restocked. Everything you need and everything you want disappears into boxes. Then there are the countless, heartbreaking goodbyes.

Once the preparations are over, the really hard stuff starts. The family has to make a trek across country to a new house (more paperwork and more cleaning), unpack, make new friends, and find another doctor, dentist, school, and hairstylist. Just thinking about it wears me out.

Whenever I think about moving, I can't help but wonder about Noah's wife. Most people know the account of

3

Noah found in Genesis, but not many of us have given her much thought. The story doesn't even tell us her name. However, based on my own experiences with moving, I believe there's a lot more to her than the Bible lets on.

If Noah and his family were the only righteous folks around, they must have lived in a tough neighborhood full of graffiti, gangs, violence, and vicious crime. Still, they worshiped God—an island of warm faith in a sea of cold callousness. Noah's wife was a loyal and steadfast helpmate as they resisted the overwhelming temptation to join the sin and lawlessness.

It couldn't have been easy. She undoubtedly met intense ridicule for the choices she and Noah made—especially the one to embark on a shipbuilding career of mammoth proportions. Only a courageous and determined woman would be able to hold a family together and protect them under such circumstances. The fact that she raised three godly sons in this unhealthy environment demonstrated her devotion to both God and her family.

There's little doubt that she worked very hard, helping to not only build the ark, but also to produce and pack food and other necessities. God may have brought the animals two by two, but someone had to collect everything else, and I'm quite sure it wasn't the moving company.

Once the flood came, she must have played a major role in organizing and overseeing management of the ark, from setting a feeding schedule for the animals to cleaning the boat. When the waters receded, there was still more work to do, and Noah's wife rose to the challenge again.

While I have been known to complain about the work involved with a big move, Genesis does not record Noah's wife grumbling about the job. She didn't even question Noah about the overwhelming task set before her. She proved herself to be trusting, skilled, organized, patient, hard working, and smart.

That's my kind of hero.

What about her confidence in God? Every time our family gears up for another move, panicky thoughts race through my head. Will the house sell? Will the kids find new friends? Will we find our favorite stores in the new town, or will we have to settle for something like Betty's Barnyard Cooking, Clothing, and Gifts? As the big day approaches, I find myself questioning God. Do you really know what you're doing, changing my world like this?

We may think moving away from our family and friends is hard, but we can send an e-mail or make a phone call to catch up when we feel homesick. While we might not find the stores we're used to visiting, we'll find something. Things were vastly different for Noah's wife. Everything she knew—not just the people, but the places as well—was obliterated from the face of the Earth.

With complete trust in God, she climbed aboard the ark and watched her whole world wash away. She knew He was with her, and she found the courage to face it all. And at the end of the trip, He marked her new address with a dazzling rainbow of promise in the sky. What joy she must have felt when she first laid eyes on her new home—a land cleansed of the past wickedness and ripe for future goodness.

We've all faced situations that threaten to flood our lives. It might be a new job, an ailing parent, financial struggles, or health issues, but like Noah's wife, we can weather the storm. Part of facing the unknown requires dropping an anchor of faith into the depths of God's sovereignty.

Noah's wife led the way. She showed us we can stand as courageous, capable, and intelligent women willing to work hard to reach our goals—and willing to trust God over every wave. She confirmed that God never fails to carry us to a new place of healing or opportunity.

Sometimes we might not even have to pack.

—Lori Z. Scott

No Disadvantage

*There was no sparkle in Leah's eyes, but Rachel had a
beautiful figure and a lovely face.*
GENESIS 29:17

When I was in elementary school, I was not one of the
beautiful children. My hair was brown and unruly. I was
the shortest and skinniest kid in the class, had crooked
teeth, and wore glasses. I was a Leah, surrounded by
plenty of Rachels, and I saw myself as being at a disadvantage right from the start. This attitude only exacerbated
the isolation and emotional pain I felt as a result of being
"different."

But the Lord looked after me. He helped me to see
that I had my own redeeming qualities, including reasonable intelligence and some musical ability. Before long,
I attracted friends with those same qualities. While my
looks were sometimes an irritation for me, they no longer
dictated my worth in my mind, or anyone else's.

It can be difficult in our society, but I strive to keep
that same attitude today.

What you see as a disadvantage may be, in fact, a blessing.

—KIM SHEARD

How Did You Get So Big, Jezebel?

*So Jezebel sent this message to Elijah: "May the gods strike
me and even kill me if by this time tomorrow I have not
killed you just as you killed them."*
1 KINGS 19:2

Just as Elijah left Mount Carmel, the scene of God's victory over the impotent Baals, the wicked queen Jezebel placed a bounty on his head. In Elijah's mind, she grew bigger than God, and he ran for the hills. Why did Elijah panic? Why would he capitulate so easily?

Then I think of the Jezebel moments in my own life, when even a small problem suddenly looms large—larger than God's ability to provide solutions. I forget how many prayers He has answered. Just like Elijah, I make a run for it, to nurse my doubts and let the "what-ifs?" shake my faith.

The next time I face a problem, I'm determined not to let Jezebel get so big. Instead, I'll remember the God who protected Elijah. And me.

No one is bigger than God.

—SUZANNE WOODS FISHER

Influence for the Future

She said, "Give me another gift. You have already given me land in the Negev; now please give me springs of water, too." So Caleb gave her the upper and lower springs.

JOSHUA 15:19

When Acsah's father awarded her hand in marriage to Othniel for his prowess on the battlefield, Acsah appeared to be viewed more as chattel than as a person in her own right.

Acsah soon proved she had a strong will and a keen intellect. She may not have had much influence as a woman in her society, but she used what power she had with her father and her new husband to obtain precious land and thus provide a secure future for herself and her family.

When my children started school, I worried about sending them out into a confusing, and sometimes frightening, world. I realized it was critical for me to make effective use of the strong influence I still had while they were in the early grades. I decided it was also vital to keep the lines of communication open, so that as they got older we could discuss any situation openly and honestly.

You have more power than you think.

—SBT

No Experience Necessary

So Ruth went out to gather grain behind the harvesters. And as it happened, she found herself working in a field that belonged to Boaz, the relative of her father-in-law, Elimelech.

RUTH 2:3

Many people think that they need to be remarkable or involved in some kind of ministry or missionary work for God to use them. The Bible is full of stories in which God makes use of ordinary people. People like Ruth.

As He also proved in the story of Ruth, He uses people right where they are. Ruth was a widow in a strange new place, gathering grain behind the harvesters. Not very glamorous or important, but God had a plan for her that included becoming a part of the genealogy of Jesus Christ.

I see myself as very ordinary, but I know God can use me. Despite the fact that I live on a 300-acre farm, miles from my nearest neighbor, I also know He can use me right where I am. There are opportunities to do God's work everywhere—even in the middle of nowhere!

*It doesn't matter who you are or where you are—
God can use you.*

—SBT

Leadership God's Way

Deborah, the wife of Lappidoth, was a prophet who was judging Israel at that time.
JUDGES 4:4

God placed Deborah in a leadership position to guide Israel to victory against its enemies. When Israel's commander, Barak, refused to go into battle without her, she agreed to accompany him, but prophesied the Lord would give Israel victory through the hand of a woman because of his hesitation.

Sometimes, God places me in leadership roles in community service where I strive to overcome uncertainty in trying my best to make good decisions. I have learned the importance of doing things God's way. He guides me toward wisdom when I let Him lead as I work with neighbors, business owners, and professionals in the community.

When being in charge is a challenge, I know that doing things God's way brings the best results. My Bible stays close when God puts me in charge, because I know He is working through me.

How do you handle your leadership roles?

—ALEXANDRA ROSE

The Power of Words

There was a man named Jabez who was more honorable than any of his brothers. His mother named him Jabez because his birth had been so painful.
1 CHRONICLES 4:9

"Mom, I'm sorry I caused you so many problems when I was a baby," my youngest son announced. He had overheard me tell someone the story about his childhood illness and how the constant throwing up, crying, and lack of sleep created stress in our family. Until that moment, I hadn't realized how much my comments bothered him. Yeah, but how often has he heard that story, I thought.

Abruptly, I felt as if I could have been the mother of Jabez. He must have had moments when he disliked the name his mother had given him in childbirth. Jabez wanted and needed to hear something more positive—just as my son did.

"I'm sorry, sweetheart," I replied and hugged him. "Please forgive me. Now, let me tell you about some of the ways you've brought joy into my life."

Lift up those you love with your words.

—LAURA BROADWATER

A Second Chance

"Where are your accusers? Didn't even one of them condemn you?" "No, Lord," she said. And Jesus said, "Neither do I. Go and sin no more."
JOHN 8:10,11

When I was sixteen, I took my driver's test. The examiner and I got in the car, and she directed me through each step. I successfully performed a three-point turn and safely stopped. Then I started again at a stop sign and backed up. The last item on the test required me to parallel-park in a space between two rubber poles. I had practiced parallel parking more than anything else and executed the maneuver without any difficulty.

However, I decided to back up a tiny bit more so the car would be straighter in relation to the curb. I hit the pole behind me and automatically failed the test. I was humiliated.

"Come back again next week," the examiner said in a kind voice. "You can always have a second chance."

Those were very welcome words to me. Imagine how the adulterous woman felt when Christ blessed her with a second chance.

Rejoice in every second chance God gives you!

—KIM SHEARD

13

Miracle Babies

She came along just as Simeon was talking with Mary and Joseph, and she began praising God. She talked about the child to everyone who had been waiting expectantly for God to rescue Jerusalem.

LUKE 2:38

A couple brought their baby girl to church the other night, and I was the first in line to hold her. I couldn't resist taking a deep breath and inhaling the unique and intoxicating scent that only babies possess. One look into her milky blue eyes told me how blessed I was to be cradling one of God's most amazing miracles, and I thought of how He came to Earth as a baby just like the one I now held.

When Mary and Joseph took the infant Jesus to the Temple in Jerusalem for a purification offering, Anna, an eighty-four-year-old prophetess, saw the baby and realized her most fervent desire. Decades of devotion were rewarded as she gazed upon and recognized the long-awaited Messiah. Just as I see a miracle when I look into a baby's eyes, Anna had the ultimate honor of acknowledging the greatest miracle of all.

Every baby is a reminder of the helpless infant who grew up to be the Savior of us all.

—SBT

God's Servant

Welcome her in the Lord as one who is worthy of honor among God's people. Help her in whatever she needs, for she has been helpful to many, and especially to me.
ROMANS 16:2

I grew up as the only child of a shy mother who didn't participate in social gatherings. It has taken me many years to learn how to function effectively in groups. I want to be included and to be helpful, but sometimes I don't know how to initiate that process.

Recently, we moved to a new church in a small community. Whenever an event such as a funeral dinner or Bible school needs to be planned and carried out, Cindy circulates a sign-up sheet with a list of jobs that need to be done and items that need to be donated. Getting involved is as easy as writing my name. I am automatically included, and at the appointed time and place, I know what to do.

I often think of Phoebe when I hear the phrase, "What would we do without Cindy?" I am grateful for the Cindys of the church who, like Phoebe before her, show the rest of us how to effectively carry out the work of the church.

Sign up and get involved!

—JEAN CAMPION

Knowing What's Right but Doing What's Wrong

It's only the fruit from the tree in the middle of the garden that we are not allowed to eat. God said, "You must not eat it or even touch it; if you do, you will die."
GENESIS 3:3

Like Eve, there have been so many times I thought I knew what was right. I understood what God desired of me, yet I did not do it. I let someone or something convince me to go against the Lord's teachings.

Over time, I've learned there are those who would encourage me to do things I know I shouldn't. I have come to realize there are false prophets who would steer me wrong.

As I have matured in my Christian walk, I have spent time in daily prayer and Bible study, developed friendships with fellow Christians, and made church services a must. I have taught Sunday school and become a newspaper devotional columnist. I have sought God's will. When I fill my heart with God's desires, it is easier to resist the behaviors that displease my Lord.

Learn to recognize what's right, and endeavor to avoid what's wrong.

—BETTY KING

Apology Accepted

Then David comforted Bathsheba, his wife, and slept with her. She became pregnant and gave birth to a son, and they named him Solomon. The Lord loved the child.

2 SAMUEL 12:24

Thankfully, David and Bathsheba's story didn't end with the death of their first child. When David found the humility to say "I'm sorry—I was wrong," his fellowship with God was restored. I can't help but wonder if he used the same words to comfort his grieving wife and restore their relationship. Perhaps Bathsheba found it easier to love a humble man of God with human frailties than a legendary king.

As with most couples, my husband, Tom, and I have had our share of disagreements. For a long time, I felt like I was the only one who ever apologized. I realized that a direct confrontation would achieve little, so I turned to God for help. About a week later, I heard some very special words. "I'm sorry," Tom said. "I was wrong."

I originally fell in love with my husband for his many remarkable qualities, but the day he became less than perfect, I fell in love with him all over again.

When we harbor unrealistic expectations of others, we set ourselves up for disappointment.

—SBT

17

Promises in the Wilderness

*The angel of the Lord said to her, "Return to your mistress,
and submit to her authority."*
GENESIS 16:9

Traits we notice in others often reflect our own. So it is with Hagar and me. She's not one of my favorite women of the Bible, but I've learned from her. When she obeyed the angel's command, her renewed servitude was made bearable because of God's promises.

God's promises for better things ahead consistently help me to endure, although sometimes He leaves me in the "wilderness" longer than I want. On two occasions, I have pleaded to be delivered from jobs I disliked. I felt the same sense of helplessness Hagar must have experienced when Abraham banished her and she faced death for herself and her precious son, Ishmael. Instead, God rescued them and later made Ishmael the father of a great nation.

God rescued me as well, but only after I had the opportunity to witness and see lives changed at both jobs, followed by a call to walk off my second job and write for Him. That was thirty years ago.

Thank God for His perfect timing!

—COLLEEN L. REECE

Childlike Trust

Holding her hand, he said to her, "Talitha koum," which means "Little girl, get up!"
MARK 5:41

Childhood trauma kept me from growing up in many ways. I remained frightened, but eager to trust. "Can you see your child-self with the children around Jesus?" a therapist once asked.

I closed my eyes and leaned back in the chair. Me, with Jesus? Not a chance. But I could make a picture of myself lying alone, terrified, with my mother weeping and my father absent. Then I was in some eerie waiting place, with no one around.

Through the darkness came a shining voice. "Little girl!" And I knew Jesus loved me just like the sick girl whom he healed. I was safe with Him. Without thinking, I reached for His hand. "Little girl, get up!"

I did as He said and He led me into the sunshine. I opened my eyes and found myself standing in my therapist's office, hand outstretched, smiling. "I can trust Him!" I said. "He will stay with me and take care of me, no matter what!"

Trusting in God's love gives you strength for any difficulty.

—ELSI DODGE

Needless Nagging

She tormented him with her nagging day after day until he was sick to death of it.
JUDGES 16:16

Using the power her sexuality gave her, Delilah harassed Samson until he relented and confessed to her the secret of his great power. Armed with this knowledge, the Philistines were able to bring down one of their most powerful enemies.

My family's deep and abiding love for me places me in a position of power—an authority I can use to either build them up or tear them down. I can nag my husband or children and risk creating feelings of anger and resentment in both my family and myself. My aim is achieved, but at what cost?

I would far rather appeal to the Lord for His help. I have learned that He can bring about changes in my family that no amount of nagging can accomplish. The second option requires time, patience, and faith, but the blessings will leave little doubt that you have made the right choice.

Stop nagging and start praying!

—SBT

A Crock Full of Blessings

Charm is deceptive, and beauty does not last; but a woman who fears the Lord will be greatly praised.
PROVERBS 31:30

"Sue, what's in that ceramic pot on the porch?" I asked my friend.

"That's not a pot," she replied. "It's a crock full of cabbage. I'm making sauerkraut."

"Did you know you could buy that in cans at the grocery store?"

She grinned. "I know, but my family can tell the difference!"

For eighteen years, I've teased Sue that she's the "Proverbs 31" woman. She cans vegetables, makes French bread from scratch, sews her children's clothes, and leads a Bible study every week.

As we sat in the coolness of the back porch, sipping sun tea and snapping green beans, I couldn't help but ask, "Why do you do all this?"

"For me," she said, "it's one of the ways I worship God."

For the first time, I saw the real Sue—the one with an all-consuming love for God who served others from her heart. And just like the Proverbs 31 woman, she was more than capable. She was worthy of praise!

Serving God should be the motivation for everything we do.

—CONNIE K. POMBO

Of Mountains and Molehills

Now I appeal to Euodia and Syntyche. Please, because you belong to the Lord, settle your disagreement.
PHILIPPIANS 4:2

As I listened to the Bible teacher, I realized I didn't completely agree with her teachings. Years earlier, I would have left that Bible study and joined one that mirrored my beliefs down to the last detail.

I thought about her comments all afternoon. Did her view of scripture make me love Jesus any less? Was He still my Savior, even though she interpreted this particular scripture differently than I did? My fundamental beliefs had not changed, and I knew she was a wise teacher, full of the love and joy of the Lord. By evening, I asked God to lead us all into truth, so that we might be in harmony with the Lord and each other.

I continued to sit under her teaching, gleaning nuggets from scripture, for many more years. There were times we didn't agree on minor points, but we learned to "minor on the minors and major on the majors."

God longs for all women to be sisters in Christ.

—SALLY JADLOW

My Home, His Church

*Please give my greetings to our brothers and
sisters at Laodicea, and to Nympha and the
church that meets in her house.*
COLOSSIANS 4:15

My husband, Gary, agreed to plant a new church, and
the district gave us ten days to find a large enough house.
We searched all week to no avail: rent too high, house too
small, no parking.

Then Saturday morning, we prayed again. "Lord, we
need an extra bathroom for our live-in grandma, large
bedrooms, and an office. We need a huge living room for
services, a large kitchen, a building for a bicycle business,
and parking space." In my heart, I dedicated my home to
the Lord. Two hours later, we drove to that house.

"Oh, no," my husband groaned. Waist-deep weeds
overwhelmed the house. Old car bodies languished in
the wraparound driveway. Inside, the house needed paint,
wallpaper, and, most importantly, cleaning.

"Thank you, Jesus," I shouted. "Hon, the Lord knew we
could clean and paint. He gave us a perfect house church."
In the years that followed, many people, including my parents, accepted Christ as their Savior in that home.

God answers all prayers—big and small.

—KATHERINE J. CRAWFORD

23

Forgotten Victims

But when the local prince, Shechem son of Hamor the
Hivite, saw Dinah, he seized her and raped her.
GENESIS 34:2

Dinah's brothers reacted to her tragic experience with rage that rapidly exploded into a desire for revenge. The Bible contains a detailed account of their retribution, but it says little or nothing about Dinah following her attack. Her brothers appeared to be more concerned with their family honor than they were with their sister's well-being.

When my daughter was very young, she came home from a friend's house in tears. Her friend's father had returned from a long fishing trip. Unfortunately, he was intoxicated and became verbally abusive toward the two little girls. Instantly, I was overwhelmed with a ferocious anger, and for a few moments, I couldn't think clearly.

My fury lost its momentum when I realized it was my daughter who had lived through the experience, and my focus rapidly shifted to her. Revenge would solve nothing. I had a daughter who needed me.

Pride can get in the way of helping people.

—SBT

Sharing Joy

Elizabeth gave a glad cry and exclaimed to Mary, "God has blessed you above all women, and your child is blessed."
LUKE 1:42

Elizabeth's greeting to Mary speaks volumes about her character. Some women in her situation might be jealous, but Elizabeth felt and expressed nothing but joy. It's no surprise that Mary spent months at the home of her relative. Elizabeth's loving and generous spirit would make any visit a blessing.

It's not always easy to be happy for someone else. A good friend of mine lost her husband to colon cancer several years ago. She told me that when she hears about someone recovering from the same type of cancer, she wants to be happy for them but, sometimes, she can't help feeling a tiny spark of resentment. Why did her husband have to die? she wonders.

Then she realized every survivor reflected the advances medical science was making in the battle against cancer. Someday, one of her loved ones might be celebrating a victory instead of becoming a victim.

Joys shared are doubled!

—SBT

Cut from the Same Cloth

*So Peter returned with them; and as soon as he arrived, they
took him to the upstairs room. The room was filled with
widows who were weeping and showing him the coats and
other clothes Dorcas had made for them.*

ACTS 9:39

I learned to sew at an early age by making doll clothes from fabric left over from the skirts and dresses my mother made for me. When I first heard about the seamstress Dorcas, I learned that women in the Bible weren't so different from women today. They lived in families, cooked, cleaned, and kept house. And many liked to sew.

Sometimes the thread that draws us together as women is, quite literally, thread. We gather in sewing circles and quilting bees, sharing scissors and fabric, stories and laughter. We spend quiet times alone with our handiwork, listening to nothing but the rustle of cloth in our hands and the current of our private thoughts. With our hands, we create something new, something that is uniquely our own, yet something that links us together throughout the ages.

Follow your creative spirit and do the things you love.

—PATRICIA MITCHELL

Fool's Gold

And regarding Jezebel, the Lord says, "Dogs will eat Jezebel's body at the plot of land in Jezreel."
1 KINGS 21:23

Recently, my son Timothy spray-painted some rocks from my garden. Even though the shiny nuggets looked like the real thing, they were nothing but simple stones covered with gold paint.

Queen Jezebel had a hard time separating herself from what looked like spiritual truth but wasn't. Surrounded by people who told her what she wanted to hear, she ended up worshiping false gods. When Elijah—a real man of God—showed up with the truth, Jezebel resisted.

My prayer is that, by God's grace, I will always walk in the truth, even when it's painful or inconvenient for me. I don't want to get caught up in what appears to be beautiful, but isn't real, according to God's word.

Appearances can truly be deceiving.

—JENNIFER E. WHYMAN

Brave Enough to Be Humble

*It isn't right to take food from the children [the Jews]
and feed it to the dogs. She replied, "That's true, Lord,
but even the dogs under the table are allowed to eat
the scraps from the children's plates."*

MARK 7:27,28

The Syrophoenician woman proved that it's possible to be bold and humble at the same time. She approached Jesus with a fearless request of healing, but was modest enough to acknowledge her lowly cultural status and even referred to herself as a dog.

I have to work up a lot of nerve to go forward in a courageous way, and once I do, I have a hard time sustaining my bravery in the face of humility. Thankfully, God knows this, and I am amazed at the ways He equips me to face the challenge.

He places people in my life who model the two characteristics I strive to balance. He puts passions in my heart that I can't ignore and must tackle boldly, but He never lets me become prideful. As He teaches me to blend the two, I see myself growing in ways I never believed possible.

*God can help you see the beauty of courage
and humility working together.*

—DIANNE DANIELS

A Gift for Everyone

And the king loved Esther more than any of the other young women. He was so delighted with her that he set the royal crown on her head and declared her queen instead of Vashti.
ESTHER 2:17

God has gifted each of us with special talents. My brother is a skillful artist, and my husband is a wonderful singer. I have taken great pleasure in watching my children's gifts evolve, although I wonder sometimes if my youngest boy has been "blessed" with the ability to talk twenty-fours a day.

God endowed Esther with great beauty. Without knowing her story, this particular gift might be viewed as frivolous or insignificant, especially when compared to David's courage or Solomon's wisdom. But just like David and Solomon, Esther put her special quality to excellent use. In a series of events with the unmistakable mark of God's perfect planning, Esther's beauty saved thousands of lives.

We may not know what our gifts are, or we might feel that whatever talents we have are inconsequential. Whether it's a good sense of humor, a smile that lights up a room, or a compassionate heart, we can use our gifts to glorify God.

Discover your special gift and use it!

—SBT

Agape Love

*Then the Lord said to me, "Go and love your wife again,
even though she commits adultery with another lover. This
will illustrate that the Lord still loves Israel, even though the
people have turned to other gods and love to worship them."*
HOSEA 3:1

Hosea married Gomer knowing she was a promiscuous woman. She bore him three children and then left Hosea to raise them while she conducted numerous adulterous relationships. Hosea never stopped loving her, and when he found her for sale at a slave auction, he paid the price and brought her home. The marriage of Hosea and Gomer is a picture of God's love for Israel and of Jesus' love for us all.

Most people will agree that love is complicated—and sometimes confusing. I have known brotherly love, love for my friends, and, of course, the deep and abiding love I have for my husband and children. We may obtain earthly glimpses of unconditional love in the feelings we have for our children or spouse, but only God truly demonstrates what the Greeks called agape love. No matter what we do, He will never stop loving us, and if we stray, He will never cease to long for our return.

*If you have wandered from God,
He is waiting for you with open arms.*

—SBT

Pain Is Gain

His wife said to him, "Are you still trying to maintain your integrity? Curse God and die." But Job replied, "You talk like a foolish woman. Should we accept only good things from the hand of God and never anything bad?"

JOB 2:9–10

It's hard to watch the people we love suffer. Perhaps that difficulty was the motivation behind Job's wife's seemingly cruel comments. My suffering plateau as a wife and mom is extremely low. A skinned knee can send me into a fit of nauseous empathy. Fortunately, I have become slightly more courageous over the years.

Two years ago, my fourteen-year-old daughter, Brittany, underwent surgery to remove a brain tumor. I couldn't bear to think of what she might endure. As I look back at Brittany's illness and recovery, I see that her trial has produced amazing character within her—character that can only be harvested from hardship, and, yes, suffering.

Even though I may get weak in the knees from time to time, I have learned to be less driven by my emotions and more by the faith that God is in control during good times and bad.

Spiritual maturity comes from both blessings and trials.

—BETH DUEWEL

Contagious Faith

*But Ruth replied, "Don't ask me to leave you and
turn back. Wherever you go, I will go; wherever
you live, I will live. Your people will be my people,
and your God will be my God."*
RUTH 1:16

In spite of the fifteen-year difference in our ages, Sandy and I had formed a close friendship at my last job. Still lonely in a new city, I eagerly anticipated the comfort and connection her letter would provide. Instead, I received a startling surprise. She wrote, "You probably never realized it but I had a problem with alcohol, but your example encouraged me to seek God again."

Alcohol? I had never attributed Sandy's perpetual high spirits to anything more than her good nature. Now, she was once again active in a local church and, amazingly, I had helped bring her back. In spite of my problems with a dying marriage, I ministered to my sister in Christ.

Like Naomi with Ruth, I discovered that my life didn't have to be the model of perfection for God to speak through me.

Don't be surprised if God speaks through you.

—DARLENE FRANKLIN

Courage in the Face of Evil

*It was Mary Magdalene, Joanna, Mary the
mother of James, and several other women
who told the apostles what had happened.*
Luke 24:10

In Bible class, my husband and I talked about being grateful to worship and give offerings openly and unafraid. Then we read two quiet verses about Joanna and our gratitude suddenly seemed insignificant.

Joanna was married, wealthy in her own right, and her husband was Herod's steward—the same evil tyrant who had ordered the murder of John the Baptist. Joanna saw Jesus crucified. She was there when they sealed his body in the cave. Her Lord was dead. Early on the first day of that amazing week, she ignored the deadly risks and returned to the tomb. I confess I might still be in hiding, but, because of her courage, she heard the words, "He is risen."

When I witness to a friendly neighbor, I fear ridicule, but a little-known follower of Jesus not only heard, but also ran to spread the good news. I want to be the kind of woman who is in a hurry to tell the world about God.

Ask God to increase your courage to follow Him.

—Liz Hoyt Eberle

He Hears Your Cry

Jacob's well was there; and Jesus, tired from the long walk, sat wearily beside the well about noontime.
JOHN 4:6

In the years before I gave my heart to Jesus, I depended on others, and because they were only human, they invariably let me down. Hurt and confused, I became determined to depend only on myself and, once again, I encountered disappointment and defeat.

For a certain woman of Samaria, it was just another day laboring under the burdens of shattered expectations and crippling failures. Even though she saw little or no hope in her future, her heart had cried out its disappointment, and someone had heard her.

On His way from Judea to Galilee, Jesus made a detour to Samaria. This woman, mired in sin and rejected by her neighbors, was important enough for the Lord to seek her out. Why? Because He knew He had something she needed.

The years had left her with a mind dulled from disillusionment and eyes that saw only a bleak horizon. And yet, a tiny spark of faith led her heart to call out for help. Jesus went out of His way to prove there was something more—much more.

Cry out to Jesus and He will hear you.

—SBT

Flammable Feelings

For Herod had arrested and imprisoned John as a favor to his wife Herodias (the former wife of Herod's brother Philip).
MATTHEW 14:3

Herodias knew how to carry a grudge. Angered by John the Baptist's comments about her marriage, she nurtured an ember of resentment until it exploded into a wildfire of rage. Obsessed with revenge, she was eventually responsible for the beheading of John the Baptist.

Some years ago, one of my husband's employees accused him of shortchanging her paycheck. He refused to become upset and provided proof that he was innocent of her charges. However, when she began spreading vicious rumors about our family, I became very agitated.

We lived in a small town—the kind where everyone knows everyone else, and her gossip found fertile ground. I quickly developed a full-fledged resentment. I didn't consider having her beheaded, but I harbored certain fantasies where she got what I thought she deserved. This was before I discovered the bliss that forgiveness can bring. No one died as a result of my bitterness, but it left its scars.

A flicker of resentment can be snuffed out by forgiveness.

—SBT

Adjusting Our Focus

One of them was Lydia from Thyatira, a merchant
of expensive purple cloth, who worshiped God. As
she listened to us, the Lord opened her heart, and she
accepted what Paul was saying.

ACTS 16:14

My late sister was a professional seamstress who appreciated fine material. She often designed and sewed entire wardrobes for her wealthier clientele, who trusted her to choose their fabrics. She took great delight in such endeavors and described in detail the various materials she had picked out.

Unlike my sister, I tend to be overwhelmed by the wide variety of available choices in a fabric store and have trouble making a decision. I remember feeling frustrated and asking her, "How can I keep from getting distracted by all the other colors when I've already decided I want green?"

Her reply was simple and straightforward. "Well, don't look at any other colors except green!" Maintaining a focus is easier said than done, but for Lydia, who concentrated on purple fabrics, it was the key to her livelihood.

The more I focus on God, the clearer His will becomes.

—ALMA BARKMAN

Only the Best Will Do

*She replied, "In your Kingdom, please let my two
sons sit in places of honor next to you, one on
your right and the other on your left."*
MATTHEW 20:21

Sometimes, I think I know what's best for my children.
When my son Dylan announced his intention to join the
military as a chaplain, I couldn't resist telling him that he
could just as easily serve the Lord in a safer environment
than the armed forces. Then I remembered that God has
a perfect plan for everyone, including my children. His
plan for Dylan may consist of following a way of life which
may test my faith and my heart.

Salome believed she knew what was best for her
beloved sons, two disciples of Jesus. When she requested
positions of honor for James and John, she assumed Jesus
planned to establish a kingdom on earth. Only after she
witnessed the crucifixion and resurrection did she realize that her desires for her sons were but a pale shadow
matched with the brilliance of what God had in store for
them.

*Placing our children's lives in God's hands means giving
them only the best.*

—SBT

FEBRUARY

I Am Not a Paragon

Who can find a virtuous and capable wife?
She is more precious than rubies.
PROVERBS 31:10

It's Mother's Day again, and the sermon is bound to be on the woman of Proverbs 31. I am not that woman. I will never be that woman. The truth is, I don't even want to be that woman! For one thing, she's a wife and mother, while I'm single, divorced, and a senior citizen.

She sews beautiful clothes and other items, selling what she's made. My mother gave up trying to teach me to sew, and I can barely replace a button.

She gets up early and cooks attractive and healthy meals. I use the microwave and read while I eat. She is a financial whiz, she gardens, and she stays busy all the time. I hire a financial adviser, walk around the dandelions, and sit down with a book every chance I get. If the description of the Proverbs 31 woman is God's idea of perfection, I'm out of luck.

But Jesus died for me—lazy, overweight, single me. So I know God loves me. Does He really want to fit me into the mold of a woman I'm not?

Reading the proverb again, I ask for insight and look for truth instead of a guilt trip. Then I notice something. Though Solomon lists all the culturally appropriate marks of a good wife, he never states she is God's ideal—the ideal wife, maybe, but not the ideal woman. He concludes, "A woman who fears the Lord will be greatly praised." (Proverbs 31:30b).

So God smiles on the woman who fears the Lord, who loves Him with everything she has, and who does everything for His glory. What kind of woman is that?

"I like the way you tell stories from the Bible," a woman told me. "I understand it that way."

"Can you explain rounding numbers to my class?" a fellow teacher asked. "When you do it, the kids remember better!"

"I'm so glad you came with me to the school meeting," a parent said. "I always get panicky when they hand me all that paperwork, and I don't understand what they're saying."

Two women approached me after Sunday school. "Thanks for saying what you did," they said. "I was thinking the same thing but didn't want to say it."

And then there's my Meandering Moose. Tormented by panic and anxiety, I bought a recreational vehicle so I would have a safe place to hide while on vacation. When God healed me from my panic attacks, a friend said, "How wonderful that the Lord has taken the frightened turtle and turned her into a strong moose!" Moose are big, awkward-looking, and run freely through nature. I am big, awkward, and travel joyfully through God's glorious creation.

I named my RV, "The Meandering Moose," and I drive across the land while my beagle sleeps on the passenger seat and my cat attacks the windshield wipers when it rains. I play "I Spy" with God, looking for His fingerprints around me. A flower reflects His infinite attention to detail. A mountain mirrors His grandeur. A passing ambulance reminds me of His love and care. A rainbow? His promise never to destroy the world by flood again. A car accident? I pray for all involved: the injured, their families, the paramedics, doctors, and nurses.

God provides an abundance of delightful situations when I'm alert to His guidance. My, that sounds spiritual and profound. Well, maybe it just sounds self-centered and pious, but it is fun to watch what He does!

One summer, I was driving through eastern South Dakota, enjoying the air-conditioning and singing praise and worship songs, when I crested a little hill and slammed on the brakes. There was a house on the highway in front of me, loaded on an enormous trailer, slowly making its way to some new location, and I was fourth in a line of vehicles behind it.

As cars piled up in my rear-view mirror, I watched the power company personnel lifting electric lines with padded poles while the house crawled along below them. After a while, the house pulled onto the edge of a dirt road leading into a field. The drivers in front of me whipped around the blockade, their cars tilting as the tires left the highway.

Then it was my turn. Would my heavy RV sink into the soft shoulder? Would I roll down the slope into the field? I inched forward, my knuckles white around the wheel. Eventually, a man came around the corner of the house to find out what was holding things up. His eyes widened, and then he began to direct me, waving me forward, gesturing: a bit more to the right, come on, a little farther, now left again. . . .

I waved my thanks as I finally passed and pulled in front of the house. The cars behind me streamed around me and disappeared over the next rise. My shoulders ached. I shook the tension from my fingers, one hand at a time, as I drove. "Okay, Abba, You're in charge of the highways, too," I prayed. "You know what You want me to do and when You want me to do it!"

I told the people in my tour group, the clerk at the gift shop, and my friends back in town how God had sent me a Wizard of Oz–style house to slow me down. Rather than complain about the annoyance, I chose to laugh and praise Him. I felt my headache receding.

There are many times each day when my arthritic hip protests loudly. There are too many steps to climb into the rig, I'm too tired to walk the dog, or it's too hard to bend down to connect my electricity. When people comment on my limp or my cane in a national park or museum, I'm sorely tempted to absorb the sympathy.

More and more, however, I am focusing on the good He brings me, rather than the inconveniences I encounter. "I love my turtle-headed cane," I say. "The Lord led me to it a couple of years before I needed a cane to walk!" I laugh when I tell people, "Yeah, I'm in a fair amount of discomfort now, but it's worth it to see this waterfall God made!" Instead of griping about the mosquitoes, I marvel at the amazing sunset.

I'm sure the Proverbs 31 woman would choose the positive attitude, the encouraging word, and the self-denying action without thinking twice about it. I, however, have to make a conscious decision each time. Too often I forget and fall back into complaining mode. When I do make a godly choice, the pain in my hip subsides, the world looks brighter, and gratitude flows through me. Then I can snap the leash to the dog's collar and head up the trail in a campground with a smile, singing as I look for what God has prepared next for me.

What does the woman whom God smiles on do? She doesn't necessarily sew, or garden, or raise a brood of courteous children. Whatever she does, she does with her whole heart, regardless of limitations, handicaps, or unfortunate circumstances. And she does everything for God.

No, I can't measure up to the Proverbs 31 paragon, nor should I try. But I can learn a lot from her, once I set aside my prejudices and let God open my eyes. And who knows? Maybe she would enjoy an RV road trip!

—ELSI DODGE

Taken for Granted

David replied to Abigail, "Praise the Lord, the God of Israel,
who has sent you to meet me today!"
1 SAMUEL 25:32

Have you ever felt taken for granted? So many of the tasks that fill our day are remarkable only if we don't do them. No one pays much attention to the clean, folded clothes in their drawers, but there's little doubt they would notice if they found the drawers empty and the clothes in a heap by the washing machine.

Abigail knew what it felt like to be taken for granted. She was prepared to spend her life serving a husband, Nabal, who didn't appreciate her, but God had different plans. He never took Abigail's loyalty and diligence for granted, and He completely changed her life. David eventually married Abigail.

As long as we glorify God in all we do, it doesn't matter whether we spend our days trying to save the world or trying to save fifty cents at the grocery store. When we work to please the Lord, He sees, He smiles, and His response is a resounding, "Well done!"

God appreciates you.

—TRACY DONEGAN

Christian Credibility

So Hilkiah the priest, Ahikam, Acbor, Shaphan, and Asaiah went to the New Quarter of Jerusalem to consult with the prophet Huldah. She was the wife of Shallum son of Tikvah, son of Harhas, the keeper of the Temple wardrobe.

2 KINGS 22:14

Huldah's story in the Bible isn't very long, but she played a significant role in the history of her people. It was her prophecy that restored her nation to God and revived their faith.

When the high priest Hilkiah discovered the Book of the Law, he wasted no time in letting the king know the nation was in grave danger. The fact that Hilkiah sought Huldah's advice strongly suggests she had a reputation for being a faithful woman of God—someone who could be trusted to relay His word.

I will never be a prophet, but if I spend my time in prayer and in learning God's word, I, too, can gain a reputation for being a passionate woman of God.

Does your reputation reflect your love for God?

—SBT

The Legacy

*I remember your genuine faith, for you share the faith that
first filled your grandmother Lois and your mother, Eunice.
And I know that same faith continues strong in you.*
2 TIMOTHY 1:5

The apostle Paul was quick to credit Timothy's grandmother and mother for the firm foundation in scripture Timothy received early in life. Just as Proverbs dictated, Lois and Eunice trained young Timothy "up in the way he should go," and gave him a gift that would never fail him.

My mother died in 1989, and I count among my most treasured possessions some of the lovely things I inherited. Far more precious than the material things, however, was the spiritual legacy she left me. She taught me to pray, to rely on God, and to love my neighbor. I may have wandered from these teachings, but eventually I returned to them and found them as familiar as my mother's embrace.

I know life's storms may blow my children off course in their journey through life, but I pray that the spiritual lessons I have tried to teach them will bring them back to the loving arms of the Lord.

What will your legacy be?

—SBT

A Fearless Future

Eli's daughter-in-law, the wife of Phinehas, was pregnant and near her time of delivery. When she heard that the Ark of God had been captured and that her father-in-law and husband were dead, she went into labor and gave birth.

1 SAMUEL 4:19

Her husband and father-in-law were dead, and the Philistines had captured the Ark of God. Suddenly, Ichabod's mother was facing a very uncertain future. Perhaps she saw herself confronting the problems and challenges of life alone. She allowed her fear to deplete the strength she needed to deliver her son and, having lost the will to live, she died in childbirth.

The future used to terrify me. My husband often teased me that if I didn't have something to worry about, I would invent something. I still have moments of fear and worry, but now I have a source of courage that has never failed me. God has promised me that I will never face anything alone. All I need to do is look back and see how He has kept this promise countless times.

I can face the future knowing God will be right there beside me.

—SBT

Royalty with a Heart

When the princess opened it, she saw the baby. The little boy was crying, and she felt sorry for him. "This must be one of the Hebrew children," she said.
EXODUS 2:6

While watching the news years ago, I was troubled to see so many war-victim children. I also knew of far too many hurting children right in my neighborhood. Their vulnerability bothered me, and I knew I should do something. So I founded Orphans First, a nonprofit organization helping suffering children. It wasn't much, but it was something I could accomplish within my power.

Pharoah's daughter had immense authority. She could use it to do anything she wanted—and I'm certain she often did. However, the fact that she acted on behalf of a needy child speaks volumes to me about her character. She didn't hesitate, but allowed her compassion to move her to act, and she adopted a child who would otherwise have been killed.

God favors this kind of compassion. Working with suffering children over the years, I've seen many find homes, receive education, and be loved.

When we show compassion, we reflect God's heart— and lives are changed.

—JANEY L. DeMEO

Perfect Submission

If she says, "Yes, have a drink, and I will draw water for your camels, too," let her be the one you have selected to be the wife of my master's son.
GENESIS 24:44

It was hard for my daughter to watch her two younger brothers marry and start families of their own. She often wondered if God had forgotten that she, too, had this desire. She never complained, but as her mother, I felt her pain.

Yet my first-born waited, and trusted God for His timing, even to the point of accepting singleness as His Will. She served God in whatever capacity He brought her way, reflecting her inward character of love and submission to her Savior.

"Your daughter is an inspiration to me," a friend said. "Her walk with the Lord is so beautiful!" In many ways Melissa reminded me of Rebekah, cheerfully and diligently serving the Lord and her family while remaining content and open to God's plan.

Maybe God hasn't brought Melissa's Isaac into her life right now, but because she knows He has a perfect plan for her, she remains content, trusting that He will reward her obedience and answer her mother's prayers.

Perfect submission produces His perfect will.

—MARIBETH SPANGENBERG

A Brand-New Me

When Jericho is conquered, you will let me live,
along with my father and mother, my brothers and sisters,
and all their families.
JOSHUA 2:13

Some people go through a profound emotional experience when they accept Jesus as their personal Savior. Others, like me, feel nothing whatsoever. Before I had my first child, a friend told me that nothing about my life would ever be the same.

Little did I know that my decision to follow the Lord would have the same effect. However, I'm not sure any friendly words of wisdom could have prepared me for the life-changing events that were about to occur.

Rahab had no way of knowing the significance of her decision to trust the Lord. She was looking for a way to save her life and the lives of her family, but when she told the spies that she believed in the power of their God, she became a new person.

Her life was about to be transformed in ways she had never imagined. The proof is right there in the Bible. All we have to do is find her name on the family tree of Jesus Christ.

Are you a new person in Christ?

—SBT

Deadly Attachments

Then the Lord rained down fire and burning sulfur from the sky on Sodom and Gomorrah.
GENESIS 19:24

Lot's wife was given the opportunity of a lifetime. Even though God had vowed to destroy Sodom, he agreed to spare the lives of Lot—the last righteous man in the sin-filled city—and his family. Angels sent to rescue the reluctant family dragged them from the city and warned them not to look back. Instead of looking forward to God's salvation, Lot's wife turned her head for one last glance at her home with all its earthly enjoyments. She paid for her disobedience with her life.

I've never been much of a camper. I like my own bed and indoor plumbing, not to mention my computer and DVD player! However, pleasures can become problems when they overshadow my devotion to God and interfere with my Christian walk. If I can't imagine living without something, perhaps it's time for me to take a careful look at my dependence on it. Maybe it's time for a camping trip with my boys!

Take a break from your "attachments,"
and spend the time with God!

—SBT

Balancing Act

The angel of the Lord appeared to Manoah's wife and said,
"Even though you have been unable to have children, you
will soon become pregnant and give birth to a son."
JUDGES 13:3

When an angel appeared to Manoah's wife, she was understandably startled, but she remained calm and remembered everything the angel told her. Her reaction was quite different from that of Manoah who was present when the angel visited a second time. While his wife viewed the extraordinary event in a practical and sensible light, he was overcome with doubt and fear.

My husband, Tom, and I sometimes have contrasting views of the same situation, and our reactions can be very different. A few years ago, we had an ice storm and lost power for several days. I perceived it as a disaster, but Tom considered it a blessing in disguise. He turned out to be right.

We spent three wonderful days getting to know each other again without the distractions of modern life. Our unique personalities have created some friction over the years but, like Manoah and his wife, we've learned to accept the differences and cherish the balance God created when he brought us together.

Rejoice and find balance in your differences.

—SBT

The Greatest Gift of All

*I remember your genuine faith, for you share the faith that
first filled your grandmother Lois and your mother, Eunice.
And I know that same faith continues strong in you.*
2 TIMOTHY 1:5

The last part of the year is a busy time around our
house. We have birthdays in September, October, November, and December and, of course, there's Thanksgiving
and Christmas. Lots of wish lists and gift giving. Although
I try to make sure everyone gets something they want, I
don't worry about buying the perfect gift anymore. I've
learned that the most important thing I can share with
the people I love is my devotion to God.

Lois and Eunice were two women who probably didn't
think they had much to offer, but they had a genuine faith
that they passed on to young Timothy—Lois's son and
Eunice's grandson. It was women like these who made me
realize I had a gift to offer more precious than any jewels.
I'll probably still spend way too much time shopping this
holiday season, but I won't spend any time looking for the
greatest gift of all.

The greatest gift I have to offer is my faith.

—SBT

Loving Again

May the Lord, the God of Israel, under whose
wings you have come to take refuge, reward you
fully for what you have done.
RUTH 2:12

Becoming a widow while raising an infant son certainly wasn't my plan but, for a time, it appeared God had given me a different path to follow. After months of crying myself to sleep, I decided to accept His will. "Lord, if you want me to be single for the rest of my life, I know you will give me the strength. I will trust your plan, even though my heart feels like it's breaking in two."

I wonder how Ruth felt when she looked into the eyes of Boaz, the kind man who sought her out, the man who would become her husband and the father of her son. I do know what happened when I met my special someone. Several years after my own loss, I looked into the eyes of Jim, the man who became my husband and a loving father to my son Jared and our own son, Joel. I am thankful God has allowed me, like Ruth, to find love again.

God knows the needs of your heart.

—SUSAN KELLY SKITT

Worthy Wisdom

Anna, a prophet, was also there in the Temple.
She was the daughter of Phanuel from the tribe of
Asher, and she was very old.
LUKE 2:36

I admired Miss Helen from the moment I met her. My elderly friend lived in humble circumstances, but she made all visitors feel as if they had wandered into a palace. Her optimism and cheery attitude never failed to lift my spirits, and underneath her fragile appearance lay a determined spirit.

However, it was her keen intellect that engendered my greatest respect.

One would never suspect that this modest, unassuming woman possessed the mind of a trained theologian. However, she didn't just know the Bible thoroughly and completely; she lived by God's word and put Him first in all aspects of her life.

I'm certain many viewed Anna as simply an old widow with little to offer.

However, like my friend, Miss Helen, Anna lived her entire life for God, and he rewarded her devotion by granting her the gift of prophecy and allowing her to know the infant Jesus as her savior.

Our elderly friends may have more
to offer than we ever imagined.

—SBT

Affairs of the Heart

When a certain immoral woman from that city heard he was eating there, she brought a beautiful alabaster jar filled with expensive perfume.
LUKE 7:37

The woman had a notorious reputation, and her lavish display of affection disgusted Simon the Pharisee. He didn't realize he and this woman had something important in common. They were both sinners in need of grace, but there was one big difference. The woman was painfully aware of her sins and desperate for forgiveness and repentance. Overwhelming gratitude had brought her to Simon's home to show Jesus how much she loved Him.

On the other hand, Simon lived in blissful ignorance of the sins that wouldn't allow him to see the power and beauty of the scene between Jesus and the woman. He was too busy judging the woman to see the amazing power of God at work.

Too often, I've found myself experiencing feelings of superiority and pride, and I remind myself that when I came to Jesus, He didn't look at my life. He only looked at my heart.

It wasn't my perfection that brought me to the Lord.

—SBT

57

Unlikely Blessings

*Soon Pharaoh's daughter came down to bathe in the
river, and her attendants walked along the riverbank.
When the princess saw the basket among the reeds,
she sent her maid to get it for her.*
EXODUS 2:5

In an effort to control the growing population of Israelites, the pharaoh of Egypt ordered the murder of all male Hebrew infants. However, his daughter wasn't thinking of her father's terrible edict when she found a crying baby in a basket floating down the Nile River.

When God used the daughter of a powerful pagan leader to help bring His children out of bondage, He proved, once again, that the greatest blessings often come from the most unexpected sources.

Some months ago, I agreed to watch my friend's foster son after school. I was often physically and emotionally drained by the time my friend picked him up. Then, one day he appeared with two small chickens. His teacher had hatched them at school for a science project, but now they needed a real home.

Since then, our population of chickens has steadily grown, along with our affection for them. How could I have known that a difficult, challenging child would bring us so much pleasure?

God loves to use the unlikely and the unexpected.

—SBT

A House of Service

The churches here in the province of Asia send greetings in the Lord, as do Aquila and Priscilla and all the others who gather in their home for church meetings.
1 CORINTHIANS 16:19

Several years ago, my mother, afflicted with Alzheimer's, came to live with us. Her care prevented me from participating in activities outside my home, so I began looking for a different way to serve the Lord.

I felt led to start a neighborhood interdenominational women's Bible study that met in our living room. Some of the woman who attended became Christians and several other women, who hadn't attended church for years, returned to worship with a church family.

Our group distributed neighborhood flyers with a gospel message and the times of local church services to every doorstep at Christmas and Easter. We also put on a Christian-themed Easter egg hunt at our local park. God was able to take my limited time and use it for His glory right in my own home, just as He did with Priscilla.

Can you make your home available for God's glory?

—DORI CLARK

Endless Suds

So she did as Elijah said, and she and Elijah and her son
continued to eat for many days.
1 KINGS 17:15

When I peeked into the washing machine, the agitator stopped. Sudsy water still covered the laundry. How could that be? I shook the jug of detergent and then unscrewed the lid. It had been months since I had bought laundry detergent, yet the same jug still produced enough to clean our clothes.

For almost a year, my son and I had survived day by day. Friends bought us groceries or left gift cards in the mailbox. Church members helped us through the grief of divorce, but no one thought to replenish the laundry detergent. Yet here it was, still making suds load after load.

Then I remembered the widow of Zarephath and how God had blessed her because she was kind to His prophet, Elijah. Her flour was not used up, nor did her oil run dry. She and her son survived the famine, because God performed a miracle. And in 2004, my son and I survived because God kept us in suds.

God's miracles are the same today as they were centuries ago.

—R. J. THESMAN

The Search for Satisfaction

The woman was convinced. She saw that the tree was beautiful and its fruit looked delicious, and she wanted the wisdom it would give her.
GENESIS 3:6

Eve was a woman who truly had it all. Made in the image of God, she was the perfect woman, born into the perfect world—a paradise where suffering and death were unknown. God gave her the perfect husband and placed them in the perfect home, a garden filled with delicious food, free for the taking. Except for that one tempting tree. When the serpent approached Eve, she knew the fruit was off limits, but she still allowed him to tempt her.

At times my focus is drawn away from the things I have to the few things I still desire: the lovely country home, that snazzy red sports car, a vacation in the Caribbean. I am no different from Eve when I fail to be satisfied with God's gracious provisions.

We must learn to be contented and grateful for God's abundant blessings.

—SUSAN E. RAMSDEN

Making Excuses

But Martha was distracted by the big dinner she was preparing. She came to Jesus and said, "Lord, doesn't it seem unfair to you that my sister just sits here while I do all the work? Tell her to come and help me."
LUKE 10:40

Martha was straightforward and outspoken, a hospitable friend and a hard worker. She was also a perfectionist and a bit of a worrywart. Like anyone, she had her good qualities and her faults. Above all, she considered Jesus a friend. She was comfortable enough to go straight to Him with her questions and concerns.

Sometimes, I find myself thinking up excuses as to why I can't spend more time with Jesus. I'm too busy, or I'm faced with other pressing events or circumstances. I may try to convince myself that I'm serving others, but it's more likely I'm seeking attention and gratification for myself.

Despite these faults, I consider Jesus my best friend. I know I can come to Him with all of my concerns. When I make the time in my busy life to commune with Him, He is always there to listen to my requests, complaints, or worries.

No more excuses—make time for Jesus.

—BETTY KING

Under Scrutiny

But when they conveyed the king's order to Queen Vashti, she refused to come. This made the king furious, and he burned with anger.

ESTHER 1:12

Vashti was the queen in a society that placed a high value on modesty in a woman. When her husband commanded her to appear at his feast so he could parade her beauty before his drunken friends, she refused. It took great courage to disobey her husband, but this was not the act of a willful, rebellious wife. This was a woman determined to maintain her honor and dignity. She was not going to let herself be devalued by anyone or anything.

When I chose to follow Jesus, I also made a decision to adhere to a lifestyle that reflected my faith. When people discover that I'm a Christian, I may come under their scrutiny. If I behave in a way contrary to what the Bible teaches, I run the risk of debasing my faith and my God.

Do your actions bring shame or glory to Jesus?

—SBT

Common Ground

In the meantime, Saul's daughter Michal had fallen in love with David, and Saul was delighted when he heard about it.
1 SAMUEL 18:20

Infatuated with David's looks and his status as a hero, Michal pictured him as the perfect husband based on superficial criteria alone. In the years that followed, it became obvious she never really knew the heart of her husband. Her disillusionment with God grew, but David's passion for the Lord had never been greater. During his triumphant return to Jerusalem with the Ark of God, Michal watched her husband dancing and leading the procession, and she was filled with nothing but disgust. Perhaps she realized that she and David were worlds apart when it came to worship, and maybe they always had been.

Much like Michal, when I was a young woman, I found myself drawn to attractive and popular people. I rarely took the time to find out what was on the inside, so it should have been no surprise when these people failed to fulfill my expectations. It was only when I began to look past appearances and find common ground based on my faith that I began to discover real friendship and true love.

Real relationships start with a mutual love for the Lord.

—SBT

Eliminating Envy

When Rachel saw that she wasn't having any children for Jacob, she became jealous of her sister. She pleaded with Jacob, "Give me children, or I'll die!"
GENESIS 30:1

Envy is like a virulent strain of bacteria, infecting everyone with whom it comes in contact. Jacob and Rachel loved each other very much, but as the years passed, their love was poisoned by Rachel's jealousy over her sister's ability to bear children.

Instead of praying to God for a baby, she pleaded with Jacob and blamed him for her barren condition. Eventually, God gave Rachel a son, but not before envy had taken its toll.

Recently, I visited a woman in a beautiful, custom-built home. The house was impeccably decorated and spotless. Suffering from a bad case of jealousy, I returned to my elderly farmhouse, tripped over my sons' toys, and slumped into a chair that smelled liked a dog.

I was miserable until I recalled that the woman I envied had no children and had told me on numerous occasions how bored she was. It was then I realized that I wouldn't trade my messy, busy house and my precious family for anything.

Conquer envy by counting your blessings.

—SBT

A Wedding and a Miracle

The next day there was a wedding celebration in the village of Cana in Galilee. Jesus' mother was there and Jesus and his disciples were also invited to the celebration.

JOHN 2:1–2

We do not know the bride's name, nor do we know the identity of her groom. We do know that Jesus was an invited guest to their wedding and that He performed his first miracle of turning water into wine during the celebration. As is often the case in a small town, the bride and groom had most likely known each other since childhood.

This past spring my daughter married her high school sweetheart. Like the town of Cana, our hometown witnessed the union of two young people who had grown up together. There was great joy. No wine flowed from the Master's hand, but we did have the involvement of many townspeople and friends of the family. Rhea and Craig were not only blessed by the Lord that day, but also by the presence of beloved family and friends.

Do we invite the Lord in all our preparations?
Is He our treasured guest?

—LaRose Karr

An Amazing Resume

*Look! I am about to cover the earth with a flood
that will destroy every living thing that breathes.
Everything on earth will die.*
GENESIS 6:17

"Preacher's wife: several hundred years farming, 120 years boat-building, one year zookeeping on gigantic houseboat, extensive sailing experience. Skilled in waiting and relocating. Competent and caring wife, mother, and mother-in-law. Free from dependence on creature comforts, worldly concerns, and outside opinions. Strong faith and family ties. Prepared for any emergency. Eyes fixed on God and the world to come."

I love this woman. I don't even know her name, but what a resume!

The most strategic military moves pale in comparison. Noah's wife stepped onto that ark leaving nearly everything and everyone behind, forever. After a harrowing ocean ordeal, her journey ended in a strange, new land. There was no welcoming committee, no friends, and no house waiting for the family. How did she do it? The last sentence of her resume reveals her secret.

Encouraged by her faith, her fortitude, and her focus, I'm proud and humbled to be her descendant. Aren't you?

Don't forget to include God in your resume.

—SANDI BANKS

Making a Stand for God

Go and gather together all the Jews of Susa and fast for me.
Do not eat or drink for three days, night or day. My maids
and I will do the same. And then, though it is against the
law, I will go in to see the king. If I must die, I must die.
ESTHER 4:16

Queen Esther was an orphaned Jewess who married the king of Persia. The plight of the Jews forced her to go before the king without first being summoned, an act that could have lead to her death. First, she asked her cousin Mordecai to order the Jews to fast for her.

The girl who rose from Jewish orphan to Persian queen is a beautiful example of God's handiwork. He brought her from obscure origins to play a vital role in the survival of the Jews in Persia's 127 provinces. Esther saved her people in an amazing act of courage and faith.

While living in Iran as a Christian woman many years ago, challenges to my faith reinforced my spiritual commitment. While I am no modern Esther, I feel that God placed me in Iran as an opportunity to model my beliefs in a sincere and humble way.

Are you prepared to stand for your faith in your home
and community?

—ALEXANDRA ROSE

Making Eye Contact

"Mary!" Jesus said. She turned to him and cried out,
"Rabboni!" (which is Hebrew for "Teacher").
JOHN 20:16

Possessed by seven demons, Mary Magdalene was a tortured, desperate woman, isolated by the disgust and derision of those around her. Only Jesus looked into her eyes and saw the person she was meant to be. Mary's seven demons were no match for the Son of God, and He healed her.

Jesus' last hours found Him deserted by many who had followed Him, but now feared for their lives. Mary's devotion remained steadfast as she heard Pilate condemn Him to death, as she watched Him carry his cross to Calvary and, finally, as she watched Him die. His ravaged body may have repulsed some people, but not Mary. She looked into His eyes and saw her Savior.

I have been guilty of turning away from the tormented and of rendering the unpleasant invisible. My growing love for God has made it possible for me to look into the eyes of suffering and see the value of a life.

Do you walk away from brokenness?

—SBT

True Security

> *He brought part of the money to the apostles, claiming it was
> the full amount. With his wife's consent, he kept the rest.*
> ACTS 5:2

As members of the early church, Saphhira and her husband had pledged to pool all their resources with their fellow believers. However, when they sold some land, they gave only part of the money to the church. Grieved by their dishonesty, God struck them dead.

We'll never know for sure why they felt compelled to withhold some of their profit, or why they lied. Perhaps they still viewed money as the security they needed. They couldn't bring themselves to fully trust the Lord, and instead of asking God and their brothers and sisters in Christ for help to overcome their problem, they chose to lie.

God's abundant blessings have taught me that if I put my trust in Him, He will ensure that my needs are met. When matched with faith, money is powerless.

Real faith provides real security.

—SBT

Never Enough

On the days Elkanah presented his sacrifice, he would give portions of the meat to Peninnah and each of her children.

1 SAMUEL 1:4

Peninnah's entire identity and self-worth were wrapped up in motherhood. In a society where having children was a woman's primary purpose, she had been fortunate enough to have a large family.

But they weren't enough for her. She didn't feel loved by her husband, and that emotional void turned her into a bitter, angry woman. She took out her resentments on an obvious target—Elkanah's first wife, the barren Hannah.

Peninnah's ancient problem is still relevant in our modern society. Many mothers expect children to fill the emotional gaps in their lives and make them feel significant. If we depend on our family for our identity, we could end up like Peninnah, a bottomless pit of "never enough."

Our identity rests with God.

—SUZANNE WOODS FISHER

God Has No Timetable

They had no children because Elizabeth was unable to conceive, and they were both very old.
LUKE 1:7

Years ago, the phone rang in our suburban kitchen. It was my friend Elsie, calling from her farm home. "Would you mind if I stayed with you for a few days?" she asked. "I have appointments for some medical tests to be done in the city."

When she arrived, she explained that she was going to give the specialists one more chance to determine the cause of her infertility. Elsie and her husband desperately wanted children but, in those days, there was little doctors could do to help her conceive.

I was preparing supper several years later when I received another phone call from Elsie. "Guess what?" she exclaimed. "I'm pregnant—can you believe it? Married for twenty-eight years and we're going to have a baby!"

Their blond, blue-eyed boy was born March 17, St. Patrick's Day, and they named him Kelly. Far from being the "luck of the Irish," this child was, indeed, a gift from God.

When we say, "Too late!" God may be saying, "Just wait."

—ALMA BARKMAN

MARCH

Back on God's Path

Deborah, the wife of Lappidoth, was a prophet who was judging Israel at that time. She would sit under the Palm of Deborah, between Ramah and Bethel in the hill country of Ephraim, and the Israelites would go to her for judgment.

JUDGES 4:4–5

I had always wanted to be a doctor. I cared for frightened birds and saved mice from neighborhood cats. My mother, taught to believe that a woman's place was in the home, insisted I should be content as a housewife. To please her, I avoided math and chemistry classes in high school and majored in theology in college.

As the years passed, I grieved through my mother's early death from cancer and celebrated my marriage to a wonderful man and the birth of my precious son. My dream of becoming a doctor never left me and, then, in my mid-forties, my own health issues led me to a wonderful integrative naturopath. As her gentle care healed my body, I realized what I needed to do. I would become an acupuncturist.

Could a middle-aged woman start her life over? I had a master's degree in counseling, but I would have to take math and science before pursuing an acupuncture degree. The enormity of my decision frightened me. It would impact my immediate family and change the life we'd built. I needed help.

I found a source of inspiration in Deborah, one of my favorite women in the Bible. The period of the Judges was a difficult time for the people of Israel. They had strayed far from the path God set for them and experienced the harshness of slavery again and again. Deborah, a prophetess and Israel's only female judge, demonstrated fortitude and fearlessness when the Israelites were forced to serve the Canaanites, under an army commander named Sisera.

Following God's will meant they would have to confront the Canaanites, but Deborah wasn't afraid. Despite the difficulties they would face on the path to freedom, she had complete confidence in the outcome. It was God's path, not hers. When she reminded the Israelite leader, Barak, that God had shown the Israelites a way to freedom, he refused to gather an army and face the Canaanites unless Deborah went with him. Her strength and commitment grounded him and helped him fulfill God's plan.

As I read the account of Deborah, I saw many parallels between the Israelites' predicament and my own. The Israelites had strayed from God's will and become trapped in a lifestyle that required them to obey the Canaanites. In trying to please my mother, I had wandered far from my goal of helping others.

My lack of courage had led me astray, not the fact that Mother and I disagreed about my role as a woman. If I had pursued my dream, God would have showed me how to reassure Mother. Just as my anxiety grew when I commenced the courses I needed to take, Deborah's path to freedom became blocked with her people's increasing fear. I didn't need to wonder what Deborah would do if her obstacles were algebra and the periodic table of elements instead of Canaanite soldiers. I knew she would confront my challenges with the same bravery with which she faced the enemy.

Knowing God was on their side, Deborah told Barak to march against Sisera and his army. Since God had already defeated the Canaanite army, all they had to do was follow His instructions. The outcome was dramatic. Barak and his army defeated the Canaanite army so soundly that Sisera fled the battlefield in panic.

I realized God had prepared my battleground, just as He had gone out before Barak. My conflict was already won. Though I didn't finish the algebra course as easily as Deborah achieved victory for her people, my dream of becoming an acupuncturist became clearer with each assignment I completed. It didn't matter how many classes I needed, or how long they would take, I was moving in the right direction, at last.

Now, whenever an obstacle appears in my life, I think of Deborah. She taught me to move into life's challenges with bravery, and it comforts me to know that her inspiring example is waiting whenever I need it. No matter where life leads me, I have no need to fear. I think my mother would have agreed.

—KRISS ERICKSON

The Real Source of My Strength

Then Hannah prayed: "My heart rejoices in the Lord! The Lord has made me strong."
1 SAMUEL 2:1

The other day, a little boy at church asked me what was wrong with my hands. I wear splints on both hands because arthritis has ravished the joints, especially in my thumbs. I explained that the splints strengthen my hands so I can do everyday activities.

"Does it hurt?" he asked, his eyes full of concern.

My usual answer is, "Only when I do something," but that didn't seem appropriate. "Not too much when I wear these," I replied.

My days seem to be filled with things I can't do. I can't turn the knob to open the door. I can't wring out the washrag. I can't pour the juice if the pitcher is too full. While there are people who are willing and able to help me, I want to continue to do as much as I can myself.

Fortunately, I can still type. It doesn't take strength to type—just perseverance. Hannah gained the strength to wait on God for a son—the great prophet Samuel. Thanks to women like Hannah, I know that my real strength comes from God.

Let the Lord be your source of strength.

—JEAN CAMPION

Lost and Found

*One of them was Lydia from Thyatira, a merchant
of expensive purple cloth, who worshiped God. As
she listened to us, the Lord opened her heart, and she
accepted what Paul was saying.*

ACTS 16:14

Lydia appeared to have it all. She was a successful businesswoman and the mistress of her own household. No doubt, many of her neighbors and friends considered her to be an extremely lucky woman who seemed to have it made—some may have even been a bit envious. Despite all this, a yearning for something more brought her to the river to pray with the other women. The message of salvation she heard from the apostle Paul that day filled the emptiness within her and satisfied her deepest need.

God knew about Lydia's spiritual hunger, and He knows about our longings, too. He can be everything to everyone searching for purpose and meaning in life. All we have to do is open our hearts and ask the Lord to fill our emptiness, banish our hunger, and fulfill each and every one of our needs.

Is something missing in your life?

—SBT

Grateful to Give

Jesus called his disciples to him and said, "I tell you the truth, this poor widow has given more than all the others who are making contributions."
MARK 12:43

Last Sunday, the pastor of our church asked us to contribute to a special offering to help someone in our congregation. Excuses poured into my mind. Our payday was ten days away, and even though I was quite certain we would be all right financially, part of me wanted to refuse his request. What if we needed that money for something important?

When Jesus watched the widow put her last two mites into the offering, he declared that she had given more than anyone else. She didn't worry about the money because she knew God would provide for all her needs.

With a flicker of shame, I recalled the countless times God had blessed us in times of need. Then I smiled and reached for my wallet.

Trust in the Lord and be a cheerful giver.

—SBT

God Supplies

Jericho and everything in it must be completely destroyed as an offering to the Lord. Only Rahab the prostitute and the others in her house will be spared, for she protected our spies.
JOSHUA 6:17

Rahab's request to spare her life and the lives of her family reminds me of my own appeal to God. Even though Rahab was a prostitute and I am a wife and mother, we both sought divine intervention for our families and ourselves.

At the age of twenty-nine, I was diagnosed with multiple sclerosis. I was busy raising four small children, and I knew the disease would have a devastating effect on my life, especially in respect to my family. So I begged God to keep me on my feet until my children were raised. I still had problems, but most were more of an inconvenience to me than to my husband and children.

When my last child got married, I walked down the aisle with the bride's mother to light the unity candle. I used a cane, but I was on my feet. It wasn't until a few years later that an electric wheelchair became a necessity.

Take all your needs to God.

—BETTY KING

Where He Leads Me

Moses accepted the invitation, and he settled there with him. In time, Reuel gave Moses his daughter Zipporah to be his wife.

EXODUS 2:21

My best friend, Kathy, confided to me that she was moving to New York. Her husband had been accepted at Nyack Bible College where he was going to study for the ministry.

She shed tears of frustration as she exclaimed, "A wife is supposed to support her husband wherever God leads, isn't she? But how will we live? I'll have to go to work, and I've never worked at a paying job." I shared her anguish as we prayed together for God's direction and for her submission to His will.

After they were settled in their new community, I received Kathy's excited call. "I have a job! I'm a grocery store cashier. Can you believe it?"

Yes, I could believe it. And it was a job she held until they left Nyack. Our prayers had been answered, and with her fears surrendered, God blessed her with a means to care for her family.

God goes wherever you go.

—IMOGENE JOHNSON

Corporate Christianity

*When Athaliah, the mother of King Ahaziah of
Judah, learned that her son was dead, she began
to destroy the rest of the royal family.*
2 KINGS 11:1

I entered the working world scornful of office politics. "Buttering up people is hypocritical," I said. "My work can stand on its own merit." Over the years, I developed a deeper understanding of corporate life. Office politics can have a negative connotation, but it includes important lessons on how people can work together for the common good.

Treating others with courtesy and respect, even those with difficult personalities, is a smart political move. It's also a wise spiritual move. God uses each one of us, no matter where we happen to work, as His light on Earth. If we backstab or cut down others to get ahead, our morals are no better than those of Queen Athaliah.

How we treat those promoted above us, how we deal with those below us, and how we react to competition all speak more loudly about Christianity than anything we may say about Jesus Christ.

Wherever you work with others, let your faith do the talking.

—PATRICIA MITCHELL

Providing the Path

But now Tamar tore her robe and put ashes on her head.
And then, with her face in her hands, she went away crying.
2 SAMUEL 13:19

Tamar's brutal rape by her half-brother Amnon destroyed her life and left her with little or no hope of ever realizing her dreams. The failure of her full brother Absalom and her father, David, to acknowledge the crime and deal with it in a just manner hindered any chance of recovery she may have had.

Horrible things can and do happen to decent, godly people. Tamar's rape was devastating, but perhaps more damaging was the isolation and lack of support she experienced after the incident. I can only hope that she found comfort in the healing presence of God. Criminal or victim, He will never abandon one of His own or refuse their request for His mercy and grace.

My responsibility is to be there for those who are suffering. I need to acknowledge their pain, to listen and love without judgment, and to lead them to the fresh beginning that only God can provide.

Are you providing a path to God for those who are suffering?

—SBT

Defusing Fear

I am one who is peace loving and faithful in Israel. But you are destroying an important town in Israel. Why do you want to devour what belongs to the Lord?

2 SAMUEL 20:19

Here was a woman who faced a grave predicament with insight and courage. A man named Sheba had rebelled against David and was hiding within the gates of Abel. The armies of Joab and David were prepared to destroy the whole city, but the wise woman negotiated with Joab and saved the inhabitants of her city.

She could have let fear control her response or waited for someone else to solve the problem, but God called her to act and she came forward. Her courage gave birth to the wisdom that allowed her to negotiate for a less violent answer to the crisis.

I have discovered that fear does not come from God, but courage is readily available. I only have to ask. By choosing courage over fear, I enable God to work through me and help me grow. Fear produces nothing but more fear.

Are you ruled by fear?

—SBT

The Real Issue

Coming up behind Jesus, she touched the fringe of his robe.
Immediately, the bleeding stopped.
LUKE 8:44

When I was only thirty-one years old, I injured my back. Three years later, I needed surgery, and for the last fifteen years my back has been temperamental. Sometimes, I wonder why this happened to me at such a young age. It didn't seem fair.

Then I think of the woman who suffered for twelve years with a bleeding disorder. She heard that Jesus was coming, and it was said he performed miracles. She knew in her heart he could help, and her hope grew strong. What if she could just touch him?

Perhaps there were times when she felt it wasn't fair to be ostracized for something that wasn't her fault. Maybe she thought she was too young for such a devastating problem. But when the good news came, she wasted no time in running to the man who could lift her burden. The real issue is that she didn't just need healing. She needed a Savior.

Do you need a Savior?

—LaRose Karr

Who's There?

When she recognized Peter's voice, she was so overjoyed that,
instead of opening the door, she ran back inside and told
everyone, "Peter is standing at the door!"
ACTS 12:14

The Jerusalem believers gathered throughout the night, fervently praying for the imprisoned apostle Peter. A knock at the door surely signaled another member of the early church. Rhoda certainly didn't expect Peter, and when she heard his voice, she was too excited to welcome him inside.

How often do I fail to follow through when God answers my prayers? The difficult boss unexpectedly leaves the company, a spring hailstorm provides a new roof, the rejection letter leads to a new direction, and the child matures from a difficult stage to an easier one. If I had been paying attention, I would have heard God knocking at my door. How many blessings come into my life that I fail to recognize? Yes, God is at the door, but do I even recognize Him?

Welcome God into your life when He knocks at your door.

—SUE LOWELL GALLION

Second Best

There was no sparkle in Leah's eyes, but Rachel had a beautiful figure and a lovely face.
GENESIS 29:17

As I gazed into my daughter's beautiful blue eyes, I decided to name her Leah. Although I had always loved that name, in the weeks preceding her birth, I wondered if it was a good choice.

The Leah of biblical times was always second best. Her plain looks could not compare to the beauty of her younger sister, Rachel. To make matters worse, her father had tricked Jacob into marrying Leah, even though Rachel was Jacob's first choice.

As I read her story, I always imagine how unwanted and unloved Leah must have felt, living in the shadow of her beautiful sister. God saw she was unloved, so he opened her womb and blessed her with sons. At long last, Leah stepped out of Rachel's shadow.

In contrast to the biblical Leah, my Leah knows she is loved, and I'm happy to report that she has always liked her name.

God sees you as worthy of His Son's sacrifice.

—DONNA J. SHEPHERD

Heroes

From the window Sisera's mother looked out.
Through the window she watched for his return,
saying, "Why is his chariot so long in coming?
Why don't we hear the sound of chariot wheels?"
JUDGES 5:28

It was a humanitarian mission in Baghdad. The young medic had a day off, yet he gladly volunteered to man the Humvee's rooftop gun. According to his comrades, moments before the blast, the son of my heart looked skyward, that megawatt grin lighting his face. Had his body not taken the hit, the doctor, seated below, would have died.

I have raged against those who triggered that bomb. Strangely, I have found comfort in reading about Sisera, an enemy of ancient Israel. He had a mother—a mother not very different from me.

I imagine her now: pacing beside the window, rationalizing his delay, picturing his heroism and glorious exploits, and anticipating a joyous reunion. She helped me humanize the enemy by giving them identities—and hearts.

And so I endure while another bereft mother, long dead, helps me to forgive.

For behold, the Lord God made us all.

—LAURIE KLEIN

Guilty Secrets

Many Samaritans from the village believed in Jesus because the woman had said, "He told me everything I ever did!"
JOHN 4:39

There are things I haven't told a soul. Embarrassment, guilt, and lack of opportunity are three of the reasons that have kept me from sharing them with another human being. Occasionally, I find it hard to believe that God knows every detail about me, including those dark moments I have kept hidden.

Yet, His love for me remains undiminished and unconditional. My momentary doubts lose what little power they have when matched with God's promise that nothing can separate me from His love.

Jesus offered the Samaritan woman a priceless gift knowing full well who she was and what she had done. With her dwindling hope restored and her faith ignited, she rushed to tell anyone who would listen what had happened. Tongues that once wagged with gossip about the woman now helped her spread the word that the Messiah had arrived.

You have no secrets from God.

—SBT

Time to Kneel

Her sister, Mary, sat at the Lord's feet,
listening to what he taught.
LUKE 10:39

Mary of Bethany is probably best known as the sister of Martha and Lazarus. The Bible reveals little about Mary's personal life, but brief accounts found in the four gospels speak volumes about her character.

Mary drew her strength from Jesus and could usually be found at His feet, worshiping not only His words, but also His presence. There were no distractions for Mary. When it came to her Lord, everything else remained a distant second.

God knows my day is filled with an endless list of things I have to do. It seems like I just get started on something, and one of my children appears as if by magic, needing my immediate attention. God is well aware of every little thing going on in my life, but He also knows I could find time to put the world aside and kneel at my Lord's feet, just as Mary did.

Do you take time each day to kneel at the feet of Jesus?

—SBT

A Family Treasure

But Ruth replied, "Don't ask me to leave you and turn back. Wherever you go, I will go; wherever you live, I will live. Your people will be my people, and your God will be my God."
RUTH 1:16

My son Dylan's girlfriend is a treasure. Bobbijo has always been a joy to have around, and it wasn't long before we thought of her as another precious member of our family.

I felt a bond with Bobbijo the first time we met, and I know she felt it, too. As time passed, the affection and respect we had for each other grew. On Valentine's Day, she gave me a card, and the words she had written inside brought tears to my eyes: "I love you as if you were my own mother. I will always love you, and when I'm not with you, I think about how much I care for you."

When Naomi's son married Ruth, Naomi had no idea of all the blessings that lay ahead—blessings that would blossom from Ruth's devotion to her beloved mother-in-law. I don't know what the future holds for Dylan and Bobbijo, but I do know that whatever happens, I will always have a loving daughter named Bobbijo.

As our families grow, so does our joy!

—SBT

The One Who Lifts Me Up

One Sabbath day as Jesus was teaching in a synagogue, he saw a woman who had been crippled by an evil spirit. She had been bent double for eighteen years and was unable to stand up straight.
LUKE 13:10–11

After a week of agonizing back pain, I consulted a massage therapist who told me it wasn't really a back problem at all. Slumping had weakened my abdominal muscles, and they were no longer helping my back hold me erect. I hadn't even realized my posture had deteriorated until she stood me in front of a mirror to demonstrate. She recommended that I commit to daily stretching exercises, gradually increasing in intensity, so that I could regain my strength.

The nameless woman in Luke hadn't been crippled by an injury or a disease, but by an evil spirit. I can be incapacitated by an attitude that keeps me looking down at my circumstances, rather than up at the Living God.

Like my gradual slumping, before I'm even aware of what's happening, I can find myself without the strength to look up. I must stretch my faith muscles daily and look up to the One who strengthens me.

Look up to God, the true source of your strength.

—LINDA DARBY HUGHES

God's Unending Supply

*"But now a creditor has come threatening to take my two
sons as slaves." "What can I do to help you?" Elisha asked.
"Tell me, what do you have in the house?"
"Nothing at all, except a flask of olive oil," she replied.*
2 KINGS 4:1–2

When he became unable to work, my young husband
had no health insurance. That meant our family of six
had to live on my small income. His monthly medications
alone cost more than twice what I earned. We had four
children to shelter, feed, and clothe. No matter how we
figured it out on paper, it was clear we weren't going to
survive financially. But we did make it—through God's
unending supply.

At first we panicked, but God found the most unusual
ways to supply our needs. It all happened one day at a time.
Doctors gave us samples of medications, friends brought
groceries, strangers left money for clothes, and someone
even made it possible for us to go on a family vacation.

Our needs were met, seemingly out of nowhere. We
learned to trust God to provide whatever was needed for
that day. The spiritual principles I learned from our experience remain with me to this day.

God will provide all of your needs for today.

—EVA JULIUSON

Small Things with Great Love

There was a believer in Joppa named Tabitha (which in Greek is Dorcas). She was always doing kind things for others and helping the poor.
ACTS 9:36

In the days of the early church, many of the families of Joppa depended on the sea for their living. Sometimes, fishermen lost their lives during winter storms, leaving their widows and children destitute. A widowed disciple named Dorcas, known for her good deeds and generosity, had compassion for these poor families. Skilled as a seamstress, she decided to make cloaks, robes, and tunics for those stricken by poverty.

I can only imagine her joy when she saw how her friends' spirits brightened when they received her brand-new garments. In addition to humble gratitude, they must have experienced renewed self-esteem and hope for a brighter future because of the great love this dear woman demonstrated.

My friend Penny makes dolls with her church group for impoverished orphans in India. She is a modern-day Dorcas, glorifying the Lord as she quietly provides comfort and delight to His children through this generous and practical act of love.

As Mother Teresa said, "In this life we cannot do great things; we can only do small things with great love."

—SUSAN E. RAMSDEN

The Invisible Women

So don't be afraid; you are more valuable to God than a whole flock of sparrows.
LUKE 12:7

My mother often spoke of growing up during the Great Depression. "Sometimes I felt invisible," she said. My mother was one of ten children, and I can well imagine how difficult that must have been.

I am reminded of King David's daughters—women whose names are not even recorded. Surrounded by so many siblings, most of whom were powerful men, I'm sure they sometimes felt invisible. Yet, we know they were privileged daughters of a great king. There was no denying their royal lineage.

Occasionally, I feel invisible and unimportant. Then I remember that I am the daughter of a king. Although, I might be invisible to the world, I am of a royal lineage.

Are you resting in the assurance that your heavenly father knows you by name?

—MARY CATHERINE ROGERS

The Eye-Opener

Then God opened Hagar's eyes, and she saw a
well full of water. She quickly filled her water
container and gave the boy a drink.
GENESIS 21:19

Abraham wasn't happy about it, but Sarah insisted and God agreed—it was time for Hagar and Ishmael to leave. So Abraham gave them food and water and sent them away, and they wandered in the desert until their water ran out.

Sobbing uncontrollably, Hagar left Ishmael in the shade of a bush and collapsed. The Angel of the Lord appeared and promised Hagar that Ishmael would be a great nation. Then he directed her to a well of life-giving water.

Although I accepted Jesus as my Savior when I was in elementary school, it wasn't until six years ago that I truly dedicated my life to Christ. I can't do anything about the years I struggled without purpose or meaning, but when I was ready, God opened my eyes. Like Hagar, I found the well of life-giving water. It had been there all along.

Open your eyes and find your salvation.

—SBT

Made for Each Other

Then the Lord God said, "It is not good for the man to be alone. I will make a helper who is just right for him."
GENESIS 2:18

One of my most vivid memories of childhood is my mother and father washing the dinner dishes together every night. I can still see them standing in front of the sink, my mother's hands immersed in the soapy water, my father turned slightly to face her as he methodically wiped each dish.

If I passed the kitchen or played nearby, I could hear them talking. Their conversation was sometimes animated, sometimes hushed and murmuring, but it was a comforting sound that left me feeling all was right in my little world.

When I read about God creating Eve—the perfect helper for Adam—I always think of my parents. My father grew up as a loner, a solitary man with solitary pursuits, but God arranged for him to meet my mother. Despite the differences in their personalities, God knew they would make a perfect match.

God provides the necessities of life, but He also blesses us with the needs of our heart.

—SBT

God Is Committed

His wife said to him, "Are you still trying to maintain your integrity? Curse God and die."
JOB 2:9

When Job, the richest man in his area, was beset by Satan's trials, he suffered in body and soul, losing children, servants, and herds that provided income. Instead of blaming God, he held fast to his faith. After finding him covered in boils from head to foot, his wife urged him to give up on God and life. Job refused and did not sin.

In grief and despair over their shared plight, Job's wife lost sight of God's plan and providence. She couldn't understand Job's integrity and admonished him to give up. She was a destroyer, not a builder, of faith.

There have been times when I could hardly watch others' suffering. Privately, I wondered why they stayed faithful to God and renewed their hope in His promises. Now, instead of questioning, I remind myself to thank God for their commitment to Him—a devotion that inspires those around them, including me.

Encourage someone overwhelmed by her burdens.

—ALEXANDRA ROSE

The Faith of a Captured Child

One day the girl said to her mistress,
"I wish my master would go to see the prophet in Samaria.
He would heal him of his leprosy."
2 KINGS 5:3

When I read the Old Testament account of Naaman, I can't help but wonder what would have happened to the tender faith of my children if they had been snatched from all things familiar when they were very young.

Naaman, the captain of the army of the king of Aram, was a highly respected and valiant warrior. He also suffered from leprosy. When his army captured a little girl from Israel, the unnamed child became his wife's servant. The girl remembered and believed her mother's teachings, and she found the courage to share her faith with her new mistress.

The king also believed the child and sent Naaman to the prophet Elisha whose servants would not allow Naaman inside.

Instead, they told him to take a bath in the Jordan River seven times. Outraged, Naaman left and his own servants convinced him to try the bath. Coming out of the river, his flesh restored, Naaman proclaimed his newfound belief in God to everyone present.

Do your children take their faith wherever they go?

—LIZ HOYT EBERLE

His Faithful Workers

*Give my greetings to Tryphena and Tryphosa,
the Lord's workers, and to dear Persis, who has
worked so hard for the Lord.*
ROMANS 16:12

As a newspaper reporter, I've met many remarkable women. In her seventies, Doris is the church greeter, rain or shine. "I've lived here all my life," she told me. "I was married in this church and raised my kids here."

Marvel, eighty, plays the piano for two congregations on Sunday. "Fifteen years ago," she said, "I volunteered to fill in until they found someone. I've been playing ever since."

Betty started playing the church organ in 1950 at the age of seventeen. Today, she plays the same pipe organ in the same historical church. Her fingers are still nimble, and the congregation is blessed by her music.

Myrtle learned to play the piano as a child and became a teacher in her teens. She played for her church until her eyesight failed. At eighty-eight, she still transposes music for a local musical group.

Opal, ninety, has been married for seventy-two years. She still drives her crippled niece to the nursing home where the two present felt board stories. Like Tryphena and Tryphosa, they've worked hard for the Lord and will soon be welcomed into His presence.

Applaud the faithful workers in His service.

—KATHERINE J. CRAWFORD

Gale-Force Love

When Sarah was 127 years old, she died at Kiriath-arba
(now called Hebron) in the land of Canaan. There
Abraham mourned and wept for her.
GENESIS 23:1–2

Assuming Sarah married at the approximate age of fifteen, by the time she died, she and Abraham had been husband and wife for 112 years. We live in a society where golden and diamond anniversaries are remarkable, making Sarah and Abraham's accomplishment truly amazing.

Abraham grieved deeply when she died and went to great lengths to purchase land so he and Sarah could be buried in the same place. Their profound commitment is a moving testament to the power of human love.

It's difficult to imagine a love more devoted and long-lived than the one between Abraham and Sarah, but their feelings for each other were a breath of air when compared to the hurricane of God's love—an unconditional, unchanging love that defies mortal description. May God's love rule our marriages for the long term as well.

God is love.

—SBT

It's All Part of the Plan

If you keep quiet at a time like this, deliverance and relief
for the Jews will arise from some other place, but you and
your relatives will die. Who knows if perhaps you were made
queen for just such a time as this?

ESTHER 4:14

When Mordecai first told Esther of Haman's plot to destroy the Jews, she reminded Mordecai that anyone who approached the king without an invitation risked being put to death. Mordecai brushed her hesitation aside and appealed to her faith.

With Mordecai's encouragement, Esther became determined to save her people even if it meant her own death. She no longer saw herself as a beautiful girl who just happened to become queen, but one of God's children and part of His great plan.

There was a time when I believed in coincidence, when I saw my life as a random series of events. Now I know that just as God placed Esther in a position of power for a reason, He has ordered my life for His specific purpose.

Confusion and even shame about things I've done have been replaced by the understanding that God has brought me through it all to be right here, right now.

Nothing in your life happens by chance.

—SBT

The Gutsy Hostess

But when Sisera fell asleep from exhaustion, Jael quietly crept up to him with a hammer and tent peg in her hand. Then she drove the tent peg through his temple and into the ground, and so he died.

JUDGES 4:21

When my husband and I began fighting for religious freedom in France, it was scary. Speaking out against discrimination put our lives in potential jeopardy. Perhaps our efforts would backfire, and we would antagonize the sleeping giant who might retaliate. Somehow, I knew we should stay the course we had chosen, no matter what it might cost us.

Jael exemplifies a willingness to take chances to conquer evil. She dared to bring the escaping enemy, Sisera, into her tent, wait until he slept, and take a peg and hammer to kill him—even though he could easily have woken up and killed her first. Or, she could have misjudged her strength and failed. The danger was enormous, but she felt compelled to do what was right despite the risk.

When we take risks to do what is right,
our courage pleases God.

—JANEY L. DEMEO

103

MARCH 28

Where Is My Security?

*But because the midwives feared God, they refused to obey
the king's orders. They allowed the boys to live, too.*
EXODUS 1:17

I had a decision to make. I had a good job with good
pay and promising prospects, but I knew God was calling
me to make a tremendous leap of faith. He wanted me to
step into His purpose for me as a full-time writer. Did I
trust Him enough to leave my security?

I looked to the Hebrew midwives, Shiphrah and Puah.
They had been called by God to bring new life into the
world, but their personal security was based on obey-
ing the orders of the pharaoh. Because they feared God,
they continued to walk in their calling, delivering every
Hebrew baby, despite the pharaoh's command to kill all
male Hebrew newborns.

I had my answer. I trusted God with my own security, and I knew my obedience would give birth to greater
blessings for my family and my readers' lives.

Your security rests in the Lord.

—LESLIE J. SHERROD

The Notebook of Joy

Then she lived as a widow to the age of eighty-four.
She never left the Temple but stayed there day and night,
worshiping God with fasting and prayer.
LUKE 2:37

Unlike Anna, my grandmother didn't move into the temple when my grandfather died in 1945, but she seldom missed church and she prayed daily. She would often show me the spiral-bound notebooks in which she faithfully wrote her prayer requests. She also recorded the victorious answers to her many petitions. "Don't stop praying for your father," she said the last time I saw her alive. "I've been praying for his salvation for years."

The day Grandma died, my sixty-nine-year-old father accepted Jesus as his Savior. She never got the chance to write the joyful answer to one of her most fervent prayers in her spiral notebook, but I rejoiced when I pictured her seeing my father in heaven someday.

Write down your requests and keep your pen handy—
God answers prayers.

—KATHERINE J. CRAWFORD

Fierce and Formidable

So David obtained the bones of Saul and Jonathan, as well as the bones of the men the Gibeonites had executed.

2 SAMUEL 21:13

In an attempt to appease the Gibeonites, King David allowed seven of Saul's sons to be executed. Rizpah couldn't prevent the death of her two sons by Saul, but afterward, she took sackcloth to the mountain where the bodies lay exposed to the elements and covered them. Then, day and night for six long months, she protected the bodies from predators.

When David heard about Rizpah's vigil, he was deeply touched by her devotion, commitment, and courage. This time, he was moved to an act of mercy. He ordered the bodies removed from the mountain and arranged for a proper burial.

Rizpah lost any power she might have had when Saul died, but that didn't stop her from publicly grieving and giving her sons what little honor she could. It doesn't sound like much, but it changed the heart of a king.

At times, I may feel limited by circumstances or lack of influence, but that shouldn't prevent me from doing what I can to effect a change in an unacceptable situation.

Never underestimate yourself.

—SBT

Healing a Heartache

*Zechariah and Elizabeth were righteous in
God's eyes, careful to obey all of the Lord's
commandments and regulations.*
LUKE 1:6

Like most people, I've experienced my share of disappointments. Following the birth of my youngest son, I suffered several miscarriages, and I couldn't help but wonder why God allowed them to happen.

Instead of sinking into self-pity, wondering what might have been, I turned to my husband and God. It was my husband's love that kept me going, and God's love that opened my eyes to the multitude of blessings He had already bestowed upon me.

Elizabeth was no stranger to the pain of disappointment. Her husband, Zechariah, must have loved her very much. He could have divorced her because she was barren, but he didn't, and I suspect she often turned to him for the comfort she needed. And, of course, she sought the solace and love of her God who eventually provided her with the ultimate consolation—a son!

Turn to God for His healing love.

—SBT

APRIL

Guided by the Finger of God

*If you keep quiet at a time like this, deliverance and relief
for the Jews will arise from some other place, but you and
your relatives will die. Who knows if perhaps you were made
queen for just such a time as this?*

ESTHER 4:14

he year was 1939, and an old country doctor had all but dashed the hopes of an expectant mother. "I cannot find your baby's heartbeat, so be prepared for a stillborn child. And because of severe complications with your other two deliveries, I'm going to attempt a cesarean section, but the outcome is very uncertain." Despite the doctor's dire predictions, the young mother survived the surgery and delivered a healthy baby girl.

At precisely the same time, several hundred miles away, another rural mother had been laboring in prayer for the soul of her youngest son. Her prayers were answered when he was delivered at age fourteen of his stubborn resistance and began a new life as part of the family of God.

Neither the baby girl nor the teenage boy would have met without the finger of God moving in the background. How do I know? I was that little girl.

Without God's intervention, the chance of our paths crossing would have been extremely remote at best, but He makes all things possible. Perhaps that is why the unlikely story of Esther resonates with my own.

Esther is the only book of the Bible in which the name of God is not mentioned. It is the intriguing story of a Jewish orphan girl with refugee roots who is raised by her cousin Mordecai. Despite the fact she is young, poor, and from a different ethnic, religious, and cultural group, the king of Persia chooses her to replace his deposed queen Vashti.

Eventually, Esther risks her life by using her favored position in the royal household to prevent the slaughter of her people. It is a dramatic example of how God fulfills his purposes through the far-reaching plans He has for each person who is committed to Him.

The teenage boy I mentioned earlier, the young man who had responded to God as a result of his mother's prayers, continued to grow in his Christian faith. He attended Bible college and became a teacher. As the years passed, his mother became anxious for him to marry and establish a home of his own. Concerned that he seldom dated, one day she exclaimed in exasperation, "Is there no girl who will have you?"

"I will marry when I find the right one," he replied.

In the meantime, I was enjoying my childhood, admiring my older brother, and, at times, envying the attention my pretty, dark-haired sister received. Six years my senior, she had become a stubborn, independent teenager who challenged authority at every level. Nobody was going to tell her what to do or whom to date, including our father. Frequently grounded for disobedience, she eloped the day she turned eighteen.

Much like the king of Persia after he had banished his first queen for insubordination, my father's anger gradually subsided, but he seemed to regret the authoritarian discipline he had inflicted. Unfortunately, it was too late. Having suffered the consequences of being too strict with my sister, he cautiously offered me wider latitude when it came to making choices.

At age fourteen—"going on twenty"—I was handling the farm machinery with the ability of an adult. Shouldering such responsibility and acquiring good grades in school had earned me the respect and admiration of the local community. I wanted to maintain that reputation by making wise choices.

Observing the pain my older sister had brought upon herself, I had secretly decided early in my life that I would live by a higher moral code. Believing in a Creator God from the time I was a toddler, I knew in my heart of hearts that Someone had made the colorful birds, the shady trees, the dainty flowers, the cattle that grazed down in the pasture, the fluffy clouds overhead, and the stars in the velvet sky.

I wasn't completely aware of it at the time, but I realize now it was that Someone who had equipped me with a moral compass. Although my father did not believe in God, he respected the Christian lifestyle that I had chosen to live.

The day came when a young man with values similar to mine drove into town in his 1946 Chevy to become the principal of the high school I attended. He had not applied for the position and felt woefully inadequate. The minister of education had prevailed upon him, however, and the relatively inexperienced teacher had reluctantly agreed to accept the job.

As the months went by, not only were his transparent Christian convictions and lifestyle attractive to me, but I was also "finding favor and kindness with him" more than the other girls. Like Esther, though, I had not yet made known to him "my kindred or my people," for fear of the consequences. I was too young, too poor, and from a nonreligious background. I knew my father would never agree.

From my point of view, there were far too many obstacles standing in the way of a possible relationship to even daydream about it. But not from God's perspective. He had planned all along that the baby girl born at the same time as the teacher was born again would one day meet.

On a beautiful spring day, that teacher asked me for a date. I stood in front of my father to ask permission, and like Esther when she fearfully approached the king, I "obtained favor in his sight." He granted my request. I was stunned, elated, fearful, disbelieving, and honored—all at the same time.

This year, surrounded by four children and nine grandchildren, we will celebrate fifty years of marriage. More than five decades ago, when I joined my future husband in becoming part of the family of God, I didn't realize the unique position of a Christian mother, nor the courage required to take a stand at pivotal points of parenting. At those times God's word reminded me that, as one of His children, a daughter of the King of Kings, I had access through prayer to rich spiritual resources.

"Who knows whether you have not attained royalty for such a time as this?" (Esther 4:14). Mordecai's profound question gave me the courage to humbly approach God's throne of grace on behalf of our family. They have been spared much pain because of His mercy, and I have been accorded much pleasure in the plan God had for me.

—ALMA BARKMAN

My Need, God's Purpose

And she made this vow: "O Lord of Heaven's Armies, if you will look upon my sorrow and answer my prayer and give me a son, then I will give him back to you. He will be yours for his entire lifetime."

1 SAMUEL 1:11

During our difficult transition from the mission field to America, I felt as if my life was in complete disarray. Everyone around us had decent paychecks, houses, cars, and college funds. We had nothing. I needed to trust that God would provide for us as He always had. I decided to seek His will for my situation—just as Hannah did.

Hannah was barren and desperate for a child. Then, one day, her focus shifted. I believe she finally understood the true reason for her need—to acknowledge God's desire. She longed to be a mother, and God needed a man to represent Him and teach His Word.

Hannah's epiphany resulted in her vow to dedicate her child to God's service, and it wasn't long before she was cradling her new son. Others may seem to have more, but if I focus on God, He will fulfill my needs in accordance with His perfect plan.

Your needs are God's opportunity to demonstrate His will for you.

—JANEY L. DEMEO

If Only

*When the child's nurse heard the news, she picked him
[Mephibosheth] up and fled. But as she hurried away, she
dropped him, and he became crippled.*

2 SAMUEL 4:4

When Mephibosheth was five, the Philistines invaded
Israel. His father, Jonathan, went into battle and left his
son with a nurse. Soon, the nurse heard that Jonathan
was dead and the battle had been lost. She took the boy
and fled, but she dropped him. The fall caused a lifelong
injury to his feet.

The Bible doesn't tell us how this accident influenced
the nurse, but I know how my negative past has affected
me. It has a way of coming back to haunt and condemn
me. When I was sixteen, I vowed I would never speak to
my friend LaVonne again because she "stole" my boyfriend.
She moved away, and I never saw her again. Why didn't I
send her an apology? Why didn't I make an effort to renew
our friendship?

Did Mephibosheth's nurse also spend the remainder of
her life filled with regret? We can't reverse past mistakes,
but we can, with God's help, put our past behind us.

Because Christ has forgiven us, we can forgive ourselves.

—JEWELL JOHNSON

Deborah Understood

Then Deborah said to Barak, "Get ready! This is the day the Lord will give you victory over Sisera, for the Lord is marching ahead of you." So Barak led his 10,000 warriors down the slopes of Mount Tabor into battle.

JUDGES 4:14

Several years ago when my daughter graduated from high school, I gave each of her friends a journal at graduation. In one I wrote, "I can't wait to see what you will become! Remember Deborah!"

The Bible describes Deborah as a prophet and a judge, but that was only the beginning for a woman who refused to be ruled by fear. I've seen people paralyzed so much by apprehension that they miss important things in life. They fail to notice a sunset just around the bend, or a friendship that may have been dear to them if only they would have opened their heart.

If your heart is faint, or fear grips your life, turn those hindrances over to God. He willingly takes on all our cares. Deborah predicted victory when her army of 10,000 soldiers went into battle. She was able to do this because she knew God had gone ahead and prepared the way.

Ask the Lord to prepare a path for you today.

—LaRose Karr

Precious Time

"Take this baby and nurse him for me," the princess told the baby's mother. "I will pay you for your help." So the woman took her baby home and nursed him.
EXODUS 2:9

When Jochebed put her son in a basket and set him adrift on the River Nile, she trusted God to keep the baby safe. Her faith was rewarded when, in a miraculous turn of events, she found herself serving as a wet nurse for her own child.

Jochebed wasn't given much time, but she made it count. She raised her son for God until he was weaned and went back to Pharaoh's daughter. In approximately three short years, Jochebed instilled in him the values he would need in the years to come as his people's leader.

Some people might claim that three years isn't enough time to accomplish such an important job, but the truth is that none of us knows how much time we have. We say that time is precious, but then we wish the day away at work and come home to a host of frivolous, meaningless activities. I think the time has come for us to match our words with our actions.

Do you treat time as a priceless gift?

—SBT

117

Spiritual Separation

Saul then said to his advisers, "Find a woman who is a medium, so I can go and ask her what to do." His advisers replied, "There is a medium at Endor."
1 SAMUEL 28:7

When Saul chose to disregard God's command regarding the Amalekites, he had no way of knowing how dearly he would pay for his decision. Faced with the vast and powerful Philistine army, he cried out in vain for God's help. Desperate for answers and frantic with fear, he finally consulted a medium.

Fear and desperation can be powerful and destructive forces. They can cloud your mind, and make you feel distanced from God. As in Saul's case, the actions that result from these feelings often make things worse and only serve to exacerbate the sense of spiritual isolation.

The only way to combat fear is with trust, and the best way to restore your fellowship with God is to seek forgiveness for any sins you may have committed and then promise to trust and obey Him to the best of your ability.

God has the answers you need.

—SBT

Passing the Blame

Then the Lord God asked the woman,
"What have you done?" "The serpent deceived me,"
she replied. "That's why I ate it {the fruit}."
GENESIS 3:13

It's easy to blame Eve, and perhaps we all have. Yet, this passage reminds us of our own sinful nature and the need for total honesty in our communication with God.

Eve stood before the Almighty and passed the blame for her sin to the serpent. How presumptuous, we might think. But upon reflection, haven't I done the same thing during prayer? I've had the audacity to blame others for my shortfalls. "My husband is hard to live with, so I have a right to be grouchy. My kids' lack of appreciation drives me to overeat."

A Christian woman must be accountable for her behavior without pointing the finger at others. I am learning to accept responsibility for my sins in a quest for spiritual growth.

Passing the blame for your sins damages
your fellowship with God.

—ALEXANDRA ROSE

Relentless in Your Need

*A gentile woman who lived there came to him, pleading,
"Have mercy on me, O Lord, Son of David! For my daughter
is possessed by a demon that torments her severely."*
MATTHEW 15:22

My German shorthaired pointer, Freckles, is the poster dog for persistence. Typical of the breed, he desires constant contact with his humans, and he must be able to see one of us at all times. He is also young and energetic and wants to fetch, swim, or run as often as possible.

He may be only a dog, but he has no trouble communicating his desires to us. He nudges, whines, and displays sad eyes until we give him what he wants, which is usually attention—that is, if he's already been fed. He never gives up.

Just as Freckles won't let us brush him off, the gentile woman whose daughter was possessed by a demon wouldn't let Christ dismiss her request. She was clear and unrelenting in what she wanted from Jesus, and she got it!

Be persistent in your prayers.

—KIM SHEARD

A Daughter of the King

But when Jacob woke up in the morning—it was Leah!
"What have you done to me?" Jacob raged at Laban.
"I worked seven years for Rachel! Why have you tricked me?"
GENESIS 29:25

After working for his future father-in-law, Laban, to marry Rachel, Jacob celebrated his wedding, but awakened the next morning beside Leah, Rachel's older sister. Laban smoothed things over by allowing Jacob to marry Rachel a week later.

Imagine Leah's chagrin at being used as her father's pawn in tricking Jacob. After having a husband for just a week, she had to share him with a younger, beautiful, and more beloved wife. And yet, her union with Jacob produced the majority of the twelve tribes of Israel.

When someone else receives honor or praise, I feel as though I will never measure up. I worry that I will never be good enough, that I will always be second best. Then I remember that God has already made me good enough. With Him, there is no second best. I am a daughter of the King.

When you feel second best, remember the ways in which
God has made you special.

—ALEXANDRA ROSE

Dancing Days

*Then Miriam the prophet, Aaron's sister, took a
tambourine and led all the women as they played
their tambourines and danced.*
EXODUS 15:20

"I have great news," my husband said as he walked
through the front door. He took a deep breath and reached
out to take my hands. "The insurance company called,
and we're going to get the full replacement value on the
house and all of the contents."

Still holding hands, we started jumping up and down,
dancing and singing around the house we had rented
after fire destroyed our home. Over the past six months,
we had prayed endlessly for financial stability and release
from the grief of losing all of our belongings. This news
was our deliverance!

Our celebration brought the kids running to see what
was going on. We told them the wonderful news, and it
wasn't long before we were all dancing and singing praises
to God.

Discover the joy in dancing and singing praises for the Lord.

—CARA STOCK

Someone Is Waiting

But when she told them that Jesus was alive and she had seen him, they didn't believe her.
MARK 16:11

I can see Mary running through the streets of Galilee to share the news. Jesus was alive! After everything He had done for her, she couldn't wait to tell the world. She went to those mourning His death, no doubt anticipating their joyous reaction. Instead, her words were met with disbelief.

When I first became a Christian and became aware of everything Jesus had done for me, I was in awe. Full of gratitude and excitement, I tried to tell everyone. "Jesus isn't dead. He's alive, and He wants to bring life to you!" I was surprised when many didn't believe me. In fact, some rejected and ridiculed me.

At first I was hurt but, then, I understood that many people would never accept the gospel message. I couldn't afford to take it personally. My job was simply to keep sharing my good news with Mary-like enthusiasm. Someone, somewhere, was ready to believe.

Share the good news of Jesus—you never know whom God has prepared to listen.

—RENEE GRAY-WILBURN

Faith in Action

She was baptized along with other members of her household, and she asked us to be her guests. "If you agree that I am a true believer in the Lord," she said, "come and stay at my home." And she urged us until we agreed.

ACTS 16:15

After hearing the apostle Paul's message, Lydia enthusiastically embraced the gospel of Jesus Christ. She and her entire household were baptized that day, and she wasted no time in putting her words into actions and proving her commitment to the Lord. She invited Paul and his followers to her home, and even after the men were imprisoned and beaten, she continued to offer them her hospitality.

The woman who cleans our church had surgery recently, and our pastor asked for a volunteer to take her place while she convalesced. My hands remained in my lap, and I stared at the floor. It wasn't the work I was trying to avoid, but I found myself reluctant to disrupt my routine—to step out of my comfort zone. Then I remembered that giving thanks to God involves so much more than mere words, and I raised my hand.

What can you do to demonstrate your faith?

—SBT

Faith Insurance

Mary stayed with Elizabeth about three months and then went back to her own home.
LUKE 1:56

It's no secret that God wants His believers in church. The main reason, of course, is to worship, but there's another very important purpose: for meeting with our Christian brothers and sisters.

The camaraderie I find at church lets me know I'm not alone. My church family rejoices with me when I share my triumphs, and they provide much-needed support when I find myself struggling. The fellowship at church nurtures and safeguards my fellowship with God.

Mary and Elizabeth knew the importance of companionship. Connected by family and faith, they also shared the joy of experiencing the miracle of pregnancy. No doubt, much of the time they spent together was filled with worship and praise.

I'm quite certain they also spent hours sharing their hopes, dreams, and fears. And there was lots of time to talk about babies, just as pregnant women have done since the beginning of time.

Protect your faith by spending time with believers.

—SBT

Special Delivery

Then Queen Esther, the daughter of Abihail, along with Mordecai the Jew, wrote another letter putting the queen's full authority behind Mordecai's letter to establish the Festival of Purim.

ESTHER 9:29

After Queen Esther and her cousin Mordecai were successful in overturning Haman's evil plot to annihilate the Jews, she authorized a decree creating the Festival of Purim. She didn't want her people to forget that, once again, the Jewish race had been preserved by an act of divine deliverance. The Festival of Purim, a two-day period of celebration and remembrance, is still observed by Jews all over the world.

Six years ago, my son Gabriel returned to Canada to live with his biological father. Six long months later, God delivered me from the anguish of worry when Gabriel stepped off the airplane and back into my life. When He sent His son to die on the cross, He delivered me from my sins—for all time.

Esther was right. I must never forget what God has done for me. My remembrance honors God, but it also reminds me that there is always hope.

Remember a time when God delivered you.

—SBT

Handle with Care

Meanwhile, a Jew named Apollos, an eloquent speaker who knew the Scriptures well, had arrived in Ephesus from Alexandria in Egypt.

ACTS 18:24

Priscilla and her husband, Aquila, were great supporters of the apostle Paul's ministry. However, it was their encounter with Apollos that spoke so eloquently of their spiritual maturity and sensitivity toward less-experienced believers.

Apollos spoke passionately about the message John the Baptist had brought, but his presentation of the gospel was limited. Priscilla and Aquila took him aside and quietly explained the coming of the Messiah more accurately. Apollos became a gifted preacher and eventually traveled to Corinth to advance the work Paul had begun there.

Imagine if Priscilla and Aquila had corrected Apollos publicly and crushed his blossoming spirit and eager new faith. How many people would have missed his message?

I returned to church six years ago with some misguided ideas, and I'm certainly glad no one patronized me or made me feel foolish. I may have found it very difficult to remain, but these believers accepted me for who I was and helped me to grow.

Handle new believers with tender, loving care.

—SBT

Before and After

*Rahab the prostitute is another example. She was shown
to be right with God by her actions when she hid those
messengers and sent them safely away by a different road.*
JAMES 2:25

Home, financial security, culture, possessions—Rahab left it all behind to serve Israel's God. Scripture presents her in a vivid before-and-after scenario and leaves no doubt that she's another "Exhibit A" for faith. Then there's her gene pool. Ultimately, this bad girl of the Bible figured into the lineage of Jesus! First, though, she had to live through culture shock: bewilderment, fear, frustration, and shame.

I know those feelings. I left everything for mission work in rural Thailand. I am obviously Nordic, so blending in was impossible. Frequent laughter at my expense rankled my pride and hurt my feelings. I bemoaned the strange foods and customs, the difficult weather, and language, not to mention the plumbing.

Cranky as I was, God helped me to forgive myself. Then He graciously worked through me, anyway. Now, I have Asian "spiritual siblings." Rahab, too, must have marveled, "Who would have thought God could use the likes of me?"

God loves to extend the family tree.

—LAURIE KLEIN

Let Go and Let God

But Mary kept all these things in her heart and thought about them often.

LUKE 2:19

The angel Gabriel told Mary that the child she carried had a special mission and, yet, she raised him in the same way any caring, devoted mother would today. She educated him, took him to the temple, and watched him grow to manhood. Then she let go.

The angel didn't grant Mary a vision of the future, nor did she have an uncanny sense of her child's destiny. So how did she know when to let go? How can we know? One thing we can do is follow Mary's example of taking everything to the Lord in prayer, keeping His wisdom in our heart, and giving the matter a great deal of thought.

When Jesus left home to begin His ministry, Mary had the same concerns we have when our children strike out on their own. Even though her son was the Messiah, she dealt with her worries and fears just as we do. She placed her child in God's hands and prayed.

Let go and let God fulfill His plan for your child's life.

—KATHERINE J. CRAWFORD

Common Ground

Now I appeal to Euodia and Syntyche. Please, because you belong to the Lord, settle your disagreement.

PHILIPPIANS 4:2

It's been said that if Mom isn't happy, nobody in the family is happy. While I've witnessed the truth of this statement in my own home, I would like to add that discontent amongst any family members can be more infectious than any flu bug. A minor skirmish between two of my children can quickly erupt into a full-scale war with other siblings choosing sides. Before I know it, the entire household is in upheaval.

The Apostle Paul was well aware of this principle as he struggled to provide strength and leadership to the early church. We don't know what happened to cause the disagreement and subsequent rift between Euodia and Syntyche, but Paul knew their division could spread quickly, potentially causing great harm to the entire congregation.

Just as I attempt to make peace by asking my children to seek common ground and focus on the positive aspects of our wonderful family, Paul pleaded with the two women to find unity in the Lord.

Conflict can be conquered by focusing on the Lord.

—SBT

Wherever Together

But Ruth replied, "Don't ask me to leave you and turn back. Wherever you go, I will go; wherever you live, I will live. Your people will be my people, and your God will be my God."
RUTH 1:16

As a military wife, I learned early that moving to new and exotic places was part of the wedding vows. Whether the move involved parched and dry lands or rainforest destinations, the answer on my lips was the same. "I'll go wherever God sends us, honey."

That affirmation made it possible for my husband to accept the challenge of moving to a new duty station, knowing his family would be there. Many times, as I unpacked our treasures and tried to make the new house a home, my mind would focus on something else I'm fond of saying. "I can do anything for a few years!"

The clock begins ticking when we start unpacking. No matter what happens, or how hard things get, the army will be sure to move us out of there in a few years. Our surroundings might change, but one important thing remains constant. We will be off to the next destination together, knowing that it's all part of God's plan for our lives.

Love can take us places we never dreamed of going.

—JENNIFER DEVLIN

Divine Makeovers

About three months later, Judah was told, "Tamar, your
daughter-in-law, has acted like a prostitute. And now,
because of this, she's pregnant." "Bring her out, and let her
be burned!" Judah demanded.

GENESIS 38:24

When Tamar realized the line of Judah was in danger of dying out, she posed as a prostitute, seduced her father-in-law, Judah, and became pregnant. At first Judah ordered her burned, but when confronted with proof of his paternity, he acknowledged both his sin and Tamar's twin sons as his own.

God used a woman to ensure the line of Judah would survive to become the forebears of our Messiah. The Bible is full of stories in which He uses the broken, the desperate, and the sinners to accomplish His plan. In Tamar's story, God proved, once again, that He could transform defeats into victories and bring blessings out of tragedy.

He is still in the business of creating joy out of sorrow. When my daughter left home, I was heartbroken. Many months later, she returned with a renewed love for her family and her faith. Now, I understand that God needed those months my daughter and I spent apart to work on her heart.

Remember God's promises and keep your hope alive!

—SBT

Foolhardy Ambition

Once when Jezebel had tried to kill all the Lord's prophets,
Obadiah had hidden 100 of them in two caves. He put fifty
prophets in each cave and supplied them with food and water.
1 KINGS 18:4

Jezebel is considered by many to be the most evil woman in the Bible. She expressed and demonstrated nothing but scorn for God and His people, particularly His prophets. One of her greatest sins lay in her foolhardy desire to usurp God's power by manipulating people and situations in accordance with her ambitions.

When I become self-centered and influence people or arrange circumstances to suit my plans, I'm not allowing God to be in control. Not only do I create an impediment to my own spiritual growth, but I also prevent others from fulfilling their potential.

Experience has taught me that, without exception, God's plans are superior to mine. Why would I want to offend Him by using the intellectual and emotional gifts He has given me for anything but compliance with His will?

Self-seeking manipulation dishonors God.

—SBT

Good News Travels Fast

He took his twelve disciples with him, along with some women who had been cured of evil spirits and diseases.
LUKE 8:1–2

When I was thirty-two, I asked Jesus to come into my heart. Soon afterward, I heard about a man who had been delivered from a twelve-year addiction to heroin. He had hit bottom and cried out to Jesus to take away his desire for drugs. The Lord answered his prayer.

When I heard this, I asked God for deliverance from my sixteen-year addiction to cigarettes. He chose to answer me in the same way, and just like the ex–drug user, I began telling others about Jesus, too.

We don't know how Jesus helped Joanna, but we do know she began following Jesus and supporting His ministry. I doubt she spent much time reflecting on her past and the misery she had endured. Instead, I believe she focused on her future with Christ—a future filled with sharing the good news about her Savior.

Jesus can deliver us from any difficulty.

—CONNIE STURM CAMERON

Hemmed with Love

So Peter returned with them; and as soon as he arrived, they took him to the upstairs room. The room was filled with widows who were weeping and showing him the coats and other clothes Dorcas had made for them.

ACTS 9:39

Gertrude had found her niche. She loved the Lord, and she loved to sew. When a Nicaraguan missions program revealed a need for children's clothing, Gertrude knew this was a ministry meant for her.

The article describing the mission included a simple pattern for a reversible, jumper-type dress, so while other members of our senior missions group cut out the fabric patterns, Gertrude sewed. To date, her offerings of time and materials have resulted in more than fifty dresses for this project.

While not everyone can be a foreign field missionary, we can all have a mission, whether it is serving at the community clothes closet, a soup kitchen or, like Gertrude, in our sewing room. God's call is to serve Him with our gifts and talents in whatever way we can.

Let your little light shine!

—IMOGENE JOHNSON

The Real Deal

There are many virtuous and capable women in the world,
but you surpass them all!
PROVERBS 31:29

The virtuous woman—Martha Stewart meets Mother Teresa in one impossible-to-reach standard. I can't look at her daily routine without feeling inadequate. Who can keep up with her? But if I make the mistake of focusing on the list of everything she does, I miss the point. An inventory of accomplishments has little to do with real virtue.

She doesn't worry. She doesn't fear present circumstances, or the future. Instead, she fears the Lord and Him alone. It is that devotion to Him, first and foremost, that results in blessings in every other area of her life and the lives of those she touches.

What makes this woman truly remarkable is her strength of character. She has pledged herself to living in God's will. Day in and day out, in good times and bad, she strives to live according to a higher standard.

Real virtue is a matter of the heart.

—PAULA WISEMAN

Family Favorites

*Isaac loved Esau because he enjoyed eating the wild game
Esau brought home, but Rebekah loved Jacob.*
GENESIS 25:28

Rebekah was a godly woman with human weaknesses. After twenty years of infertility, she gave birth to twins. Instead of being the blessings she expected, her sons became a source of disappointment and heartbreak.

She loved Jacob, while her husband, Isaac, favored Esau. Unwilling to let God's plan for her sons unfold as it should, she took matters into her own hands. Her conspiracy to rob Esau of his birthright brought her nothing but misery and tore her family apart.

Many children grow up thinking their parents preferred one sibling over another. I was deeply hurt—and defensive—when my husband accused me of giving preferential treatment to our oldest child. I denied it until I heard one of my other children echo my husband's opinion.

Like Rebekah, I had put my son on a pedestal, and in the process, hurt my other children and God. Unlike Rebekah, however, I was blessed with the opportunity to recognize the problem and take steps to prevent it from continuing.

Do you play favorites?

—SBT

Matching Towels and Other Misplaced Priorities

But Martha was distracted by the big dinner she was preparing. She came to Jesus and said, "Lord, doesn't it seem unfair to you that my sister just sits here while I do all the work? Tell her to come and help me."

LUKE 10:40

My husband comes from a family of ten children, and they often gather for holiday meals and other special occasions. Not long after I married Tom, we invited the family to come to our house for Thanksgiving. That's about all I remember. I promptly went into a frenzy of cleaning, meal planning, and shopping. I wanted everything to be perfect but, in my zeal, I definitely lost sight of what was really important.

I did my best to spoil my family's eager anticipation by worrying about what kind of vegetables to serve or if the bathroom towels matched. And while everyone sat around the table after dinner, enjoying the special fellowship that families share, I was in the kitchen cleaning up.

Like Martha, I brewed up a fine case of resentment because no one was helping me. And like Martha, I needed a gentle scolding, just as the Lord gave her for misplacing her priorities.

People rarely remember the menu, but they never forget the special time they had.

—SBT

The Genuine Article

So Hilkiah the priest, Ahikam, Acbor, Shaphan, and Asaiah went to the New Quarter of Jerusalem to consult with the prophet Huldah. She was the wife of Shallum, son of Tikvah, son of Harhas, the keeper of the Temple wardrobe.

2 KINGS 22:14

My husband and I live near the rock house his grandparents built 130 years ago. While cleaning out the decaying, old home, we found some lovely dishes and rushed them to an antiques dealer. They turned out to be nice imitations.

In Old Testament times, officials discovered a scroll during a repair of the temple. The priests read it and thought it might be the Book of the Law that God had given Moses. They read it to King Josiah, and he said, "Inquire of the Lord . . . about this book."

The priests took the document to the prophetess Huldah, an obscure woman and a minor character in the Bible. She had dedicated her life to the study of God's word and instantly recognized the scroll as the genuine word of God. Without hesitation, she announced, "Tell the man who sent you, this is God's Law!"

Studying God's word teaches me to recognize the truth.

—LIZ HOYT EBERLE

Salome's Scars

But at a birthday party for Herod, Herodias's daughter performed a dance that greatly pleased him, so he promised with a vow to give her anything she wanted.
MATTHEW 14:6–7

A glance at the scar on top of my foot takes me back to when I was nine. I was cutting out paper dolls with my best friend Hilda. She sat on my floor, holding scissors, and when I hurried to join her, it happened. In a matter of moments, the scissor's blade was imbedded in my foot with blood everywhere. I still cringe at the memory.

My scar can't compare to the one Salome carried, for whether she meant to or not, Herodias wounded his daughter with her heartless and foolhardy request. Salome's injury wasn't physical like mine, but it still inflicted permanent damage.

Even though Jesus forgave my friend, I'm certain that memory never faded. I am so thankful that our spiritual scars can be healed through the Lord's mercy, love, and grace. What a healing balm!

You can be healed with His love.

—IMOGENE JOHNSON

Willing Workers Wanted

*All the women who were willing used
their skills to spin the goat hair into yarn.*
Exodus 35:26

God gave Moses detailed instructions to construct the Tabernacle. It was a massive task and required many people to complete it. Those women whose hearts were moved by the Lord's command spun the fabrics needed.

Notice that not every woman in Israel took on this job—only those who were eager to serve God in any capacity. He gave them the desire to produce the materials of blue, purple, scarlet, fine linen, and goat hair.

These women remain nameless, yet their contributions were invaluable. God calls each of us to do those things He's placed in our hearts. We may never have recognition here on this Earth, but our obedience and faithfulness will never go unnoticed by our Heavenly Father.

No task is insignificant when we work for God.

—Susan J. Reinhardt

Father of the Year for Eternity

The angel replied, "The Holy Spirit will come
upon you, and the power of the Most High will
overshadow you. So the baby to be born will be
holy, and he will be called the Son of God."
LUKE 1:35

One day, when my son Connor was ten years old, he complained of a stomachache. He didn't appear ill, but I kept him home from school. Later that day, he told me the pain had moved to his lower right side. Suspecting appendicitis, my husband and I took him to the hospital where he underwent emergency surgery for a ruptured appendix.

While I waited, I tried not to think about how close we had come to a potentially fatal medical crisis. And then, abruptly, I understood. Connor didn't belong to me. I had been given the honor of being his earthly mother, but his destiny had always been in the hands of his Heavenly Father.

It had taken me ten years to come to this realization, but Mary knew it from the moment the angel Gabriel announced her pregnancy. The child she carried belonged to God, and although she would experience the joys and sorrows of motherhood, the ultimate fate of her son rested with God.

Your child belongs to God—the greatest Father of all!

—SBT

All the Answers

*When the queen of Sheba heard of Solomon's fame,
which brought honor to the name of the Lord, she
came to test him with hard questions.*
1 KINGS 10:1

The queen of Sheba was a pagan ruler who valued wisdom above power. Curious about the remarkable things she had heard about Solomon, she decided to pay him a visit, intent on exhausting him with her questions. Instead, she left with all of her questions answered and something she had not expected—immense respect and admiration for both Solomon and his God.

The day I began to talk, I began to ask questions. Like the queen of Sheba, I've always valued wisdom and knowledge. I may not have had Solomon around when I began asking questions about God, but I had a wonderful substitute. A very wise woman at church told me that all the answers to all my questions could be found in God's word. And she was right. I may still have a lot of questions, but now I know where to look.

Open your Bible and find the answers!

—SBT

143

MAY

A Door in the Wall

And I will bless her and give you a son from her! Yes, I will bless her richly, and she will become the mother of many nations. Kings of nations will be among her descendants.
GENESIS 17:16

*M*y nine-year-old nephew wobbled and jerked as he made a painfully slow, unsteady arc around my parents' condo parking lot. He fell once, his bicycle tipping him onto the pavement as a glint of sun bounced off the bike's racing red paint.

I called out from the front steps. "Keep going! It just takes time."

When I was a child, I wondered about grownups. Why did they just sit on the benches at playgrounds, instead of stretching their feet toward the sky on swings and whooping their way down a slide?

Even in middle school, my curiosity continued. The adults stood motionless and watched, hands on hips, eyes hidden behind sunglasses. On the other hand, we ran around kicking soccer goals and feeling the wind push us faster. Why don't they play? I used to wonder.

When I turned thirty-nine, I felt the doors closing, one after another, like some TV game show gone wrong. I wasn't married; I wasn't even close to starting a family. I wanted a life on the other side of those doors I saw slowly easing shut.

What I wanted was love and a vision for the future no longer blurred with tears of loneliness. I wanted love and ears no longer echoing with the creaking of an empty house. I wanted love and arms no longer aching with the need to hold. Most of all, I wanted to transform my broken heart into one that beat so strongly, nothing could ever break its rhythm again.

Sometimes, I could see past what I perceived as my seemingly tragic life. I reminded myself that Christ made all things possible. I read about Sarah in the Bible and discovered that, like me, Sarah had known great heartbreak during her life.

When the Lord commanded Abraham to leave his country and go to a new land, she left behind her friends and loved ones without question. Moving away from the places and people she'd known for so long must have been excruciating. Even though it was difficult, she loved Abraham with her heart still wide-open, and she didn't hesitate to follow him wherever the Lord needed them to go. She knew that no matter how far they traveled, their love and commitment to each other was their true home.

Sarah had the best intentions when she gave her husband permission to father a child with her maidservant, Hagar. Like many of us, however, she learned that going against God's plans could result in suffering. Childless, and in her late nineties—long past any hope of her own child—Sarah received a miracle.

God appeared to her husband while he was sitting at the entrance to his tent on a hot day. He told Abraham, nearly 100 years old, that He would return in a year, by which time Sarah would have a son. Overhearing the conversation, Sarah laughed to herself. Barren for so long, she had trouble believing God's promise. But when her son, Isaac, was born, she chose a name that meant, "he laughs." No longer skeptical, Sarah laughed with a heart full of love and thankful celebration. Her son's birth demonstrated the power of God's blessings, not only to Sarah and Abraham, but also to all of us. When our hearts are flung open wide, blessings can come in any form, at any time. "GuGu, watch this!" Kenneth called to me, using the Chinese term of endearment for aunt.

Somehow, in the minutes since he'd brushed himself off and climbed back on his bike, he had mastered the skill of balancing and pedaling simultaneously. He whizzed past in one and, then, two sweeping circles around the lot. He came toward me, pretending to aim for my feet. I laughed and jumped up. Somehow, he'd learned to keep his balance, as sure and steady as the uniformity between God's love and us.

"I can do it now. I can ride all by myself!" he called out with a wide grin. I clapped for him, letting the warmth of my own smile reach his. Then I recalled my earlier words of advice: Keep going. Sometimes, it just takes time.

I thought of the love that surrounded me. It remained constant and unchanging, no matter how hard I tried to push it away. When I faced the challenges of job stress, chores, and needless worries, I forgot that nothing was more powerful than this love.

Sarah knew what love could do, and God saw something special in Abraham and Sarah. He saw their responsiveness to His plans, and the doors to their new life opened wide at a time when they considered them shut. We may have built a wall and we may think the door is closed, but God's love can tear down any wall and open any door.

—Christine P. Wang

The Green-Eyed Monster

They said, "Has the Lord spoken only through Moses?
Hasn't he spoken through us, too?" But the Lord heard them.
NUMBERS 12:2

As a young girl, Miriam's courage and quick thinking saved her brother Moses' life and allowed him to be raised by his own mother. Later, however, she succumbed to jealousy of the brother she had cared for in such a loving manner.

Scripture records the flaws as well as the strengths of God's servants so that we can learn from both their successes and failures. Miriam became resentful of Moses because of the authority God gave him. As punishment for her rebellion, she was cursed with leprosy and banished from the Israelite camp for seven days.

Miriam's story challenges me to check my motives before passing judgment on others. Is my constructive criticism actually destructive jealousy? Perhaps the critical finger I'm so quick to point should be directed at myself.

Leave judgment up to God.

—SUSAN E. RAMSDEN

A Slithering Surprise

The serpent was the shrewdest of all the wild animals the Lord God had made. One day he asked the woman, "Did God really say you must not eat the fruit from any of the trees in the garden?"

GENESIS 3:1

Years ago, my mother-in-law opened her dishwasher to find a little green garden snake coiled up among her clean spoons and forks. She cried out in fear and surprise, and her three boys came running. The snake was quickly removed and, to this day, she still doesn't know which son put the creature there.

Eve also encountered a snake as she wandered through the paradise God had created for her and Adam. Unfortunately, this snake proved to be far more deadly than the one my mother-in-law met long ago. His deception would separate Eve and her descendants from their Creator and change the world forever.

Eve's experience is a powerful reminder to waste no time in calling on God for help. He provides strength and protection in the midst of life's challenges, temptations, and surprises!

Don't let anything separate you from God's ever-present help.

—JENNIFER E. WHYMAN

The Mother Who Let Go

*But when she could no longer hide him, she got a basket
made of papyrus reeds and waterproofed it with tar and
pitch. She put the baby in the basket and laid it among the
reeds along the bank of the Nile River.*

EXODUS 2:3

Growing up in the pastorate, my children had lived
in a Christian setting their whole life. When we moved
to France, they encountered people who didn't share our
beliefs and they began questioning everything we'd taught
them. That was when I learned not only to pray, but also
to let go and trust God for my children—just like Moses'
mother.

Jochebed must have been terrified by the prospect of
her baby being killed. Yet she turned her fear into pro-
ductivity and made him a tiny, waterproof cradle that
she released into the river. She didn't know where Moses
would end up, or if he would escape death, but she trusted
God. When I learned to let go and trust God for my children, I finally found peace and, in time, they came back to
Him with a stronger faith than they had before.

God works best when we trust Him and let go.

—JANEY L. DEMEO

Waiting for the Plan

"How kind the Lord is!" she exclaimed. "He has taken away my disgrace of having no children."
LUKE 1:25

Elizabeth was an old woman when she spoke these words. She and her husband, Zechariah, had spent a lifetime together without a child to brighten their lives and carry on the family name. It's obvious from her reaction that the years had not hardened her heart or made her bitter. She transformed withering disappointment into flourishing devotion and dedication to God.

During the trials and testing that come with chronic disappointment, I find it very difficult to avoid being disheartened or believing that it's not my fault. Being only human, I'm sure Elizabeth had moments of discouragement and heartache, but she knew God had a purpose. He was preparing her for the miraculous plan He had in store. I must remember God has a reason for allowing disappointment in my life. It's all part of His plan.

Sometimes God says no, and sometimes He says, "Not yet."

—SBT

Dignity During Disaster

Go and gather together all the Jews of Susa and fast for me.
Do not eat or drink for three days, night or day. My maids
and I will do the same. And then, though it is against the
law, I will go in to see the king. If I must die, I must die.
ESTHER 4:16

When Esther's cousin Mordecai heard about the planned annihilation of the Jewish people, he tore his clothes, dressed in burlap, and covered himself in ashes. Overwhelmed by grief, he traveled through the city, moaning and wailing. Jews throughout the land behaved in much the same way as they learned of the decree.

Esther did none of these things. At first reluctant and then determined, she reacted to the news with calm dignity. The fate of her people rested in God's hands, and to demonstrate her faith in His mercy and His promises, she decided all the Jews, including herself and her maids, would fast for three days. At the end of this time, she would risk her life and approach the king.

I find it difficult to keep my emotions in check when faced with a crisis, but I can achieve far more by calling out to God than shaking my fist and cursing the Fates.

In times of trouble, relax and
remember that God is in control.

—SBT

Lemonade Faith

Once again Leah became pregnant and gave birth to another son. She named him Judah, for she said, "Now I will praise the Lord!" And then she stopped having children.

GENESIS 29:35

Leah knew how to turn the lemons of life into lemonade. She gave birth to three boys, and each time she said, "Now my husband will love me instead of my sister Rachel. She can't have children!" Sadly, Jacob never did love Leah the way he loved Rachel.

When Leah became pregnant for the fourth time, she stopped asking for the sweet fruit of love and chose to make lemonade. In a remarkable statement of faith, she said, "This time I will praise the Lord." Is it any surprise that God chose Judah—that child of Leah's faith—as the leader of the twelve tribes of Israel?

When life turns my dreams into disillusionment, I need to affirm, "This time I will praise the Lord."

How will you turn your disappointments into praise?

—DARLENE FRANKLIN

What Do You See?

*Mary Magdalene found the disciples
and told them, "I have seen the Lord!"*
JOHN 20:18

I've allowed the wonder and impact of the gospel to fade after years of familiarity with the message, and sometimes I behave like Peter and John in the early part of John 20. They went to investigate the claim that Jesus was gone. Everything checked out, but then they returned home. For them, the resurrection was just a hole in a rock.

In a very different scenario, Mary Magdalene saw her Lord. He spoke her name and assured her that He was the same Jesus she had known—the one who loved her in spite of her sins, her past, her very self. Mary got it!

She didn't run and tell folks about the empty tomb she had seen. She was too busy spreading the word that Jesus was alive. When the resurrection seems as empty as that tomb, I need to see my Lord, risen and victorious, just as Mary did.

Acquaint yourself with the miracle of the message.

—PAULA WISEMAN

A Used Woman

Jericho and everything in it must be completely destroyed as an offering to the Lord. Only Rahab the prostitute and the others in her house will be spared, for she protected our spies.
JOSHUA 6:17

In the years I worked as the director of education at a home for unwed mothers, I gained great respect for the women there. Many of them had been used by others until their bodies, souls, and spirits felt completely empty.

Thankfully, the home was run by compassionate and caring people who loved the Lord, and there were a number of young women who accepted God's gift of love and allowed Him to transform their lives.

As I watched God change and work through these women, I was reminded that He is never limited by our mistakes. He isn't looking for perfect people, just those He can use—like Rahab. She believed in God, and then she obeyed and served Him.

I want to be a "used woman" of God.

—EVANGELINE BEALS GARDNER

Unexpected Answers

But God replied, "No—Sarah, your wife, will give
birth to a son for you. You will name him Isaac,
and I will confirm my covenant with him and his
descendants as an everlasting covenant."
GENESIS 17:19

Whenever I think about Sarah, I am reminded of my aunt Charlotte. She and my uncle Jack were married for almost sixty years. They never had children of their own, although I'm sure Charlotte prayed passionately for a baby. I can only imagine Charlotte's disappointment and heartbreak as one by one her sisters-in-law and friends announced their pregnancies.

Because God has a way of working things out for His children, Aunt Charlotte and Uncle Jack were blessed by numerous nieces and nephews who looked upon them as surrogate parents. As the years passed, they were beloved by many "grandchildren." God answered their prayer, but not in the way they had imagined.

Sarah had given up any hope of being a mother when God finally answered her years of prayerful waiting with a precious son. The arrival of Isaac demonstrated to Sarah and all who read her story that God's timetable is not our timetable.

God answers all prayers in His own time and His own way.

—SBT

A Pantry Full of Promises

"What can I do to help you?" Elisha asked.
"Tell me, what do you have in the house?" "Nothing at all,
except a flask of olive oil," she replied.
2 KINGS 4:2

The prophet Elisha wanted to do what he could to help the widow of one of his students. When he discovered that her only resource was a pot of oil, he instructed her to find and borrow as many jars, pots, and pans as she could.

These were filled with oil from the original pot, and when every available container had been filled, the oil stopped flowing. From the sale of the oil, the widow had the money to pay her debts with enough left over to live comfortably.

No matter how carefully I try to manage our finances, there are times when it feels like we are down to our last "pot of oil." As with the widow, God is ready and willing to help. Some of our best meals have come from a near-vacant pantry, and the food always tastes better when I recall the Lord's promise that He will supply all my needs.

When it comes to God, one pot of oil is all you need.

—SBT

A Special Invitation

If you do not act, my son Solomon and I will be treated as criminals as soon as my lord the king has died.
1 KINGS 1:21

From a flawed and sinful beginning, David and Bathsheba's relationship evolved into a marriage based on trust and caring. As David lay dying, one of his sons Adonijah plotted to take the throne. At the prophet Nathan's urging, Bathsheba told David her life and that of their son Solomon would be in grave danger should Adonijah become king. Concerned for their welfare, David acted quickly to appoint Solomon as his successor and protect Bathsheba.

It was David's confession and repentance that allowed a solid foundation of love and respect to emerge from the wreckage of his first years with Bathsheba. Not only did he accept responsibility for his actions, he welcomed God into his marriage.

Recently, my daughter and her boyfriend have been discussing marriage. I condensed the volumes of advice I wanted to share and stuck to a few important truths. I said, "Invite God to the ceremony, and keep Him in your marriage, and you'll be okay."

Have you given God a place in your marriage?

—SBT

159

She Said Yes

Then she said to Elijah, "O man of God, what have you done to me? Have you come here to point out my sins and kill my son?"
1 KINGS 17:18

Elijah arrived at the widow's home just as she was about to prepare her last meal before she died, and he made an outrageous request. He asked for food and water, and she said yes. Later, when her son became ill and died, Elijah asked that she release her dead boy to him. Again, she said, yes.

As a widow, a son had been her only hope for a secure future. Now he was dead and, somehow, she found the faith and courage to hand the boy's body to Elijah. Presented with her greatest needs, God did not disappoint her. Elijah brought the child back to life, and the widow became the first woman to witness God's power to raise the dead.

What is your answer when God asks you to hand over your worries and hopes? Just as Elijah's widow did, try saying yes, and you will discover God's grace and power.

God is always with us in our most desperate moments.

—SUZANNE WOODS FISHER

Potent Prayers

Anna, a prophet, was also there in the Temple.
She was the daughter of Phanuel from the tribe of
Asher, and she was very old. Her husband died
when they had been married only seven years.
LUKE 2:36

"I'm praying for you," Meredith said in her quavering voice, and her reassurance eased my burden almost immediately. Meredith is a widow in our church and her ministry is prayer. Old age and infirmities won't allow her to participate as she did when she was younger, but she keeps each of us in her prayers.

The weekly prayer meeting now convenes in Meredith's home so she doesn't have to make the trip across the street to the church. Our Sunday services are broadcast into her house through the miracle of modern technology. Even though she's no longer sitting in the front pew, she has remained a valued member of the congregation. She's taught us that no matter what our age or health or circumstances may be, we can always pray.

The prayers of a righteous woman are powerful.

—JEAN CAMPION

A Caring and Cordial Heart

*She was baptized along with other members of her household,
and she asked us to be her guests. "If you agree that I am a
true believer in the Lord," she said, "come and stay at my
home." And she urged us until we agreed.*

ACTS 16:15

Lydia ran a successful business, dealing in purple cloth. She demonstrated her caring heart when she invited Paul and his companions to be guests at her family's home. One day, God spoke to my compassionate heart, and I was given an opportunity similar to the one He had given Lydia.

I spotted two college-age bicyclists resting in front of our business, and I discovered they were peddling their way across America and spending their nights camping out in tents. After inviting them in for a hot meal and friendly conversion, I felt God leading me.

Invite them home for a shower, encourage them to call their family in New York, and give them a clean, warm bed to sleep in. There was no mistaking a message from God.

The next day, after my husband and I said goodbye and wished the two boys a safe journey, I thanked God for the opportunity He had given me to show His love.

*When we are kind to others,
they can see God working through us.*

—BETTY KING

Choose to Get Along

Now I appeal to Euodia and Syntyche. Please, because you belong to the Lord, settle your disagreement.
PHILIPPIANS 4:2

Eudoia and Syntyche, two devout believers, found themselves at odds with each other. The Bible doesn't tell us why, but the disagreement obviously hurt the apostle Paul.

My friend and mentor Bernice became upset by something I did or said, and when my husband, Gary, became the pastor at another church, she refused to say goodbye. Later I received a letter from her, and I replied. Instead of hashing over what had happened, Bernice and I moved forward and built a friendship bridge.

Ten years later, Bernice heard about our move from Oregon to Nebraska. She called. "My sister in Nebraska has cancer. I desperately need to get there, can I ride with you?"

I was overjoyed. "Bernice, you are an answer to prayer. Gary is driving the U-Haul, and I have been praying for a companion driver." We had a blast. God healed our hearts and turned the long tedious driving hours into a time of memory making and laughter.

Women united can accomplish much for Jesus.

—KATHERINE J. CRAWFORD

163

Tell Them Today

*What's more, the Lord will hand you and the army of
Israel over to the Philistines tomorrow, and you and
your sons will be here with me. The Lord will bring
down the entire army of Israel in defeat.*

1 SAMUEL 28:19

Caught in a vice of desperation, Saul turned to a
medium in Endor and persuaded her to call up the spirit
of Samuel. Instead of the wisdom and assistance he hoped
to receive, he heard something far more terrifying than
the approaching enemy army.

Samuel told Saul that the Israelites would suffer
defeat the very next day at the hands of the Philistines.
Worse yet, Saul discovered that he and his sons would be
dead before the day was over. He collapsed and fell to the
ground, frozen with fear. I wonder how I would react to
the news that I only had one day left to live. Without a
doubt, the most important thing for me to do would be to
make sure my family knew how much I loved them.

Then it occurred to me that I didn't need to wait to
deliver such an important message. There was nothing
to stop me from expressing my love today, tomorrow, and
every day after that.

*Don't wait for a crisis to let your
family know how much you care.*

—SBT

Heavenly Consolation

"Why are you crying, Hannah?" Elkanah would ask.
"Why aren't you eating? Why be downhearted just
because you have no children? You have me—isn't
that better than having ten sons?"
1 SAMUEL 1:8

Hannah's most heartfelt desire was to have a son. Her husband, Elkanah, loved her very much, but when Hannah remained barren, it's obvious from his attempts to console her that he found it difficult to comprehend the depths of her despair.

I know my husband loves me, but there are times when he doesn't know how to share my emotions, and his attempts to comfort me fail. This has nothing to do with the quality and stability of our relationship, but it has everything to do with the fact that he is only human. When my mother died, and when I suffered a miscarriage, only God identified and understood my deepest feelings.

Like Hannah, it was only when I poured out my heart to God, that I found the relief and compassion I had been seeking.

Take your emotional burdens to the Lord for the soothing consolation He alone can give.

—SBT

165

Major Faith and Minor Doubts

*He went on board the boat to escape the flood—he and his
wife and his sons and their wives.*

GENESIS 7:7

Can you imagine how Mrs. Noah felt when her husband told her God had instructed him to build an ark? A gigantic boat hundreds of miles from any body of water? The Bible does not tell us her name, but it provides us with a vivid portrait of a faithful woman of God.

Have you ever been asked to do something you did not understand? As the wife of a pastor, I'm often called upon to help my husband, and on many of those occasions I've found it difficult to understand his reasoning for a certain task.

We have biblical accounts of wives who ridiculed their husbands, but Noah's wife accepted God's will for her family. She remained devoted to her husband and to God. Can we do the same? Occasionally we feel God's guidance to do something we don't totally understand. God won't ask us to build another ark, but He does want our trust and obedience.

Don't let momentary confusion cloud your faith.

—DONNA J. SHEPHERD

Drama Mama

*There were few people left in the villages of Israel until
Deborah arose as a mother for Israel.*
JUDGES 5:7

She redefined gender roles, sang like a diva, and won
a war. She also set goals, delegated as needed, and got
things done. But Deborah had something beyond remarkable leadership skills—something I badly needed.

I was directing our church musical: amateur actors
and dancers, musicians, tech crew, a choir. I was jazzed
up—but unprepared for battle. Not once during those
early rehearsals did everyone show up. How was I supposed to present the Easter story? My worries multiplied,
and my bruised ego began to ache.

Then I thought about Deborah, a "mother for Israel,"
and my frustration turned to chagrin and, from there, to
compassion. Talk about a wake-up call. I started nurturing
my people; later, they dubbed me the Drama Mama. Oh,
did I mention the nightly standing ovations? *No Greater
Love* was a hit—in more ways than one.

God's love awakens the greatness in others.

—LAURIE KLEIN

167

Your Real Name

Coming up behind Jesus, she touched the fringe of his robe.
Immediately, the bleeding stopped.
"Who touched me?" Jesus asked.
LUKE 8:44–45

Why did this woman touch only the edge of Jesus' cloak? She had been unclean for twelve years, and even her own husband couldn't hug her for comfort because that would make him unclean as well. For twelve years, she had been known by the name of Outcast, with humiliation as her only companion.

While teaching in an urban school, I endured the embarrassment of name-calling. Some of the epithets hurled at me came from students who used them deliberately. Others came from adults ignorant of their cruel behavior.

Jesus knew the woman needed to know her real name. He turned to her and called her "Daughter." There is a wealth of love and belonging in that name. That is exactly what the Father calls you and me, as well, because that is our true identity. We are the beloved and cherished daughters of the Lord.

Let the Lord heal your wounds.

—PRISCILLA BLAIR STRAPP

Fickle Finances

Jesus called his disciples to him and said, "I tell you the truth, this poor widow has given more than all the others who are making contributions."
MARK 12:43

There have been times when I've allowed the status of our bank account to determine my moods and actions. I relished in a healthy balance and exuded self-confidence. I placed my offering in the plate on Sundays without a second thought.

But five children, an old farmhouse, and a zoo full of pets are a warm invitation for unexpected expenses, the cost of which has often sucked the life out of my checkbook.

As the money disappeared, insecurity and doubt quickly stepped in to replace my earlier bravado. And when Sunday arrived, I gave my offering a second, third, and even a fourth thought. What about groceries? I wondered with a flash of panic. What about the water heater on its last legs?

The widow knew God would provide. Over time, His abundant blessings have taught me that if I trust Him as the widow did, He will make sure my family has everything they need.

Look to God for real security.

—SBT

169

A Clean Slate

Soon a Samaritan woman came to draw water, and Jesus said to her, "Please give me a drink."
JOHN 4:7

No one went to the town well at noon when the blistering heat was at its worst. No one besides a woman who chose the scorching sun over the cruel whispers of her neighbor. Through a series of bad choices, she had become a prisoner of her past. She had heard the Messiah was coming, but she probably thought there wasn't much hope for someone like her.

Little did she know that her salvation stood before her in the form of a travel-worn, weary Jew asking her for a drink. After years of living with the guilt and sorrow of a misguided life, here was someone willing to listen and help.

I am surrounded by people skilled in the art of acting as if everything is okay. Behind the façades, however, are lives suffocated by shame and loneliness. These people need to know there is someone who isn't concerned with their past—only their future. They need to know about Jesus.

Jesus doesn't care about your past.

—SBT

Led by Love

"Look," Naomi said to her, "your sister-in-law has gone back to her people and to her gods. You should do the same."
RUTH 1:15

When I met my husband, he was planning a move to Colorado. Our paths crossed one evening when I was out with some friends. We enjoyed each other's company and, soon, love blossomed. Even before we discussed marriage, he asked me if I would ever move to Colorado.

I was young, in love, and adventurous so I consented. We moved to Colorado after our marriage, and I fell in love with the state where my husband had always wanted to live. That was twenty-eight years ago.

The Moabitess Ruth followed her mother-in-law under different circumstances, but for similar reasons. She loved and trusted Naomi enough to follow her to a strange new land. Most importantly, she believed Naomi's God would be her protector and comforter under any circumstances.

Put your trust in the protector and comforter of women.

—LaRose Karr

A Heart That Ponders

*All who heard the shepherds' story were
astonished, but Mary kept all these things in her
heart and thought about them often.*
LUKE 2:18–19

I was a child when I first read about how Mary, the mother of Jesus, pondered things in her heart. That's me! I thought. It was just one of the many things I've thought about and treasured in my heart. I've had experiences that I didn't completely understand at the time. So, I've hidden them in my heart and wondered what God was doing.

The more I meditate and pray about things that happen, the more I see God at work. Over the years, I've seen Him weave everything together for His perfect plan. Life is always tempting me to stay busy, but I've learned I can accomplish much more during the times I am still before God. And as I ponder, God reveals Himself!

Be still and know that God is at work in your life.

—EVA JULIUSON

Dancing with Danger

One day Dinah, the daughter of Jacob and Leah, went to visit some of the young women who lived in the area.
GENESIS 34:1

When Dinah left the safety of her home to visit the neighbors, the son of the tribal leader raped her. Her brothers ultimately orchestrated revenge, but I have to wonder what Dinah was thinking. She had to know she didn't belong outside her family's camp. She had to know she was flirting with the enemy and dancing with danger.

But she didn't anticipate rape. And she didn't envision the ripple effect of the bad-decision stone she dropped into the pond of life. Her enraged brothers killed every man and kidnapped every woman, child, donkey, sheep, and goat in her attacker's city. Her father had to move to ensure the family's safety.

When I make a self-centered rather than God-centered decision, I dance with danger. Do I realize I might damage someone other than myself? With God's guidance, I strive to make decisions that reflect righteousness rather than selfishness.

God-centered decisions bring blessings
to you and those you love.

—REBECCA LYLES

173

Keeping Up Appearances

He brought part of the money to the apostles, claiming it was the full amount. With his wife's consent, he kept the rest.

ACTS 5:2

Sapphira and her husband, Ananias, were members of the early church, a remarkable community of believers who pooled their resources for the common good. Not content with simple acceptance, Sapphira and Ananias craved applause. They became preoccupied with appearances and approval, an obsession that eventually cost them their lives.

A few months ago, my husband, Tom, gave our son Dylan and his date a ride to a school dance. Enjoying the excitement of the occasion, I decided to go along. When we arrived at the school, Tom turned to Dylan and said, "I'm sorry I didn't wash the car. I hope your friends don't think it's a complete piece of junk."

Dylan shook his head. "I don't care what they think. The car got us to the dance, didn't it? That's all that matters."

I could tell by the look on Tom's face that he felt as blessed by Dylan's words as I did. "You're absolutely right," he replied. "That's all that matters."

All that really matters is what God thinks.

—SBT

Straight from the Heart

*But as the Ark of the Lord entered the City of David,
Michal, the daughter of Saul, looked down from her window.
When she saw King David leaping and dancing before the
Lord, she was filled with contempt for him.*
2 SAMUEL 6:16

Michal was disgusted with David's exuberant display of worship. She didn't understand the significance of the occasion, or the manner in which David chose to express his gratitude to God. She thought she was watching her husband behaving like a fool, but in reality she was witnessing true devotion.

I'm not sure I will ever dance down the aisle of my church, but I love to sing. I was not blessed with a beautiful singing voice—just ask my children—but when I'm in church, I don't care what I sound like. I sing as loud as I'm able and with as much enthusiasm as I can muster. We all worship in our own way, and as long as we come to God with a loving and grateful heart, our own way is the right way.

Does your worship come straight from the heart?

—SBT

Substitute Mom

"Take this baby and nurse him for me," the princess told the baby's mother. "I will pay you for your help." So the woman took her baby home and nursed him.

EXODUS 2:9

For fifteen years, I cared for children in my licensed home day care. At times, there were guilt and tears as mothers dropped off their most precious treasures. Their family became part of my family as we all watched our kids grow up together.

Many of these women became my lifelong friends. I was always surprised when they referred to me as an answer to their prayers, but I know it's not easy to trust your children with just anyone.

What a joy it's been to watch those children grow into young adults and to share memories when they come back to visit. When I see evidence of the things I taught them, any worries I may have had about the importance of my job melt away. I'm so grateful that their mothers chose to trust me. I consider it a great privilege to have been a part of their children's lives.

Do you know a mother who could use some support and encouragement from a "substitute mom"?

—EVA JULIUSON

Tomorrow Never Comes

One day the widow of a member of the group of prophets
came to Elisha and cried out, "My husband who served you
is dead, and you know how he feared the Lord. But now a
creditor has come, threatening to take my two sons as slaves."

2 KINGS 4:1

Part of the widow's mind was trying to deal with the present and the death of her husband, while some of her thoughts had jumped into the future, making her frantic with worry over the possible loss of her two sons to creditors. The prophet Elisha brought her thinking into the here and now when he forced her to focus on the problem at hand. He knew there was nothing the widow could do about tomorrow, but if she dealt with the situation she faced at the moment, the things she feared most might never come to pass.

When I worry about the future, I redirect the time and energy I need for today. My anxiety reflects a lack of trust in God and His promise that He will always meet my needs.

When I find my thoughts creeping into tomorrow, I need to pray and ask the Lord to keep me in today. Like the widow, if I deal with what's happening now, the future might just take care of itself.

God will take care of today, and tomorrow never comes.

—SBT

A Really Bad Hair Day

*She tormented him with her nagging day after day until he
was sick to death of it.*
JUDGES 16:16

Samson, the Jewish hero with legendary strength, fell
in love with the pagan Delilah. The Philistines bribed her
to discover the source of his strength so that they might
conquer him. Three times, Samson lied to Delilah, but
she finally wore him down with her persistence.

He confessed that his strength was in his hair, which
he hadn't cut in fulfillment of a vow to God. Because she
valued money more than relationships, Delilah betrayed
the man who trusted her.

Sometimes a person's greatest accomplishment is helping people achieve their goals. However, there are others
whose greatest failure is preventing others from reaching
their destiny. Cold and calculating, deceitful and self-
serving, Delilah pretended to love Samson, while interested only in personal gain. Her unfaithfulness brought
ruin to him and to her people.

I have been blessed with a wonderful husband and
friends who consistently encourage me. I am so grateful
to those who express joy in my successes and empathy in
my losses.

*God rejoices when He sees
His children caring for one another.*

—SUSAN E. RAMSDEN

Devoted Disobedience

And because the midwives feared God, he gave them families of their own.
EXODUS 1:21

My work with street children has taken me into some strange situations. And there have been times when it's been hard to know whose words to heed.

In India, we were warned not to give to beggars for fear of starting a riot. We decided to disobey and deliberately filled our pockets and banana bags with coins and little gifts—trivial things that most Americans wouldn't even value. And everywhere we went, we gave away all that we could.

The result? A lot of smiling beggars who had perhaps heard about the love of Jesus, but who were now able to see it in our actions. We chose to heed our inner instincts rather than fear man—just like those Egyptian midwives.

The Egyptian midwives defied the king's command to kill the Hebrew baby boys. They should have feared challenging the king but, instead, they feared God. As a result, He protected them from punishment and provided them with their own families.

When you fear God, you need not fear man.

—JANEY L. DeMEO

JUNE

Great Things for Me

Mary responded, "I am the Lord's servant.
May everything you have said about me come true."
And then the angel left her.
LUKE 1:38

I pulled my car into the driveway, shut off the engine, and sat for a moment. Half an hour earlier, I had been offered a magnificent job and the excitement of the afternoon had left me in awe of God's power.

I responded to the job as an afterthought. I wasn't qualified for the position; I didn't have the required college degree. What I did have was experience, obtained from the "school of hard knocks." The job sounded interesting so I typed the e-mail, prayed, and hit the send button. Uncertain of how I landed the job, and not entirely sure I was qualified, I accepted and went to work as the head of the human resources department for a major manufacturing firm.

As time passed, I developed strong relationships with the other employees. I met their spouses and remembered the names of their children. As people became comfortable with me, they occasionally shared their personal struggles and sought advice. After offering what I believed to be godly counsel, I bowed my head and prayed for each person as they left my office.

Those who sought advice often came back and let me know how a particular situation had been resolved. Though I never understood why some of these solutions occurred, I was confident God heard my prayers and worked things out for the good of all involved.

One evening, after a frustrating day at work, I shared my concerns with a girlfriend. I told her I was having some doubts about my ability to be effective for God in the workplace.

"You're like Mary," she said.

"Mary? Mary who?"

"Mary, the Mother of Jesus."

I must have looked bewildered because she put her teacup down and smiled. "Think about the parallels," she said. "You are the person God chose to minister to the needs of the people in your workplace. The actual job itself is only a part of the work, not the whole."

Then, she pointed out that my level of education hadn't been what the company desired when I submitted my resume. She reminded me that Mary didn't have an education either, but the job she was asked to accomplish didn't require an education. Though I may have been older than the other candidates, my age—like Mary's youth—had nothing to do with the responsibilities of the job. As with Mary, there had been nothing that set me apart from the other candidates except my love for God and a heart for His people.

"Your humble heart and your willingness to do the job are the same qualities Mary possessed when she was chosen to bear the Savior of the world," my friend said. "You may have thought you didn't have the qualifications for the job, but the criteria weren't necessarily beauty, fancy clothes, or education. Mary didn't have any of those, either."

God was aware of the struggles and stresses my coworkers faced, and He realized they needed someone who would not judge them. He placed me in my job because He knew that when He spoke, my heart would listen. He knew Mary's would too.

The following morning, my devotional focused on courage. I remembered that Mary didn't think she was qualified to undertake the job God had given her, but she yielded her will and allowed Him to use her. As a result she became one of the most important women in history.

Today, when I am faced with a difficult task—one for which I don't feel qualified—I think about Mary and her obedience to God's will. If I make myself available, He will use me and, like Mary, I will be able to rejoice and say, "The Mighty One has done great things for me."

—ELISA YAGER

Spousal Support

And Noah went in, and his sons, and his wife,
and his sons' wives with him, into the ark,
because of the waters of the flood.
GENESIS 7:7

The other day my husband called me from work and read the description for a position at a power plant in Michigan.

I tried, with little success, to share his enthusiasm. I wasn't sure I wanted to contend with a "real" winter, and when I pictured trying to organize a move for our large human and animal family, I realized I wouldn't even know where to start.

Noah didn't ask his wife if she wanted to move. He told her the world was under God's judgment and was about to be destroyed by water, but he was going to build a massive boat to save his family and two each of the Earth's creatures. Mrs. Noah didn't respond with doubts or complaints. She obeyed God by supporting her husband's leadership and faithfully helping Noah just as she always had.

Perhaps it was time for me to stand behind my husband when he made his decisions and stand beside him when he needed help.

A husband needs his wife's faith, not her faultfinding.

—SBT

Miracles on the Menu

*So she did as Elijah said, and she and Elijah and her son
continued to eat for many days.*
1 KINGS 17:15

Except for some pasta and a few condiments, our cupboards were almost bare. I needed groceries, but finances
were low, and we had to pool our resources for the children's summer camp.

Suddenly, my daughter bounced in the room and
asked if her friend could stay over for a few days because
her mother was unwell. I felt awkward, but I knew I had
to say yes. Now, what would I cook for supper, I wondered?
Then, I remembered the widow at Zarephath, and I prayed
for God to meet our needs. Somehow, I concocted a delicious pasta dish.

Victims of an extended famine, the widow and her
son were about to eat their last morsel and lie down and
die. But God had told Elijah to go to Zarephath where the
widow would feed him. She shared the little she had and,
miraculously, there was enough for her family as well—
and it never ran out.

A little faith can be very filling.

—JANEY L. DeMEO

No Excuse for Ignorance

"You won't die!" the serpent replied to the woman. "God knows that your eyes will be opened as soon as you eat it, and you will be like God, knowing both good and evil."
GENESIS 3:4–5

Eve didn't stand much of a chance when the serpent set out to ruin things in the Garden of Eden. For starters, she had never been faced with a decision, and she had yet to experience cunning and deceit, two of the serpent's favorite items in his evil inventory.

Perhaps one of the most significant factors that led to her being drawn into sin was her ignorance of God's character.

When the serpent told her God had lied, she did not know God was incapable of lying. Maybe if she had been armed with the truth about her Creator, the battle for paradise might have turned out differently.

That's why it's critical for me to pray and specifically ask God to reveal His character to me. Reading my Bible is equally important in my ongoing quest to discover as much about Him as I possibly can.

*Making mistakes is part of being human,
but ignorance is no excuse.*

—SBT

Comforting Companionship

Anna, a prophet, was also there in the Temple. She
was the daughter of Phanuel from the tribe of Asher,
and she was very old. Her husband died when they
had been married only seven years.

LUKE 2:36

Anna spent the vast majority of her long life alone, but I'm fairly certain any feelings of emptiness and longing she might have had were rare and fleeting. For Anna knew that with God in her life, she was never truly alone.

On weekends and holidays, our home is seldom empty—or quiet. My five children, their friends, and our many pets fill the house with a comforting din of chaos and confusion. Occasionally, I retreat to a safe haven like my bedroom or the bath, but most of the time I'm happy with things just the way they are.

Inevitably, Monday morning arrives and like troops going off the war, my husband leaves for work, and the children trudge out to the bus stop. Even the dogs grow quiet and subdued as the house settles into an unfamiliar silence. At first, I feel a bit lost and lonely, but it isn't long before I find comfort in the knowledge that, like Anna, I am never truly alone.

God is always with you.

—SBT

The Present Is a Gift

When the child was weaned, Hannah took him to the
Tabernacle in Shiloh. They brought along a three-year-old
bull for the sacrifice and a basket of flour and some wine.
1 SAMUEL 1:24

I wait for the school bus every morning with my eight-year-old son, Owen. When we see the bus approaching from a distance, I walk back to the house, leaving Owen to stand by himself for a few minutes until the bus pulls up.

Occasionally, I'll turn my head for one last look at my little man standing straight and tall, full of self-importance or stepping confidently into the cavernous interior of the bus. I can't help but think of the day when Owen will be returning to a home of his own, and I will have to content myself with phone calls and visits.

Hannah only had three short years with Samuel before she took him to the temple to start his new life serving God. Instead of languishing in self-pity and sadness, she chose to praise God for her son and the blissful time they had spent together. Perhaps I should spend less time worrying about the future and more time enjoying the present.

Yesterday is gone, and tomorrow will never come.
Thank God for today!

—SBT

Streams in the Desert

Thereafter, Hagar used another name to refer to the Lord, who had spoken to her. She said, "You are the God who sees me." She also said, "Have I truly seen the One who sees me?"

GENESIS 16:13

Sinking under the weight of the various roles I had accepted in my job, I felt abandoned by the people who continued to place demands on me.

Hagar felt abandoned when she found herself pregnant and lost in the wilderness. What hope was there for her, an alien to the people of God? But God not only saw her, He cared enough to make promises. He has done the same for me.

You may be feeling lost—alone in a wilderness of bad circumstances. Don't forget that the living God who hears and sees all things knows exactly where you are. Whether you belong to Him yet, you are not lost to Him, and He is whispering to you as He whispered to Hagar long ago, "Where are you going?"

Turn to God and tell Him where you have been. Tell Him where you are trying to go, and believe that He has a plan and a purpose for you.

The Lord will give you streams in the desert.

—PRISCILLA BLAIR STRAPP

Preparations and Priorities

And the king loved Esther more than any of the other young women. He was so delighted with her that he set the royal crown on her head and declared her queen instead of Vashti.
ESTHER 2:17

As a bridal consultant, I observed many women who were preoccupied to the point of obsession with the arrangements for their big day. These women appeared to care more about their weddings than the marriages to which they were committing themselves. They spent thousands of dollars on gowns, tiaras, and veils, which was great for business, but I couldn't help but question their preparations and priorities.

Esther spent twelve months completing beauty treatments preparing to meet the king, but she never lost sight of what was really important. When she became queen, she fasted and prayed for days in an effort to spare her people. Her devotion to God and her willingness to sacrifice her own life saved the Jewish nation.

Our preparations should reflect our priorities.

—EVANGELINE BEALS GARDNER

God Has Me Covered

When the Lord first began speaking to Israel through Hosea, he said to him, "Go and marry a prostitute, so that some of her children will be conceived in prostitution. This will illustrate how Israel has acted like a prostitute by turning against the Lord and worshiping other gods."

HOSEA 1:2

I've often said, "Being the wife of a pastor wasn't in my prenuptial agreement." While we didn't really have a pre-nuptial agreement, there were certain expectations. Mine never included the possibility that I would fill the role of pastor's wife, but that's where I found myself several years into our marriage.

I had known lots of pastor's wives, and I didn't seem to be like any of them—soft-spoken, patient, saintly—and submissive! My past included a divorce and other actions I felt had grieved God. Did God know to whom my husband was married when He called him into the ministry?

Of course, God was aware of my history. Something that has always helped me accept God's grace and forgiveness is remembering the wife of the Old Testament prophet Hosea. Gomer was a prostitute, yet God used her to reveal His desire to redeem His beloved children. I'm so thankful that God's love does, indeed, cover a multitude of sins.

God doesn't care about your history. He cares about you!

—KAREN MOREROD

Temporal Hurt

*King Asa even deposed his grandmother Maacah from her
position as queen mother because she had made an obscene
Asherah pole. He cut down her obscene pole, broke it up,
and burned it in the Kidron Valley.*

2 CHRONICLES 15:16

I tried to explain my reasons, but my mother didn't
understand. How could she comprehend my desire to
bring honor and glory to God when she, herself, did not
have a personal relationship with Him?

She was hurt because I didn't plan to get married in
the church of her birth, nor did I want a reception with
drinking and dancing. God had changed me, and in order
to win my family to the Lord, I knew I needed to take a
stand.

I imagine it was hard for Asa to not only speak out
against Maacah's idolatry, but to also dethrone her. She
may not have been a godly grandmother, but God's mercy
still reached down to Asa. His stand for the Lord reaped
abundant blessings. Living a life that is pleasing to God
may sometimes involve hurting those we love. Ultimately,
however, it will be a test of faith as to who is number one
in our lives.

Do you need to take a stand?

—MARIBETH SPANGENBERG

193

More Than a Magic Act

When the Lord saw that Leah was unloved, he enabled her to have children, but Rachel could not conceive.

GENESIS 29:31

God cares about each and every one of His children. Not only is He concerned with providing our necessities, but He is also attentive to our emotional needs. The same God who created the universe took the time to notice a lonely young woman struggling with the sorrow of knowing that her husband loved someone else. In order to bring comfort to Leah's grieving heart and to create something beautiful out of her sadness, He gave her children.

When my mother died suddenly, I found myself thrust into a bewildering maze of grief and isolation. The joyful anticipation with which I used to greet the day began to disappear along with my ability to make sense of my life.

Then, I found out I was pregnant. Gradually, my spirits began to lift and my feelings of loss made way for an increasing sense of excitement. Once more, God had transformed heartbreak into happiness.

God cares when you're hurting.

—SBT

Never Say Never

The angel replied, "What's more, your relative Elizabeth has become pregnant in her old age! People used to say she was barren, but she's now in her sixth month."

LUKE 1:36

When the angel Gabriel appeared to the young Virgin Mary and announced that her barren cousin Elizabeth had conceived a child in her old age, Mary was astonished.

When I discovered I was pregnant at the age of forty-two, I experienced some of Mary's amazement. I had longed for another child, but my circumstances and age prevented me from giving the idea serious thought. However, my situation changed, and I soon discovered my age was irrelevant when it came to God's plan for my life.

Like Mary, the news of my pregnancy brought more than a little anxiety. I was healthy, but increased maternal age carried so many risks. Despite my fears, I turned down genetic testing and potential reassurance, believing God would give me the baby He wanted me to have. Still, I worried, but when I saw my strong and healthy baby on the ultrasound screen, the angel Gabriel's words of comfort to Mary came back to me.

For God, nothing is impossible.

—SBT

Paralyzed by the Past

But Lot's wife looked back as she was following along behind
him, and she became a pillar of salt.
GENESIS 19:26

One hint of a familiar scent or one note of a song from long ago, and I'm jettisoned back in time. Sometimes, I recall seasons in my life consisting of nothing more than fleshly emptiness. A life void of the passion of God—a life set on the things of the world.

If I'm not careful, I can get so caught up in that scent or song that I may actually long for those particular days of my youth. How can it be when the here-and-now is so much better? Darkness has a funny way of masquerading as light—or fond memories.

It is moments like those that help me realize just how easily I could have been like Lot's wife. I might have looked back for just a moment, to take in one last whiff, or to listen to one more stanza, and ended up destroyed by a longing for the things left behind.

Don't dwell on the past; it may just destroy your future!

—JENNIFER DEVLIN

Call Me Bitter

"Don't call me Naomi," she responded. "Instead, call me Mara, for the Almighty has made life very bitter for me."
RUTH 1:20

At the shower, Grandma held the baby while aunts, cousins, and friends celebrated the precious addition to our family. I had been unable to conceive for six long years. "How lovely," I said and attempted to smile. I stroked a downy blanket that would soon cuddle my niece and rejoiced with my sister-in-law, but how I wanted a baby of my own.

Later, I cried out to God. "It isn't fair. Why can't I have a child?" No answer came, just one word. Mara. Bitter. Naomi was so bitter, she was unrecognizable. I did not want my niece to know me as her bitter aunt. I wanted to praise God and use my life to serve him.

Gradually, I learned to let go of the sorrow and resentment. God worked on my heart and gave me joy at the next baby shower and the next and the next. Four years later, it was my turn. I held my son and said, "Call me Mother."

Bitterness is a choice and so is a grateful heart.

—R. J. THESMAN

Learning from Lois

I remember your genuine faith, for you share the faith that first filled your grandmother Lois and your mother, Eunice. And I know that same faith continues strong in you.

2 TIMOTHY 1:5

After raising six children, we were surprised by the joy of being grandparents. As more and more grandchildren arrived on the scene, I felt an awesome responsibility to do whatever I could to influence their lives for Christ.

In the Bible I read about Lois, Timothy's grandmother. She had been responsible for nurturing the seed of faith God planted in her grandson's heart.

The Lord fulfilled the desire to pass on my faith by providing a fantastic vehicle to bring our grandchildren closer to God and to each other. I invited them to Cousins' Camps. The first camp had five children aged three to eight. The theme, our heritage, explored the legacy of both our physical and spiritual families.

The camps provided a chance to teach the children more about the Lord and opened opportunities to minister to them throughout the year. We are expecting our twentieth grandchild this year and have two camps each summer.

It is a privilege to pass on my faith in the Lord.

—MARION E. GORMAN

Step One

But the angel said, "Don't be afraid, Zechariah! God has heard your prayer. Your wife, Elizabeth, will give you a son, and you are to name him John."

LUKE 1:13

Zechariah knew how much his beloved Elizabeth wanted a child. He had witnessed her suffering and sorrow for many years and, no doubt, he experienced his share of disappointment and sadness. Because he loved her, he wanted her to have her heart's desire. So, he turned to God and prayed for the baby she so desperately wanted.

Part of loving my husband, Tom, and my five children is praying for their highest good. When Tom tells me about a problem at work, I may not understand all the details or his true feelings about the situation. However, I still ask God to watch over him and bless him with the wisdom and peace and mind he needs.

Like Zechariah, I want the people I love to be happy. I used to think I could make this happen on my own, but I have discovered that turning to God first is the best way to accomplish anything in my life.

God is the first step on any journey.

—SBT

No Help Required

So Sarai said to Abram, "The Lord has prevented me from
having children. Go and sleep with my servant. Perhaps I
can have children through her." And Abram agreed with
Sarai's proposal.
GENESIS 16:2

Sarai and I have a lot in common. God said she would have a child, but when it didn't happen in the time frame she expected, she took matters into her own hands. She was unable to wait for what God promised. Like Sarai I sometimes run short of patience.

When God gives me clear directions, I want to follow them immediately. If I have to wait, I start looking for ways to help God speed things up. Invariably, He lets me flounder in my foolishness until I see the error of my ways.

Unlike Sarai, I didn't have to long for children, but the fulfillment of His other promises often came after months, or even years, of preparation. God works hard to get my heart and head where they need to be to accept His gifts, and when He sees that I am ready to receive, He gives more abundantly than I could ever imagine.

God always follows through with His promises.

—DIANNE DANIELS

The Grand Lady

When she speaks, her words are wise, and she gives instructions with kindness.
PROVERBS 31:26

We hear of "The Grand Lady" often in sermons and devotions. She was successful in all areas of her life. A shrewd businesswoman valued by her husband, she helped to make him successful by protecting their good name. Her children called her blessed. She sewed and helped the needy and the poor.

When my children were young, I didn't think I was wise or esteemed. In fact, there were times I often didn't know if I was coming or going! And later, when we had teenagers and hormones raging in our home with hurricane force, I doubted that I had ever done well in my child-rearing role.

One thing I know for certain—this grand lady made her share of mistakes. Perhaps she was a frazzled young mom. Her husband and children praised her because she sought God's favor and wisdom. She lived victoriously because of His promises, and she walked by the Lord's side, holding His hand.

Whose hand are you reaching for today?

—LAROSE KARR

Thanksgiving All Year 'Round

Listen, you kings! Pay attention, you mighty rulers!
For I will sing to the Lord. I will make music to the Lord,
the God of Israel.
JUDGES 5:3

In a time when women channeled most of their energy into homemaking, raising children, and tending crops, Deborah's life was unique. As a prophetess and Israel's fourth and only female judge, she was crucial to the leadership of the Israelites.

Deborah was a powerful and respected mediator, adviser, and counselor who possessed wisdom, charisma, and an unshakable faith in God. Although gifted with strong leadership qualities, she was never power hungry or self-promoting. Her greatest desire was to serve God. Her story proves that God can accomplish great things through those who are willing to be led by Him.

As a writer and occasional public speaker, I am faced with finding God-honoring (not me-honoring) responses to the compliments I receive. Deborah's song of thanks-giving, celebrating Israel's great victory over the Canaan-ites, helps me remember the importance of recognizing God as the source of all my abilities.

In victory or defeat, give glory and praise to the Lord.

—SUSAN E. RAMSDEN

Attracting Notice

Then Boaz asked his foreman, "Who is that young woman over there? Who does she belong to?"
RUTH 2:5

The Moabite woman Ruth followed her mother-in-law Naomi home to Israel and gleaned the fields to support them both. Naomi's plan to find her widowed daughter-in-law a protective husband led to Ruth's marriage to Boaz, a union that is included in the ancestral line of Jesus.

Ruth's love for Naomi transcended the death of their husbands and any family obligation. Ruth's faithful care for her aging mother-in-law attracted the notice of Boaz, a powerful distant relative. He redeemed Ruth and her husband's property to save the family and their legacy.

Through my simple acts of service, efforts I may sometimes see as insignificant, God brings me to the attention of others. They offer praise and occasional opportunities for new skills or advancement. Other people might be watching as we do what we can to serve the Lord, and their lives might be touched.

What are you doing that may impact those who are watching?

—ALEXANDRA ROSE

Human Failings

*Give my greetings to Priscilla and Aquila, my
coworkers in the ministry of Christ Jesus. In fact,
they once risked their lives for me. I am thankful
to them, and so are all the Gentile churches.*

ROMANS 16:3–4

The apostle Paul's tribute leaves no doubt that Priscilla and her husband, Aquila, were invaluable members of the fragile, new ministry. Priscilla's deep faith emerged amid the conflict and dissent of the early church in Rome and Corinth, years before she met Paul.

She stood beside Paul as the controversies continued in Ephesus. If anything, the struggles she endured seemed to strengthen her devotion to the point where she became willing to risk her life.

Recently, our church went through a difficult period. Opinions differed and emotions flared. There were moments when I grew weary of the conflict and fought the temptation to stay home and avoid any more stress.

Then, I realized we weren't the first church to experience discord, and we certainly wouldn't be the last. We would always be less than perfect simply because we were human. So, for the reassurance I needed, I turned to my Bible—the inerrant, infallible, and inspired word of God.

Make your Bible the source of your solutions.

—SBT

A Cloud of Terror

Then Pharaoh gave this order to all his people:
"Throw every newborn Hebrew boy into the Nile River.
But you may let the girls live."
EXODUS 1:22

For any woman, childbirth is a life-changing event fraught with a kaleidoscope of emotions. Despite the best prenatal care, there isn't an expectant mother who doesn't experience moments of apprehension.

I recall staring at the ultrasound pictures of my children, narrated by the reassurances of the doctor. And yet, as the baby's birth drew near, I suffered moments of anxiety. Would my baby be okay?

Jochebed went through all this and more. Fearing that someday the increasing population of Hebrew slaves would form an army and overcome their captors, the pharoah ordered the murder of every newborn Hebrew male. Jochebed gave birth under this cloud of terror, but her courage and determination, coupled with faith in God's guidance, resulted in the happy ending every new mother deserves.

Faith is the perfect antidote for fear.

—SBT

Setting Prisoners Free

She had suffered a great deal from many doctors, and over the years she had spent everything she had to pay them, but she had gotten no better. In fact, she had gotten worse.
MARK 5:26

Once a week I visit a woman in jail who requested a Christian friend through a ministry in which I participate. For the duration of her sentence, I am committed to spending an hour each week sharing the Bible, listening to her, and praying with her.

While not all inmates are Christians, most are searching for answers. Many have been shunned by society and struggle with low self-esteem. They hunger for truth; the truth that Jesus loves them and will forgive them.

Mark gives us the account of a woman who endured twelve years of rejection. She had an issue of blood that, according to the law, rendered her unclean—and effectively isolated her from any human contact. She could not enter the synagogue with her family and friends. She was an outcast. Not only did Jesus heal this woman, but he also befriended her. And Jesus wants us to reach out to the shunned among us, too.

*Jesus wants us to befriend the outcast in His name—
even through steel doors.*

—CONNIE STURM CAMERON

One Bad Apple

"I know the Lord has given you this land," she told them. "We are all afraid of you. Everyone is living in terror."
JOSHUA 2:9

I have a particular fondness for Rahab. I love the fact that God demonstrated His grace by adding what many would consider an unlikely pick off the family tree to the lineage of Christ. Wouldn't many have considered this woman "one bad apple"?

As a teenager I did a lot of things of which I'm not proud. On the outside, I may have passed for a "good girl," but my heart was self-seeking and wild. Not the characteristics I would want for a daughter of my own. It wasn't until my mother died that I committed my life to Christ.

I would like to say that a profound revelation prompted my leap of faith but, like Rahab, my initial motivation to follow the Lord was fear. However, I soon realized that God loved me and was more than willing to transform another "bad apple" into some fine fruit!

You are God's choice fruit and worth much in His sight.

—BETH DUEWEL

A Widow's Mite

*Jesus called his disciples to him and said, "I tell you
the truth, this poor widow has given more than all the
others who are making contributions."*
MARK 12:43

My mother, a typical 1950s stay-at-home wife, was
unprepared when my father died unexpectedly at age
forty-seven. She was unskilled, with only an eighth-grade
education, but she knew how to pray. God provided her
with information about a local store in need of a clerk, so
she walked six blocks twice a day and earned a dollar an
hour. I was a senior in high school, and I vividly recall
how careful she was with the $38 and change she earned
each week.

My favorite memory is her opening a small manila
pay envelope and pouring its contents into her palm. She
would take out two $1 bills and place them in a Mason
jar. I knew the money was her tithe, and I asked her how
she could afford to spare it. Her answer was quick and
emphatic: "If I give God His part first, He will stretch
the rest." And He did—always. Like this widow with her
mite coin for the temple, she gave far more than she could
afford.

He will never leave you nor forsake you.

—IMOGENE JOHNSON

Until the End

Mary Magdalene found the disciples and told them, "I have seen the Lord!" Then she gave them his message.
JOHN 20:18

While Jesus' disciples doubted and denied, Mary believed. While they remained hesitant and bewildered, she understood. Thinking nothing of her own pain and grief, she followed Him to the cross and was there when He drew His last breath.

When my mother fell critically ill, her brother and two sisters joined my father and me at the hospital. As the hours passed, we persuaded my exhausted and distraught father to go home and rest, promising to phone him if her condition deteriorated. Later that night, one of my aunts and my uncle also left to get some sleep.

Only my aunt Charlotte and I remained. I couldn't bear to think of my mother alone, and by morning, she was gone. It was one of the hardest things I have ever done, but it was my way to pay tribute to the woman who gave me life and so much more.

Will you remain faithful until the end?

—SBT

Pleasures or Purpose

*And Potiphar's wife soon began to look at
him lustfully. "Come and sleep with me," she
demanded. But Joseph refused.*
GENESIS 39:7

Potiphar's wife, married to a wealthy and influential Egyptian, enjoyed every luxury imaginable. Lacking faith in the one true God, however, rendered her life void of meaning or purpose. With too much time on her hands, she turned to wicked pleasures, including the attempted seduction of young Joseph, brought into her husband's home as a Hebrew slave.

Sometimes I want what I don't need or what I can't have. The world would have me believe that I can't live without a new car, rooms full of costly furniture, and a closet full of designer clothes.

Unlike Potiphar's wife, I can turn to my Bible during moments of temptation. And God's own words remind me that my real treasures are not of this Earth. I may not have everything I want, but I am always given what I need.

Are you lusting for something you can't have or don't need?

—SBT

Going into Business with God

When she told the man of God what had happened, he said to her, "Now sell the olive oil and pay your debts, and you and your sons can live on what is left over."

2 KINGS 4:7

Perhaps God has allowed a circumstance into your life that proved to be the catalyst needed to propel you into an action of faith. If so, you can identify with the widow turned into an entrepreneur by the prophet Elisha.

My friend Cassandra experienced a similar situation. She found herself divorced after twenty years of marriage. Her years of keeping the home, nurturing their children, and helping her husband launch a new business had left her without the career she had set as her goal in college.

Now, however, she had no choice. Though well past the ideal employment age, and with her heart still broken, she determined to refresh her skills. Consequently she found renewed strength in God's power to sustain her, and it wasn't long before she was soaring with her own wings.

Life's lessons are often hard to learn, but God's mercies are eternal and He can turn your calamities and disappointments into vibrant life.

Let God open the door to new opportunities.

—IMOGENE JOHNSON

211

Too Busy for Jesus

But the Lord said to her, "My dear Martha, you are worried and upset over all these details!"
LUKE 10:41

Martha is often criticized for being overly concerned with details and for being bossy and irritable with her sister Mary, who dropped everything to be with Jesus. But Martha had many fine qualities too. She wanted to please, do things right, and serve others, especially her friend and Lord, Jesus.

However, like many of us, she overdid it. She tended to the details of homemaking and meal preparations so ardently that she missed the opportunity to enjoy her special guest. She had Jesus in her home, but barely spoke to Him, and then only to complain!

In the early years of my Christian walk, I put more effort into working for the Lord than into spending time with Him. As I matured, I learned that what He wants most is for me to sit at His feet, listen to His heart, and enjoy His presence. Both Martha and I have learned from her sister Mary!

Service must be balanced with worship—
truly the better part.

—SUSAN E. RAMSDEN

Needles Pricked My Conscience

So Peter returned with them; and as soon as he arrived, they took him to the upstairs room. The room was filled with widows who were weeping and showing him the coats and other clothes Dorcas had made for them.

ACTS 9:39

My friend, Sarah, suffered from kidney failure, so three times a week she was hooked up to a dialysis machine. To help pass the time, she taught herself to knit. She became so proficient that even after she received a kidney transplant, she continued knitting. Tragically, her body went into rejection, and she died from complications of the transplant.

At her funeral, samples of her beautiful work were displayed on a long table at the back of the church. Most poignant was the piece she did not have time to finish. It spoke to me of how, at any moment, I could be called away before I'm able to complete the good works I have always intended to do.

Since Sarah's death, I have made more of an effort to befriend the lonely, send cards to the elderly, and make quilts for all the grandchildren.

*In order to leave a legacy for tomorrow,
I have to be diligent today.*

—ALMA BARKMAN

The Big Solution

Jesus said, "You're right! You don't have a husband—for you have had five husbands, and you aren't even married to the man you're living with now. You certainly spoke the truth!"
JOHN 4:17–18

The woman of Samaria had made her share of errors in judgment, but Jesus took her transgressions and turned them into something positive. He commended her for being honest, and then he used her situation to demonstrate her need for salvation. The Bible is filled with accounts of God transforming mindless mistakes into something beautiful.

Sometimes my errors in judgment create a big problem in my life, but as soon as I admit my blunder, God goes to work on an even bigger solution. Because I'm human, I make mistakes, but they do nothing to change the way God feels about me. As with everything else in my life, I can bring my problems to God because He wants to help.

Make God part of the solution.

—SBT

JULY

Decisions, Doubts, and Direction

But Ruth replied, "Don't ask me to leave you and turn back. Wherever you go, I will go; wherever you live, I will live. Your people will be my people, and your God will be my God."

RUTH 1:16

hings didn't look good for Ruth, the Moabite woman. She had married a foreigner, and he died. Now she was a widow—just one step above a slave. Then her widowed mother-in-law, Naomi, heard famine conditions had improved in Israel, her home country, and she was making plans to return. Ruth had a decision of her own to make. Should she stay in Moab or go with Naomi?

If she stayed in Moab, there was a chance she'd marry again, this time to one of her own people. What opportunity would she have for marriage in Israel? Who would want her—a foreigner and a destitute widow?

Then there was Naomi's God. What of this God of Israel? Ruth wondered. For years, she had watched Naomi trust the invisible deity whom she claimed to be the only God. Should she also claim Him as her God?

Ruth and Orpah, her sister-in-law, agreed to accompany Naomi to Bethlehem, but along the way, perhaps at the border of Israel, Naomi stopped. "Go back," she urged the girls. She knew their chances of finding a husband were better in Moab. "Return to Moab," she said. Orpah turned back, but Ruth could not be persuaded.

I know something of the struggle these two women faced because at sixteen, I had to make a difficult decision.

Should I renounce my sinful past, choose Jesus as my Savior, and become a Christian? Or should I stay in my old life? I agonized for months, weighing my choices.

If I choose Christ, I'll lose my friends, I reasoned. But if I renounce Jesus, who or what will guide my life? If I stay where I am, how can I hope to meet a Christian man, have a godly home, and raise a Christian family? The battle raged within me. I cried easily, and I couldn't sleep. Should I be an Orpah or a Ruth?

One summer day, I chose Christ. To my surprise, my old friends supported my choice, and I made new friends. But now I had to learn to walk in His ways, and the transition was difficult.

Like Ruth, I made the big decision, but choosing to walk in humble obedience to God was another matter. Early in my Christian walk, I realized I needed to change my lifestyle, read my Bible, learn to pray, and go to church. I found the disciplines constraining, but Ruth learned and so did I. Each day I prayed for God to show me His will.

As Ruth and Naomi neared Bethlehem, they noticed workers harvesting the barley. Watching them, Ruth made another wise decision. She and Naomi would not starve. "I'll pick after the barley reapers, gathering what they drop," she told Naomi. Being a penniless widow may have been a humbling experience, but working in the hot sun picking up the barley stalks left by the reapers brought Ruth to a new level of humility.

It was no coincidence that found Ruth working in a field belonging to Boaz, a wealthy farmer in Bethlehem and a relative of Naomi. It was a dividend that resulted from her decision to follow the God of Naomi.

When I decided to follow Christ, I broke off my relationship with a young man named Lee. Then one evening he showed up at my door and announced he had become a Christian. I was skeptical, but after a time I discovered he had been telling the truth. Like me, he had left Moab.

It was a special and exciting time for me and Lee. We attended church, read the Bible together, and prayed, all the time conscious of God's direction in the "new land" in which we had found ourselves. The course of love didn't run smoothly for Ruth and Boaz. He sought to marry her, but according to Jewish law, another kinsman had first chance to the land that rightfully belonged to Naomi. This also included the right to marry any woman of childbearing age in the family. Boaz met with the relative at the city gate. The matter was settled when he gave Boaz his sandal, a symbolic gesture that indicated he had relinquished all rights to the land and Ruth.

The problems Lee and I encountered were of another nature. My parents liked Lee, but because our religious backgrounds were miles apart, they thought a marriage would be destined for failure. When Lee and I tried to reconcile our differences, we clashed. We broke up and reunited several times. Will we ever reconcile our points of disagreement? I wondered. What will a compromise mean to each of us, and can we live with those compromises? I wanted to be sure God's approving smile rested on our marriage.

Who can understand the ways of God? They are unfathomable! Did Ruth and Boaz know their child, Obed, would become the grandfather of Israel's great king David? More important, did they realize that their union was just one part of God's great plan for man's salvation?

Lee and I eventually worked out our differences and meshed our lives into one. Today, we follow God whole-heartedly, living by the vow Ruth made to Naomi. "Your people will be my people, and your God will be my God."

—JEWELL JOHNSON

Smiling Through the Tears

*All who heard the shepherds' story were astonished,
but Mary kept all these things in her heart and
thought about them often.*
LUKE 2:18–19

My oldest son, Gabriel, left for an extended trip to San Francisco, and I said goodbye with both tears of sorrow and smiles of happiness. Despite his promises to be home in about six weeks, my heart told me this was his first step in creating a life of his own.

When Gabriel was born, it didn't seem possible that the tiny, fragile bundle in my arms would be a grown man someday. But I knew God had a plan for his life. The time had come for me to let go.

While those around her rejoiced with amazement and wonder, Mary remained quiet and reflective in the hours after her son's birth. Was she thinking about the day Jesus would take the first step on his journey to fulfill God's plan? Or, like me twenty-two years ago, was she simply content to bask in the light of love at first sight?

Like any mother, Mary experienced both joy and sorrow.

—SBT

C-O-N-T-E-N-T

The woman was convinced. She saw that the tree
was beautiful and its fruit looked delicious, and she
wanted the wisdom it would give her. So she took
some of the fruit and ate it.
GENESIS 3:6

During a recent shopping trip together, I found myself in a teachable moment with my youngest daughter. "You have enough little pet shops. You don't need them all."

"But I don't have the squirrel," she said, her tiny mouth set in a firm line.

I decided to keep it brief. "Brooklyn," I replied, "you need to be more content." Then, in an effort to emphasize my point, I spelled out the word: "C-o-n-t-e-n-t."

I took her by the hand, and we wandered into the home and garden department, where all the items on my want list just happened to be on sale. While drooling over a new patio table and chairs, I spotted my daughter giving me a solemn stare. "What's the matter, honey?"

"I was just thinking about how to spell that word again. C-o-n-"

Needless to say, Eve and I have a great deal in common. Having enough, but wanting more. I guess actions speak louder than spelled-out words.

Contentment is knowing that we have more than enough.

—BETH DUEWEL

A Clean Slate

Jesus said, "You're right, you don't have a husband—for you have had five husbands, and you aren't even married to the man you're living with now. You certainly spoke the truth!"
JOHN 4:18

Startled by a man who appears to know everything about her, the Samaritan woman is both intrigued and embarrassed. She tries in vain to change the subject, a tactic that reminds me of the prayers in which I ask God for forgiveness, but find myself reluctant to voice my actual sins.

I find it hard to admit I've made a mistake, especially if it's one of those difficult sins I seem doomed to repeat. Even though I don't say it out loud, I wonder how He can still love me when it feels as if I am always letting Him down.

The truth is that He loves me no matter what. I cannot earn God's love, nor can I lose it. He loves me just the way I am with a love that knows no beginning or end. Once I confess my mistake, the slate is wiped clean. A fresh start feels great—just ask the Samaritan woman!

Find a new beginning with God.

—SBT

Cutting Your Losses

His wife said to him, "Are you still trying to maintain your integrity? Curse God and die."
JOB 2:9

But Lot's wife looked back as she was following behind him, and she turned into a pillar of salt.
GENESIS 19:26

These two women, although separated by time, had a lot in common. They longed for the preservation of the status quo. Neither one could accept their losses, and they both rebelled against God. Job's wife told her husband to curse God, and Lot's wife deliberately quit going God's way, because she couldn't bear to let go of her things.

Sooner or later loss comes into everyone's life—be it financial reverses, the death of a loved one, or a loss of health. When my husband and I lost what would have supported us for the rest of our lives, we knew we had two choices. We could harbor resentment against God for allowing this to happen, or behave like Job, who chose to praise God regardless of his circumstances. The moment we chose the latter, the Lord removed futile regrets and heaviness of spirit.

Rely on the Lord in every area of your life.

—RITA STELLA GALIEH

223

Rejected No More

When the Lord saw that Leah was unloved, he enabled her to have children, but Rachel could not conceive.

GENESIS 29:31

Leah was no stranger to rejection. It came first from her father, Laban, and then from her husband, Jacob, but God did not reject her. He loved and valued her so much that He blessed her with seven children—one of whom was Judah, the lineage from which Jesus was born.

Although I've enjoyed success and many wonderful relationships, I've also experienced rejection from childhood classmates, employers, and fellow believers. Through it all, God has stood with outstretched arms, patiently waiting to comfort me.

He never fails to remind me that no matter how others may treat me, or how I may feel about myself, I'll always be precious to Him. I know He will never leave me nor forsake me.

Find comfort in God's unconditional acceptance.

—RENEE GRAY-WILBURN

Multiplication of the Casseroles

*There was always enough flour and olive oil left in the
containers, just as the Lord had promised through Elijah.*
1 Kings 17:16

We watched as twice the usual number of women
filed into the fellowship hall for our monthly circle lun-
cheon.

"What in the world are we going to do?" one of the
hostesses asked while she eyed the five casserole dishes.

"I guess we should pray and ask the Lord to multiply
the food," someone replied.

And that's what we did. We dished out generous portions to eighty women, instead of the expected forty, and
we had food left over. We served seconds to almost everyone. After we cleaned up the kitchen, we found another
casserole untouched and divided it between the five hostesses for their family dinner that evening.

Later, I watched my son clean his plate. "Mom, that
was the best dinner ever," he said.

Trust Jesus with the impossible.

—Sally Jadlow

The Master Planner

Then Deborah said to Barak, "Get ready! This is the day the LORD will give you victory over Sisera, for the LORD is marching ahead of you."

JUDGES 4:14

When we moved into our house located in a new development, we hired a surveyor to mark out the boundaries of our lot. After he placed the flags in strategic points around the yard, he showed me what he had done. He took out each flag and lifted up the sod he had removed to expose an underground stake. A surveyor hired by the builder had already done the work of plotting out the parameters of our lot. The only thing our surveyor had to do was find the location of those markers in order to know where the edge of our property fell.

God has prepared a path for our lives—all we need to do is find His markers. The only way to discover the Lord's "flags" is to stay in His will through persistent prayer and the divine wisdom revealed in His word.

Follow the Lord's path, trusting that He has gone before you.

—CINDY BOOSE

Open Door Policy

When Paul and Silas left the prison, they returned to the
home of Lydia. There they met with the believers and
encouraged them once more. Then they left town.
ACTS 16:40

Our church may not have a large membership, but we treasure the close and loving relationships that have developed as a result of having a smaller group. We often refer to our congregation as our church family, and we enjoy a multitude of activities together.

Harold and Connie are constantly opening their home to the "family." They often host informal gatherings and whether it's a Super Bowl party or a baby shower, everyone leaves full of food and fellowship.

We have been to their house numerous times, and I admit I'm a bit envious of the relaxed and almost carefree way in which they host a group of three or thirty. It doesn't matter if the sink is full of dishes or the family room has a decidedly lived-in look.

Harold and Connie have obviously decided that real friends are there to see them and not their house. Perhaps I should spend less time worrying about the mess in my living room and more time enjoying my family.

Is your door open for friends and fellowship?

—SBT

It's Never Really Goodbye

Each year his mother made a small coat for him and brought it to him when she came with her husband for the sacrifice.

1 SAMUEL 2:19

I've never considered motherhood as anything less than one of God's greatest blessings, but that doesn't mean I haven't experienced sorrow and heartbreak. Hannah has always been a powerful role model for me as I've struggled to train my children, and she has been a source of inspiration and encouragement during my darker moments.

When my daughter left home last year, I thought of Hannah, taking young Samuel to live with the priest in Shiloh. My daughter and I weren't saying goodbye in any permanent sense, but things would never be as they were when she lived at home.

As time passed, Hannah's influence and love remained constant. I often think of her taking Samuel a little coat every year to remind him how precious he was to her. And so it is with my daughter. There are many ways I can let her know that I think of her often and love her as much as ever.

Changes can bring new blessings.

—SBT

Acts of Love

There was a believer in Joppa named Tabitha (which in Greek is Dorcas). She was always doing kind things for others and helping the poor.
ACTS 9:36

Dorcas lived during the time of Jesus' ministry and spent her life serving the poor. She didn't just talk about the tragedy of hungry people; she found ways to feed them. When she heard that many local widows had nothing to wear, she made clothing for them.

When I served dinner at a local mission, I felt the needs of the homeless people who lived there. Even though I couldn't serve dinner every week, I wanted to help. I love to bake, so I asked the cook if I could bring two dozen loaves of pumpkin bread twice a month. He was ecstatic.

"Where do you get these ideas?" my husband asked. I told him the spirit of Dorcas led me.

All acts of service express God's love.

—KRISS ERICKSON

Accountability Days

She fell at his feet and said, "I accept all blame in this matter,
my lord. Please listen to what I have to say."
1 SAMUEL 25:24

One day, my eight-year-old son, Owen, came home from school in tears. He had been caught misbehaving on the bus and he told me, between hiccups and sobs, that the driver would be calling me later to discuss the problem.

My first thought was that some other undisciplined child had started the trouble and persuaded Owen to join in. Then I laughed at my own foolishness. My high-spirited, exuberant son was capable of getting into hot water all by himself. And there I was, making the matter worse by freeing Owen from facing any consequences or learning something of value from his experience.

When Abigail discovered David's plan to kill her entire household because of her husband Nabal's ignorance and greed, she hurried to David's camp. One of the first things she did was accept responsibility for Nabal's actions. She may not have been directly at fault, but she made herself accountable for the actions of her household.

There is no excuse for avoiding accountability.

—SBT

Turn Toward the Wind

At this time Aramean raiders had invaded the land of Israel,
and among their captives was a young girl who had been
given to Naaman's wife as a maid.
2 KINGS 5:2

Snatched from her home and family, this girl from Israel served Naaman's wife as a slave in a foreign land. Despite her circumstances, she continued to believe in God and pointed her master in the right direction for healing from his leprosy. She has been a source of encouragement to me when facing life's challenges. Do I run from the storm or turn toward the wind and look to my Lord and Savior Jesus Christ?

Sometimes we question why God permits trouble to enter our lives. I certainly didn't understand why He allowed me to become a twenty-five-year-old widow raising a newborn son. But God has been faithful to me through the years. I know He has a plan and His plan involves pointing people to Jesus.

It's difficult to adjust to life's turning points, but I've discovered the key to living is keeping my eyes on Jesus and embracing the change.

Plant your feet firmly on the Rock of Christ and turn toward
the wind.

—SUSAN KELLY SKITT

Honored Guests

One day Elisha went to the town of Shunem. A wealthy woman lived there, and she urged him to come to her home for a meal. After that, whenever he passed that way, he would stop there for something to eat.

2 KINGS 4:8

As a farmwife with five children, finding time to write isn't always easy. A few days ago, a knock at the door interrupted my work on a current writing project. I reluctantly gave up my seat at the computer to greet a friend from church who had come to visit. It wasn't long before I realized she was troubled and needed to talk.

Longing to return to work, I listened halfheartedly to my friend while I made coffee. And as we talked, my mind kept wandering back to the piece I was writing. Later, I deeply regretted my behavior. I had been to my friend's home many times—a place where I was treated like an honored guest and not an intruder.

The Shunammite woman welcomed Elisha whenever he was in town. I'm certain there were times when his arrival interfered with plans she had made, but her hospitality remained constant and cordial. As one of God's people, she understood her role to minister to those in need.

Are you available to those in need?

—SBT

Earthly Honors

"What is your request?" he asked. She replied, "In your Kingdom, please let my two sons sit in places of honor next to you, one on your right and the other on your left."
MATTHEW 20:21

When Jesus promised each of his apostles a throne in His coming kingdom, the mother of James and John mistakenly thought He referred to a kingdom of this Earth. She gathered her courage and asked Jesus to give her two sons positions of honor on either side of His throne.

Perhaps she was overly ambitious, or maybe she just wanted to make her sons happy. It wasn't until she witnessed Jesus' crucifixion and resurrection that she realized who truly knew what was best for her sons.

For several years now, my son Connor has achieved perfect scores in the Standards of Learning (SOL) tests administered by his school district. This prompted me to imagine a life of great academic achievement for Connor.

Then it occurred to me that perhaps God had made other plans for my son. I have learned to spend less time thinking I know what's best for my children, and more time in prayer asking for God's will in their lives.

Are you seeking earthly honors for your children or God's will for their lives?

—SBT

A Walk in the Garden

When the cool evening breezes were blowing, the man and his wife heard the Lord God walking about in the garden.
GENESIS 3:8

I meandered down the narrow path by the lake. The sun filtered through the trees and the dew glistened on the leaves. Breathing in the earthy scent, I gazed across the water. It looked like a sea of glass.

When I read my Bible, I feel like I'm walking through paradise with God. For a time, Eve walked and talked with God in the cool of the day. How peaceful the Garden of Eden must have been in those days.

As a busy mom, I find it difficult to get a few moments by myself, but I need time alone with God to navigate my day. His word keeps me on the right path and helps me maintain my spiritual perspective.

Experience the peace that comes from a walk with God.

—SUSAN KELLY SKITT

The Perfect Gift

*I commend to you our sister Phoebe, who is a deacon
in the church in Cenchrea. Welcome her in the Lord
as one who is worthy of honor among God's people.
Help her in whatever she needs, for she has been
helpful to many, and especially to me.*

ROMANS 16:1–2

I felt let down after spending six hours at the "Discovering Your Ministry Gifts" seminar. "Well, that was a waste of forty dollars," I said to my friend. "I don't have a special gift. I'm just a helper, and I already knew that."

Her eyes widened. "Yes, but you don't value it," she said. "Your gift is needed everywhere."

On the drive home, I reflected on her words. I remembered the long trips to assist at the birth of a new grandchild or packing boxes for a family's move to another state. I recalled the homeless family of five who lived with us for three months. I thought about the booklet I had written for women overcoming depression and the invitations to speak at various engagements—weren't these all forms of helping?

I love being a helper. God uses me to reach out to others in deceptively simple ways. I nestled into my ministry gift like a cozy bathrobe and decided I hadn't wasted my money after all.

Embrace your unique gifts with joy.

—SANDY EWING

Teamwork

*When Priscilla and Aquila heard him preaching boldly in
the synagogue, they took him aside and explained the way of
God even more accurately.*

ACTS 18:26

In the New Testament, we read of how the apostles
preached the gospel, but little is said about the women
in their lives. With Aquila, however, it's a different story.
Aquila is never mentioned without his wife. They were a
team.

Priscilla helped Aquila make tents and the two traveled with Paul. They helped the young pastor Timothy,
among many others, and a church met in their home.
When they heard Apollos speak in the synagogue, they
took him home and explained Christ's message more
accurately. Because of their efforts, Apollos won many to
Christ.

After I remarried, I constantly referred to my kids, my
house, and my problems until, one day, my new husband
said, "I thought we were in this together."

"We are," I answered, but then I realized I had been
trying to do everything alone. Since that time, I have
been more conscious about placing an emphasis on the
teamwork aspect of our relationship.

It takes more than one strand of twine to make a rope.

—ALICIA GOSSMAN-STEEVES

My Career Counselors

You will have great joy and gladness, and many will rejoice at his birth, for he will be great in the eyes of the Lord. He must never touch wine or other alcoholic drinks. He will be filled with the Holy Spirit, even before his birth.

LUKE 1:14–15

Elizabeth was faced with an immense responsibility as the mother of John the Baptist, but she never even hesitated. God had chosen her to be a profound influence in the life of the prophet who proclaimed the coming of the Messiah.

In the same way, God chose me to be the mother of my five children. It has been godly women like Elizabeth and my own mother who have given me strength and inspiration to fulfill my role. Being a mother hasn't always been easy or rewarding, but it was their devotion and the value they placed on motherhood that became my legacy. Because of them, I have never felt as though my time has been wasted, or that I missed out on a more significant job.

Our children may never be as famous as John the Baptist, but that doesn't diminish the duty or blessing God has given us. There are few, if any, responsibilities more weighty or worthy than being a mother.

God has entrusted mothers with a vital and valuable role.

—SBT

The Best of Everything

*But Jesus, aware of this, replied, "Why criticize this woman
for doing such a good thing to me?"*
MATTHEW 26:10

Jesus knew his days on Earth were coming to an end.
On several occasions, he tried to discuss His death and
resurrection with His disciples, but His words were met
with doubt, fear, and even denial.

However, this woman heard and believed Jesus, and
in an act of selfless love and devotion, she anointed Him
with some very expensive perfume. She wanted to give
Him a special gift before He died—her way of saying
thank you for His many priceless gifts.

My gratitude to God goes much deeper than simply
saying thank-you. Like this woman, I need to show God
how much I appreciate Him. One of the greatest gifts I
can give Him is to read and cherish my Bible, to take His
word and apply it to my life. I can share my love for God
with my children and with anyone else who cares to listen
and give Him my best in everything I do.

What will you do to show your gratitude to God?

—SBT

The Hundred-Dollar Question

When the queen of Sheba heard of Solomon's fame,
which brought honor to the name of the Lord,
she came to test him with hard questions.

1 KINGS 10:1

The queen of Sheba wanted answers to some serious questions. Recently, I had an important question of my own for God. I came home from work to find someone had slipped a white envelope containing a "God Bless You" greeting and $100 beneath my door. Exciting, right?

Not really. I should have been thrilled, but I immediately questioned the gift. I called my friends and badgered them with questions. "Who would anonymously give me money? Is it really for me? Did they get the wrong door?" Instead of being filled with gratitude for someone's generosity and praising God for His blessing, I ended up with a mind reeling with theories and a stomach tied up in knots.

Finally, one wise lady answered, "Why don't you just stop questioning it and thank God?"

Always praise God—that is the one-hundred-dollar answer.

—JAMIE BIRR

Expect the Unexpected

A Gentile woman who lived there came to him, pleading,
"Have mercy on me, O Lord, Son of David! For my daughter
is possessed by a demon that torments her severely."
MATTHEW 15:22

The woman in this passage knew who Jesus was, and even though He wasn't one of "her kind," she knew He could do whatever He wanted, to whomever He chose. She understood that He was capable of stepping outside of societal norms, and she didn't hesitate to seek His help for her daughter.

My past experiences, my heritage, and the teachings of my church have all shaped my idea of who Jesus is. Sometimes, I expect certain answers from Jesus according to these assumptions.

But Jesus has a way of shaking up our preconceived notions—as He did when He sent a long-haired, tattooed truck driver to help me change a flat tire when I was stranded by the side of the road. At first I was terrified by his appearance, but my fear turned to wonder as he held my hand and prayed alongside the busy interstate. The Gentile woman knew the Lord could answer any prayer in any way he chose. That night beside the road, I learned to expect the unexpected.

If we expect only certain answers from Jesus, we may miss
His most wonderful works.

—CINDY BOOSE

Who, Me?

*Go and gather together all the Jews of Susa and fast for me.
Do not eat or drink for three days, night or day. My maids
and I will do the same. And then, though it is against the
law, I will go in to see the king. If I must die, I must die.*
ESTHER 4:16

When I was fairly new to public speaking, I sometimes
doubted my ability. Other times, I was amazed that God
had actually called me to lead in this way. One morning,
when I prayed and admitted my lack of confidence, God
spoke directly to my heart. "This isn't about ability; it's
about obedience."

I suddenly realized that God just wanted me to perform the task He had set before me. He would take care
of the details. My somewhat flawed perception of my own
abilities was not an issue with God.

I like to think of Esther as an impoverished orphan in
a foreign land. She had no training to be queen or to save
an entire nation from destruction. She just did the thing
God set before her. Like Esther, I am here, right now, for
such a time as this.

*Step forward in obedience and
God will take care of the details.*

—KAREN MOREROD

A Quest for Answers

For she thought to herself,
"If I can just touch his robe, I will be healed."
MARK 5:28

For twelve years, she had suffered from a debilitating illness. For twelve years, she had sought treatment, only to be rendered penniless by ignorant or inept doctors. And for twelve long years, she had been an outcast—judged unclean according to the religious laws of her people.

She may have lived on the edge of complete despair, but she never lost her faith in God. And when she heard about Jesus, the hope she thought was dead flickered into life once more.

Somehow, she knew if she could only touch His clothing, she would be healed. But Jesus didn't simply cure a chronic physical condition. He brought healing to her heart and soul as well.

There have been times when I have let shame, fear, or guilt block my path to the Lord. Ignoring His still, small voice inviting me to share my burdens, I look to the world for my answers. It's only when I become lost that I realize I must find my way back to Jesus.

Start your quest for answers with God.

—SBT

Rejecting Revenge

Thank God for your good sense! Bless you for
keeping me from murder and from carrying out
vengeance with my own hands.
1 SAMUEL 25:33

Married to the domineering and selfish Nabal, Abigail's life was far from pleasant. Years of abuse might have made another woman bitter or vengeful, but not Abigail. When she learned of David's plan to kill her husband, she was given the perfect opportunity to exact her revenge.

Instead, she hurried to David's camp to plead for her husband's life and the lives of those in her household. By the time she finished her speech, she had convinced David that vengeance belonged to God.

When my youngest son was in the first grade, he was plagued by bullies. Every morning found me trying to persuade a frightened and tearful little boy to get on the school bus. Part of me wanted to punish my son's tormentors, to show them how it felt to be in their victim's shoes but, like Abigail, I had to leave that part up to God. Besides, I had a son who needed to see his mother trying to please God even when things turned tough.

Honor the Lord by resisting revenge.

—SBT

In the Business of Caring

The churches here in the province of Asia send greetings in the Lord, as do Aquila and Priscilla and all the others who gather in their home for church meetings.
1 CORINTHIANS 16:19

In the Bible, God commands his followers to assemble together in worship. He understood that the Christian walk could be a lonely experience, but He knew that association with other believers could resolve the feelings of isolation. Priscilla realized these things, too, and that's one reason she and her husband, Aquila, started several home churches.

Although a church is primarily a place for believers to gather, it also has an important place in our communities. In a day when the family unit is disintegrating, the church has an obligation to step forward and provide a haven for those in need of love, healing, and acceptance.

In addition, there are people in need of more tangible things such as food, clothing, and shelter. There will always be a call for missionaries to carry the gospel all over the world, but there is also a desperate need for ministries right here in our own country. As Christians, we can show the world that we're in the business of caring for others.

Open up your hearts—and your church—to those in need.

—SBT

Righteous Mother, Righteous Son

Hezekiah son of Ahaz began to rule over Judah in the third year of King Hoshea's reign in Israel. His mother was Abijah, the daughter of Zechariah. He did what was pleasing in the Lord's sight, just as his ancestor David had done.

2 KINGS 18:1–3

I pray for the teenagers, homeless and without direction, hanging out on my city's downtown streets. I send offerings to local street ministries. What will become of these children? Amazingly, some of them do well in spite of the faith-destroying circumstances around them.

His father, Ahaz, was the most evil king in Judah, and as a child he lost his brother to sacrifice in the arms of the god Molech. However, years later, God would call Hezekiah the most righteous king since David.

The Bible doesn't tell us, but Hezekiah's mother, Abijah, must have faithfully taught him to love the one true God. She probably had priests such as Micah and her father, Zechariah, instruct her son in the Law. We can be sure she prayed for him.

A mother's influence and prayers are never wasted.

—AUDREY HEBBERT

Generosity in Genesis

When she had given him a drink, she said, "I'll draw water for your camels, too, until they have had enough to drink."
GENESIS 24:19

One of Rebekah's daily chores was hauling water. Carrying big, heavy jars of water on her head was an exhausting task and, yet, she offered to make additional trips to get more water for a stranger and his camels. I am usually too preoccupied with my own survival needs to take responsibility for someone else.

The New Testament is full of exhortations to "go the extra mile" for people, and we are often encouraged to carry one another's burdens. This means making the effort to get to know someone and the issues that are important to them.

No doubt, we are struggling with our own large and cumbersome responsibilities, but when we offer our support and encouragement, God has a way of lightening our load as well.

Be generous with your time and encouragement.

—EVANGELINE BEALS GARDNER

Baby Love

When the princess opened the basket, she saw the baby. The little boy was crying, and she felt sorry for him. "This must be one of the Hebrew children," she said.

EXODUS 2:6

There was no hatred for the Hebrew slaves in the pharaoh's daughter's heart that day—only compassion for a helpless baby. She had no way of knowing that by saving the Hebrew child, she secured her role in the preservation of God's people.

When my fourth child was born, I lived across the street from young girl with her new baby. Her husband, a fisherman, was often gone for weeks at a time. I began to invite her over and, at first, she refused, but it wasn't long before loneliness led her to my door.

One day she confessed she knew next to nothing about babies. "God will help you," I said with a big smile. "And I'd be happy to do whatever I can." I believed that by helping the mother, I was also helping the child.

Although I've lost touch with my neighbor, I'd like to think I lightened her load during a difficult time. And I was greatly blessed with the opportunity to honor God by loving a child.

All children are precious in God's eyes.

—SBT

A Kind and Caring Man

*When the Lord saw her, his heart overflowed with
compassion. "Don't cry!" he said.*
LUKE 7:13

As Jesus entered the city of Nain, he encountered a
funeral procession. He found out that the man who died
was the only son of an elderly widow and, moved by the
woman's grief, he raised her son from the dead. The crowd
who witnessed the event was understandably terrified, but
they gave the glory to God.

Jesus didn't perform this miracle for the benefit of the
crowd. He restored the young man to his mother because
he had compassion for her feelings and her situation. He
wasn't just God accomplishing a miracle; He was a kind
and tender man reaching out to a suffering woman.

Jesus knew that an older widow with no family would
be in a fragile, economically unstable position and dependent on the charity of others.

So often, after attending a funeral, we go on with our
lives, unaware that the grief-stricken are struggling with
their devastating loss. This is when they really need love
and compassion.

*Be there in the difficult days after someone endures the loss
of a loved one.*

—SBT

Full-Time Zookeepers

Pairs of every kind of bird, and every kind of animal, and every kind of small animal that scurries along the ground, will come to you to be kept alive.

GENESIS 6:20

My husband and I sometimes discuss getting away for a weekend alone together, but we keep a lot of animals that have specific needs.

I'm quite sure Noah's wife would have welcomed a day off from caring for the floating zoo even if she wasn't able to leave the ark. For her family, it was a matter of survival, whereas for my family, it's always been a labor of love. Even so, we still have something in common. We made a commitment to care for our animals and we've kept it, no matter what.

I've made many other commitments, but unlike the animals, some of these promises can be shelved without appearing to disturb the status quo. A while ago, I promised God I would set aside time every day after lunch and before bedtime for prayer and devotionals. It would be easy to skip these times, but I need to nurture and satisfy all my commitments—human, animal, and spiritual.

Are you staying true to all of your commitments?

—SBT

Something out of Nothing

One day the widow of a member of the group of prophets came to Elisha and cried out, "My husband who served you is dead, and you know how he feared the Lord. But now a creditor has come, threatening to take my two sons as slaves."
2 KINGS 4:1

When Elisha asked the widow if she had anything of value in the house, at first she said there was nothing. Then she hesitated and added, "Nothing save a pot of oil." It's fairly obvious she didn't think the pot of oil was going to be any help.

However, God had quite a different view of a seemingly insignificant item. Through Elisha, he created a miracle that not only resulted in the widow's being able to pay her debts, but also left her with money for living expenses.

I may feel like I have little or nothing to give, but God isn't counting or measuring. Throughout the Bible, He often makes much out of little, and my life is no exception. If I give Him what I have, He will give me more. If I am willing to trust Him and pour out my little jar of oil, He will refill it and continue to refill it until I have precisely what I need.

It all starts with trust.

—SBT

AUGUST

Lessons in Surrender

No one is holy like the Lord! There is no one besides you;
there is no Rock like our God.
1 Samuel 2:2

$\mathcal{F}$or several years, we had been struggling with our daughter's rebellion. Not only were matters escalating, there didn't seem to be any end in sight. We saw no sign that her heart was turning back to God. Now I was tired. Worn out from wondering what I should do next, weary of worrying, and frustrated because I didn't see any answers to my prayers. The conflict had completely exhausted me.

A few years later, my prayers were answered, and my daughter recommitted her life and heart to living for God. I was so thankful God had given her the strength to make better life choices.

If the same situation occurred now, I'm not sure I would offer up the same prayers. Not that my petitions at that time were wrong. I believe God had compassion for my desperate heart, my weariness, and my lack of acceptance for His eternal plan. Since then, however, studying and understanding the story of another desperate woman have sharpened my spiritual awareness.

When we first meet Hannah in the Old Testament, she is a desperately unhappy, barren woman. Worse yet, her husband's other wife was enjoying the abundant fruits of her womb while she mocked Hannah daily for her failure. The infertility and taunting continued year after year.

In an act of complete surrender, Hannah cried out to God for a child. She vowed that if He granted her request, she would dedicate the child to do God's work in the temple at Shiloh.

I had difficulty understanding this. Why would she pray earnestly, pleadingly, for something and then give it up? It didn't make sense to me, especially when I remembered my fervent prayers for my daughter. I wanted my daughter back so we could enjoy a close relationship.

Much like Hannah, I was pleading for a child. Why was Hannah willing to relinquish the child she so desperately wanted? Then, I recognized a hint of shortsightedness in my thinking. Hannah's life resounded with a spiritual maturity that I lacked—a maturity I was determined to achieve.

Hannah knew God was the source of all things. Her long-awaited son was one of His most precious gifts. I have acknowledged that God gave my children to me, but for a long time, I didn't share Hannah's commitment to this belief.

In the years following my daughter's teen rebellion, I gave more thought to God's miraculous gift and found myself in a state of awe that God had chosen me to parent this strong-willed child. He makes no mistakes when He blesses people with His gifts. This realization has given me a greater confidence to make it through my struggles as a mother.

Not only is God the source of all things, but He also answers our prayers in His own time. In my prayers for my daughter, I often rebelled against the Lord's timing, but that only resulted in frustration and, sometimes, bitterness. If I had trusted in His wisdom, I could have rested more fully in His hands and relieved my heart of much worry.

Some may pray for a better job, the right spouse, or physical healing. If we believe God always acts in our best interests, we can be assured that what He gives and when He gives it will be perfect.

Hannah demonstrated that all things are intended for God's glory. She wasn't abandoning her child; she was giving him back to God. She recognized that God had given her the child, so her choice to commit the boy to the Lord's service was a natural act of deep gratitude.

Today, I want Hannah's eternal perspective to inspire me. I want to realize God can be seen and worshiped in the most difficult circumstances. Most of all, I want to remember Hannah's declaration that everything belongs to the Lord and her conviction that our world is under the authority of a great and loving Heavenly Father.

There will be more struggles and times of asking, even pleading with God, for the health of my friends and loved ones, for my financial and material needs to be met, and for the strength to forgive when I've been mistreated. God allows difficulties to enter our lives. He could remove our troubles if He wanted to, but the tough times allow God to shower us with His love, mercy, and strength.

It's amazing how God's lessons travel through time. I can't help but wish I'd learned Hannah's remarkable messages sooner, but I can chose to live my life today so others will be inspired in years to come.

—KAREN MOREROD

The Good Aunt

*But Ahaziah's sister Jehosheba, the daughter of King
Jehoram, took Ahaziah's infant son, Joash, and stole him
away from among the rest of the king's children, who were
about to be killed. She put Joash and his nurse in a bedroom
to hide him from Athaliah, so the child was not murdered.*

2 KINGS 11:2

Wicked Queen Jezebel had a daughter named Athaliah
who was every bit as evil as her mother. When Athaliah's
son Ahaziah was killed she wanted power at any cost. She
decided to kill any relative who could usurp her throne.
She began systematically wiping out her family, even
intending to kill her infant grandson Joash. She would
have succeeded, but. . . .

The word *but* introduces a mighty story. Aunt
Jehosheba played an important role in saving the future
king's life. Jehosheba was the wife of a priest and wisely
hid the baby in the holy places of the kingdom.

Have you ever had a special aunt? My aunt Geneva
took care of me when I was a child and, later, I lived with
her as a teen. She never places limits on the time she
spends with her family. And if we need help, she is there
for her nieces and nephews.

*Women are mighty protectors of family, and the enemies
who get in their way should beware!*

—LaRose Karr

Amazing Love

When the Lord saw that Leah was unloved, he enabled her
to have children, but Rachel could not conceive.
GENESIS 29:31

After deceiving his father to receive the blessing meant for his brother, Jacob had to leave home and live near his uncle Laban. He worked for Laban for seven years to be able to marry his daughter, Rachel. During the wedding ceremony he was tricked and given Leah, Rachel's older sister. In the midst of this story one scripture stands out—"When the Lord saw that Leah was unloved. . . ."

Blessings, birthrights, customs, anger, jealousy, and deception were all part of this story. I ponder the intricately crafted accounts of these inadequate and flawed people. And yet, I'm not surprised by God's response to Leah's distress. She was a pawn in the game of life, but God saw her as His special daughter.

I am also one of God's special daughters, and when circumstances in my life leave me feeling unloved or unappreciated, I need to remember that I am still the blessed recipient of His love—a love that never falters or diminishes.

God's love remains constant throughout eternity.

—LAROSE KARR

Not Just a Pretty Face

When the queen of Sheba heard of Solomon's fame, which brought honor to the name of the Lord, she came to test him with hard questions.

1 KINGS 10:1

Most women long to be noticed for their beauty. I spent my college years focused more on my wardrobe than my mind. As I grew older, I realized beauty was fleeting and, now, after fifty-plus years of living, I truly appreciate the story of the queen of Sheba.

The Bible doesn't speak of her beauty. Instead, it focuses on her sharp, inquisitive mind, as well as her great wealth and adventurous spirit. She was a wise woman who respected God.

Few women have achieved her position of honor. Yet, in all of her glory and power, there is no evidence of her vanity. She is a true role model for young women. She demonstrates that the most beautiful and noticeable traits are those within, the ones that are enhanced and not depleted with the passage of time.

Are you focused on the beauty within?

—MARY CATHERINE ROGERS

The First Birthday

*When she gave birth to Cain, she said, "With the Lord's help,
I have produced a man!"*
GENESIS 4:1

Babies haven't always arrived in sterile hospital set-
tings with an assortment of medical personnel in atten-
dance. In the not-too-distant past, many babies were born
at home with the assistance of a female neighbor and perhaps a doctor. There was certainly no doctor nor even
another woman present when Eve went through childbirth.

I find it difficult, if not impossible, to imagine being
the first women to have a baby. But Eve did it with Adam
by her side, and when it was all over, she gave God the
credit for guiding her through what must have been a baf-
fling, terrifying experience.

I love thinking back to the births of my five children,
but when I stop to recall each little detail, I'm careful to
make sure God is in the picture. Just like Eve, I couldn't
have done it without His help.

We don't have to go through anything alone.

—SBT

A Good Son

And he said to this disciple, "Here is your mother." And
from then on this disciple took her into his home.
JOHN 19:27

My son Dylan recently went on a weekend field trip
with his Junior ROTC regiment. When the group stopped
to eat in Lancaster, Pennsylvania, Dylan struck up a conversation with a young girl. After she left, he noticed
she had left her money on the counter. He grabbed the
money and hurried outside where he found the girl and
her mother.

Later, he told his father about returning the money,
and Tom gave him a big hug. "You're a good son," he said
in a voice filled with obvious emotion.

During the time Jesus spent on Earth, he experienced
many things, including the powerful love a son has for his
mother. His final words to Mary never fail to move me.
He was dying, but He wanted to make certain she would
be cared for. Jesus may have been Mary's Savior, but she
knew He was much more than that. He was a good son.

Acknowledge the good things your child does.

—SBT

Turning Points

So Hilkiah the priest, Ahikam, Acbor, Shaphan, and Asaiah went to the New Quarter of Jerusalem to consult with the prophet Huldah. She was the wife of Shallum son of Tikvah, son of Harhas, the keeper of the Temple wardrobe.

2 KINGS 22:14

While repairing the rundown temple, the workers found a portion of the Book of the Law containing God's word. They gave it to the men in charge who, in turn, read the scroll's contents to King Josiah.

Upon hearing it, the king tore his robes as a sign of anguish for his disobedient nation of sinners. Then he told Hilkiah, the priest, and other dignitaries to lay the matter before Huldah, the prophetess.

King Josiah knew what to do in a crisis—he consulted a person in touch with God. With the help of her judicious counsel, he turned the nation away from wickedness.

When I suffered distress in my soul due to sin, I sought the advice of my pastor, a man of God. Many young people in the same situation turned to drugs, alcohol, or sex. The wise pastor talked and prayed with me until my sin-burdened past was lifted.

In your time of need, turn to someone in touch with God.

—JEWELL JOHNSON

When Hope Is Lost

She named the child Ichabod (which means "Where is the glory?"), for she said, "Israel's glory is gone." She named him this because the Ark of God had been captured and because her father-in-law and husband were dead.

1 SAMUEL 4:21

When Ichabod's mother heard that her husband and father-in-law were dead and that the Philistines had captured the Ark of God, she went into labor and gave birth to her son.

She named the baby Ichabod—"the glory has departed"—just before she died. Because the Ark, the symbol of God's presence, had left Israel, she thought her child had no future.

When our oldest son had an epileptic seizure at the age of fourteen, I succumbed to intense feelings of depression. As I cared for him during subsequent seizures, I felt alone and forsaken. What kind of future will my child have?

When our second son also began having seizures, the outlook for the two boys seemed dismal. Unlike Ichabod's mother, however, our family refused to abandon hope, and we struggled to sustain our faith in God to protect the boys. He didn't fail us.

God never forsakes those who place their trust in Him.

—JEWELL JOHNSON

The Power of Persistence

The judge ignored her for a while, but finally he said to himself, "I don't fear God or care about people, but this woman is driving me crazy."

LUKE 18:4–5

For two years after our Dalmatian died, my two daughters begged for another dog. I responded with what I considered common and practical reasons for not adding to a household already ruled by two cats.

My girls had youth and inexhaustible energy on their side, and their persistence wore me out. Their tenacity sent me to the animal shelter where I rescued Zoe, the four-year-old orphan that looked like a miniature golden retriever.

Christ's parable about the persistent widow is also a rather lighthearted tale. He described the judge as someone who didn't care about God or man. Yet, he finally yielded and dispensed justice to a woman who had no power other than her unrelenting determination.

May we persevere in prayer until God answers our requests.

—EVANGELINE BEALS GARDNER

A Blessing and an Honor

"Mary!" Jesus said. She turned to him and cried out,
"Rabboni!" (which is Hebrew for "Teacher").
JOHN 20:16

I wasn't very fond of my name when I was a little girl, but I grew to like it as I got older. One day, I realized that my name itself wasn't as important as the way someone said it. The first time I read the account of the meeting between Mary Magdalene and Jesus after His resurrection, I was deeply touched when He called her by name. What a glorious tribute, I thought. He not only knew her name, but He also knew everything about her, including her thoughts and feelings.

It occurred to me that I, too, am blessed and honored because Jesus knows my name and everything about me. Then I remembered the first time He called my name. It was the day I invited Him into my heart.

Listen carefully—Jesus might be calling your name!

—SBT

It's Not about Me

One day Cain suggested to his brother, "Let's go out into the fields." And while they were in the field, Cain attacked his brother, Abel, and killed him.

GENESIS 4:8

Earlier this year, in a fit of rebellion, my eighteen-year-old daughter left home. For the next few weeks, I wallowed in a toxic mixture of self-pity and guilt. My "perfect" family was now flawed, and I felt wounded and fragile. I asked God to heal my broken heart, but felt no relief.

I thought about Eve, the mother of all humanity, thrust from paradise into a tragedy I could scarcely imagine. Refusing to be suffocated by self, Eve had found comfort and strength in her faith and carried on.

I finally understood why I had found no respite. Blinded by my own misery, I lost sight of the countless mothers living with heartbreak. It was only when I began to pray for my daughter and for other women suffering in sorrow that I gained the support and encouragement I needed to carry on.

Let your suffering open your eyes to the needs of others.

—SBT

Ready, Willing, and Available

This man had a very beautiful and lovely young cousin, Hadassah, who was also called Esther. When her father and mother died, Mordecai adopted her into his family and raised her as his own daughter.

ESTHER 2:7

You don't get any more insignificant than Esther. She was a woman, she was an orphan, and she was a Jew in exile. In other words, she was perfect for God's purpose. The Bible is full of stories in which God chooses the most ordinary person to achieve the most extraordinary things. Only God could take an orphaned Jewish girl, transform her into a queen, and set the stage for her to save the Jewish race.

Esther and the other unremarkable individuals chosen by God all had one thing in common. A few of them needed a little persuasion, but eventually they all nodded their heads. "Yes, God," they said, "I'll do it."

I'm pretty sure my husband and children think I'm wonderful, but that about covers my fan club. God doesn't want to know if I'm amazing—He just wants to find out if I'm willing.

Let God know you're available.

—SBT

A Solid Foundation

The churches here in the province of Asia send greetings in the Lord, as do Aquila and Priscilla and all the others who gather in their home for church meetings.

1 CORINTHIANS 16:19

Every Wednesday night for two years, I enjoyed sitting under the teaching of a wonderful Bible study leader. Gwen was no ordinary teacher; she had come straight from the mission field to the classroom. She had spent decades ministering and doing the Lord's work with her husband by her side.

Back in our country, on a break from career missions, our powerful teacher inched through the book of Matthew for two years. No rush, no hurry. Verse by verse, truth by truth. Each week, we propped our Bibles on one knee and a notebook on the other and listened intently to the wisdom that flowed from her lips to our ears and hearts.

Serving the Lord and supporting her husband in ministry—such was the foundation for the lessons she taught. She had built her life on the rock that is Jesus Christ. Her heart overflowed in devotion to her Lord, much like Aquila's loving wife, Priscilla.

Serve the Lord in gladness, wherever He sends you!

—JENNIFER DEVLIN

It All Goes to the Same Place

*Joanna, the wife of Chuza, Herod's business manager;
Susanna; and many others who were contributing their own
resources to support Jesus and his disciples.*

LUKE 8:3

The bookkeeper regarded me with suspicious eyes. "Make sure to turn in all of your receipts," she said. She knew me. She also knew I'd probably never turn in this set of receipts, either. I rarely worried much about getting reimbursed for supplies and items for programs.

I believe we can give to the Lord in so many different ways. We support ministries, contribute supplies, and even give our tithes and offerings. When my friendly bookkeeper gives me a hard time about receipts, I have a simple answer to explain my motives. "It all goes to the same place anyway!"

Contributing to the furthering of the gospel and filling the many needs of God doesn't happen only in church. Just like Joanna, who supported the ministry of Jesus and the disciples out of her own wealth, we too can contribute to our community of faith in a variety of ways.

*Use the talents and resources the Lord has blessed
you with to be a blessing to others.*

—JENNIFER DEVLIN

Grab Hold of Hope

*But when she came to the man of God at the mountain,
she fell to the ground before him and caught hold of his
feet. Gehazi began to push her away, but the man of God
said, "Leave her alone. She is deeply troubled, but the
Lord has not told me what it is."*

2 KINGS 4:27

"I'm calling to let you know that your son has left the facility," the woman on the phone said. I was heartbroken. It had only been one day since my son had arrived at a Christian center to receive counsel and treatment for his alcohol addiction. Now, he had run away. And I was told that there was nothing I could do. Wrong.

I knew the story of the Shunammite woman. Just as the Shunammite woman grabbed hold of the prophet Elisha's feet, I knelt at the feet of Jesus. Despite being told to give up on my son, I refused to let go of the hope I knew Jesus could provide. Today, my son is a loving, vital part of our family—the family he virtually abandoned for many years.

There is always hope with Jesus.

—CHARLOTTE KARDOKUS

The Eeyore of Ur

His wife said to him, "Are you still trying to maintain your integrity? Curse God and die."

Job 2:9

She never saw the glass half full, or even half empty—it was drained dry. Job's wife had been the unwilling recipient of the devil's attack against her husband because of his righteous life. Previously, she'd happily shared Job's blessings of wealth, a large family, and good health.

But when the going got tough, our girl lost faith in the provider of those blessings. Hope disintegrated. She became the distributor of gloom and doom, just like Winnie the Pooh's friend, Eeyore.

Sometimes, we lose sight of everything God has done and focus only on what He didn't do. Our attitudes nosedive and negativity imprisons us. Job's response is the key to escaping the shackles of Eeyore-ism. "I know that my Redeemer lives." Job's wife discovered the truth of her husband's declaration when God restored all she had lost and more.

With God, your glass is overflowing.

—Debora M. Coty

Childlike Trust

*Mary asked the angel,
"But how can this happen? I am a virgin."*
LUKE 1:34

When I was a little girl, I pictured Mary as someone much like my mother—mature, even matronly, in appearance and bearing. It was a shock to discover, years later, that she was barely a teenager when the angel Gabriel paid her a visit.

Her age is only one of many remarkable things about Mary. I think Mary's most amazing quality is her simple acceptance of the angel's announcement.

She asks only one question, posed in a voice of childlike trust. There is no hesitation, no arguing, and no bargaining. Her unshakeable trust in God leads her to risk her reputation, her marriage, and her life to answer most eloquently, "I am the Lord's servant. May everything you have said about me come true."

When my life gets turned upside down, I tend to complicate things by worrying, questioning, and even panicking. Peace comes only when, like Mary, I respond to God with the pure and simple trust of a child.

Be as a child and trust the Lord.

—SBT

Baby Steps

"I know the Lord has given you this land," she told them. "We are all afraid of you. Everyone in the land is living in terror."

JOSHUA 2:9

Unlike the other residents of Jericho, Rahab chose to believe the stories she had heard about the Lord. She took a huge step of faith, and God blessed her in numerous ways. He not only saved her life and the lives of her family, He also gave her an honored position in the genealogy of His son.

My son's girlfriend, Bobbijo, took the test to get her learner's license twice and failed both times. She was understandably discouraged, but the lure of a driver's license proved too powerful, and she began to study again.

This time, I told her to pray and put the situation in God's hands. I reminded her that we were all behind her 100 percent but, more important, God believed in her. He would be with her every step of the way. For Bobbijo, it was a small step of faith, but she took it and was rewarded with a passing score.

Even the tiniest steps of faith please the Lord.

—SBT

A Good Reputation

One day the girl said to her mistress,
"I wish my master would go to see the prophet in Samaria.
He would heal him of his leprosy."
2 Kings 5:3

When my daughter was three years old, she had an extraordinary memory. One day, I lost my keys and, without hesitation, I asked her if she had seen them. Within moments, she put them in my hand. I knew I had gone to the right person for help.

When a little maid advised Naaman, suffering from leprosy, to see a prophet from her homeland for help, the great warrior was willing to go before kings, seek a stranger, and bathe in dirty water for healing—all based on the recommendation of a little girl.

That says a lot about Naaman's trust in her words, and it says even more about this young lady's reputation. Whether it's locating lost keys or facilitating physical healing, our reputations precede us when giving others advice.

Based on your reputation,
would someone follow your advice?

—Leslie J. Sherrod

The Intercessor

Then Deborah said to Barak, "Get ready! This is the day the Lord will give you victory over Sisera, for the Lord is marching ahead of you." So Barak led his 10,000 warriors down the slopes of Mount Tabor into battle.

JUDGES 4:14

When spouses, neighbors, or nations clash, the disagreement is often fueled by sharp, contentious words. I discovered this truth on the afternoon I enraged my new neighbor by fighting off her cat when it tried to bite and scratch me.

I wanted to retaliate. Instead, I went into my house to doctor my wounds and calm myself. I decided that our conflict was senseless, and I needed to make things right.

The next morning, I baked a luscious prune cake with walnuts, carried it next door, and rang her doorbell. When she threw open the door, her expression told me she was still very angry, but when she saw my peace offering, her face softened and tears welled in her eyes.

That day, I learned that God's solution was a lot better than mine. Soft words—and warm prune cake—will indeed turn away wrath.

Sweet words are easier to swallow.

—IMOGENE JOHNSON

Order in the House

*Charm is deceptive, and beauty does not last; but a woman
who fears the Lord will be greatly praised.*
PROVERBS 31:30

It seems like every Mother's Day I hear a sermon on that pesky Proverbs 31 woman, held up as the perfect standard—the epitome of a godly woman. Don't you get tired of hearing about her sometimes? As one of my friends pointed out, the Proverbs 31 woman had help because scripture mentions her servants. I received little comfort from that observation because having servants only meant that she administrated in a skillful manner, too.

I look up to her and long to possess her many admirable characteristics but, sometimes, I lose sight of her most important quality. God was number one in her life, and she used the gifts He had given her to the best of her ability.

Every Christian woman, married or not, should emulate her in this regard. I constantly strive to put God first—before my husband, my children, my work, or anything else. In at least one area, I can be just like the Proverbs 31 woman!

Ask God for His guidance in establishing your priorities.

—DONNA J. SHEPHERD

Road Hazards

*When Mary arrived and saw Jesus, she fell at
his feet and said, "Lord, if only you had been
here, my brother would not have died."*

JOHN 11:32

When Mary first saw Jesus after her brother's death, she responded to his presence with love and faith. She knew Jesus was capable of amazing miracles, and there was no doubt in her mind that He could have saved Lazarus. Her words to Jesus demonstrate a deep, unswerving faith—a powerful message that calls out to me more than 2,000 years later.

I find it much easier to believe when things are running smoothly, but the road of life is filled with potholes and ruts. Illness, grief, loss, or any of the other bumps that lie waiting for me down the road should not deter real faith—the kind that Mary possessed.

To keep my faith from faltering I need to commit myself fully to God, I need to read and rejoice in His word, and I need to replace my earthly worries with the things of God.

Does your faith falter when you hit one of life's rough spots?

—SBT

Behind the Scenes

Year after year it was the same—Peninnah would taunt
Hannah as they went to the Tabernacle. Each time,
Hannah would be reduced to tears and would not even eat.
1 SAMUEL 1:7

Sometimes, Hannah must have thought that if God were going to make her a mother, He would have done it by now. Hannah had no way of knowing that, despite her fears and doubts, God was at work in her life. Hannah is just one of many women in the Bible who felt God was working too slowly in their lives or, worse yet, believed He had deserted them.

I can share numerous examples of God's miraculous intervention in my life, but I have come to realize that He is most often at work on specifics and seemingly trivial details. I know that when it comes to God, nothing is inconsequential.

He is the conductor of my life's symphony, concentrating on every note, bringing dozens of sounds together to create a beautiful song. And just like His work in my life, the polished performance I finally hear takes time.

You may not see it, but God is working in your life at this
very moment.

—SBT

One Hundred Percent

She never left the Temple but stayed there day and night,
worshiping God with fasting and prayer.
LUKE 2:37

Eighty-four year old Anna was a fixture at the Women's Court in the temple at Jerusalem. Widowed at an early age, she committed the rest of her life to worshiping God. She spent her days and nights praying, fasting, and waiting for the coming of the Messiah. Many years went by, but her devotion never faltered, and her belief in God's promises never wavered.

Unlike Anna, I chose a life that keeps me far too busy to spend my days in constant prayer. However, I can make sure the time I do spend in worship gives God the glory and honor He deserves.

A few months ago, it occurred to me that, when it came to prayer, God was not getting my best, especially in church. I may have been sitting in a pew, but my mind was often somewhere else. Since then, I have committed myself to giving the Lord one-hundred percent, whether I'm singing a hymn or listening to His word.

Is God getting your best?

—SBT

Someone's Little Girl

Then the Lord said to me, "Go and love your wife again,
even though she commits adultery with another lover. This
will illustrate that the Lord still loves Israel, even though the
people have turned to other gods and love to worship them."
HOSEA 3:1

I'm sure the women in Gomer's neighborhood scorned her, looked past her on the street, and whispered behind her back. And I have been guilty of passing judgment and finding comfort in thinking, "I'd never do a thing like that!"

Perhaps I could have done such a thing, had I walked the path she walked. Maybe someone she should have been able to trust betrayed her as a little girl. Perhaps, the treachery left her tiny soul soiled, scarred, and misshapen, her ears dull and her eyes dimmed.

I've seen Gomer—and many like her—in the present day. She stumbles down the street as I hurry past, and I can't help but think she was once someone's little girl. She came into the world helpless and needy, but with the same potential as any other baby. Someone should have prayed for her. Someone should have taken her little hand and taught her how to walk in this world. Someone should have loved her.

Children need prayer, guidance,
and love to reach their potential.

—VIRGINIA DAWKINS

Stepping Stones to Providence

*May the Lord, the God of Israel, under whose
wings you have come to take refuge, reward
you fully for what you have done.*
RUTH 2:12

When I read the story of three widows in a time when women without men were most vulnerable, Ruth amazed me. I understood Orpah making a "normal" choice for her future by going back to her family and her familiar neighborhood. I related to Naomi's grief after losing her husband and two sons. But Ruth, even though her life had been forever changed by the same tragedy, behaved in a courageous, selfless manner.

She dealt with her problems by rising each morning and focusing on things she could do for others. Ignoring any risk to her own life, she concerned herself with providing for her mother-in-law.

This remarkable young woman had no way of seeing God's intended provision for her life. She wasn't aware of the happy ending to her story, an ending in which God would give her a rich husband and a prominent place in the lineage of Jesus Christ. She simply walked by faith.

Walking by faith leads into the pathway of God's providence.

—VIRGINIA DAWKINS

Pennies

While Jesus was in the Temple, he watched the rich people dropping their gifts in the collection box.
LUKE 21:1

My mom was a lot like the widow who gave two small coins. She believed that every dollar she earned making buttonholes at the local shirt factory actually belonged to God. And she believed if she gave Him the first ten percent of each paycheck, He would stretch the rest to feed and clothe her children.

One day, she accidentally dropped an envelope containing her tithe into the trash can. When she realized what had happened, she ran outside to search the garbage. To her horror, she found the dented metal can empty and the garbage truck long gone. Tears welled in her eyes as she scanned the sidewalk, grass, and shrubs.

And then she spotted a white envelope wedged in the thick branches of a shrub. She pulled it out to find God's money safe inside. Now, as an adult, I realize that God didn't really need Mom's pennies. What He treasured most was her faith in Him to supply our needs.

Express your gratitude to God.

—VIRGINIA DAWKINS

Mothers of Nations

*And I will bless her and give you a son from her! Yes, I will
bless her richly, and she will become the mother of many
nations. Kings of nations will be among her descendants.*
GENESIS 17:16

I hated Mother's Day. Every year, all the mothers at
church were asked to stand. Then they were given a flower
and praised. After six years of marriage, I was still childless, and it felt like Mother's Day had been specifically
designed as a potent reminder of my heartache.

Like Sarah, I discovered that God's timing wasn't my
own. Eventually, I became the mother of two adopted
children and then, by God's grace, gave birth to another.
These joyful events didn't solve all my problems. In some
ways, my trials were just beginning—but any mother can
tell you that!

In our global village, it takes more than just the birth
mother to raise a child. Everyone has something to offer
in the complex, often difficult job of parenting. We can
contribute in a multitude of ways, even if our involvement
is limited to simply being a positive role model. We are all
mothers of nations.

Every woman deserves to celebrate Mother's Day.

—JEAN CAMPION

Words as Weapons

So Peninnah would taunt Hannah and make fun of her
because the Lord had kept her from having children.
1 Samuel 1:6

She was the second wife, brought into the family for one purpose only—to bear children. Peninnah quickly became a mother, but endured the heartbreak of knowing that her husband, Elkanah, didn't love her. She may have been unable to do anything about her situation, but she wasn't completely powerless.

Scarred by hatred and bitterness, she sought to ease her own suffering by inflicting pain on Elkanah's barren first wife, Hannah. Her only weapons were mere words, often more deadly than any knife or spear.

If someone accused me of being a violent person, my claims of innocence would be loud and long. And yet, I have used words to wound. When I am hurt or angered, my instincts cry out for me to strike back, but God gave me much more than instincts. He gave me the power to choose. Hurting someone else displays my weakness, whereas living to please the Lord demonstrates my greatest strength.

Words should inspire—not injure.

—SBT

Her Savior's Eyes

When the accusers heard this, they slipped away one by one,
beginning with the oldest, until only Jesus was left in the
middle of the crowd with the woman.
JOHN 8:9

The teachers of religious law and the Pharisees had come up with a permanent answer to adultery—for the women, anyway. Women found guilty of this sin were stoned to death. Killing someone was certainly one way of ending his or her sinful behavior, but Jesus arrived on the scene with a kinder, gentler solution that was lifesaving in more ways than one.

The authorities sought to end the woman's sin by condemning it—and her. Jesus vanquished the same sin by forgiving it. Not only did He give the woman the opportunity to change the way she lived, but I have a feeling she also would always remember the love and mercy in her Savior's eyes.

If I am hurt by someone's actions or words, I accomplish nothing by reacting in kind. It may not be the easiest thing to do, but I need to forgive. My forgiveness will not only please God, but, as Jesus demonstrated, it will have a far more lasting effect than my condemnation.

Forgiveness saves lives.

—SBT

Stop to Think

*But since Shechem had defiled their sister, Dinah, Jacob's
sons responded deceitfully to Shechem and his father, Hamor.*
Genesis 34:13

Dinah didn't stop to think how her decision to leave the family compound might affect others. Not only did she end up as a victim of rape, but she also placed her entire family in danger.

Seeking revenge, her brothers massacred every man in the town where the rapist lived. Then, they looted the area and took the women and children as slaves. When word of their vengeful acts spread, Dinah's family was forced to flee for their lives.

Faith brings its share of rewards, but it also carries an immense responsibility. As the mother of five, I've always been sensitive to the effect my behavior may have on my children. Recently, I became aware that my conduct may also affect a fellow believer—particularly, someone with a weaker faith.

Like my children, younger Christians are watching me and, perhaps, following my example. With God's help, I need to recognize the greater good and base my actions and decisions upon it.

*Stop to think and pray before you act—
someone may be watching.*

—SBT

Learning from the Potholes

He went on board the boat to escape the flood—he and his wife and his sons and their wives.
GENESIS 7:7

Few of us learn anything when life is treating us well and the road ahead is smooth and straight. We may hit a small bump and feel a bit smug when we—mistakenly— think we've handled it all on our own. It's when we hit a big pothole, one that really shakes us up, that God enters the picture.

Most people react in one of two ways. There are those who get angry with God, and then there are others who accept their trials with the belief that God is trying to teach them something. Noah's wife was one woman who chose to make the best of what appeared to be a bad situation.

As a result, she came through her situation a better woman. She learned more about herself and her God; she acquired skills, both spiritual and practical. She chose to see her hardship as a blessing and not a curse.

What is God trying to teach you right now?

—SBT

285

SEPTEMBER

Discovering the Good Part

There is only one thing worth being concerned about. Mary
has discovered it, and it will not be taken away from her.
LUKE 10:42

I am contacting you on behalf of the church nominating committee," the friendly voice on the other end of the line said. "We'd like you to assume the position of chair of our education ministry."

I had led several ministry teams for this congregation of more than 1,000 members, but I had never considered myself qualified for the education ministry. Several seconds of silence passed. "Are you still there, Ms. Curry?" the caller inquired. "We know this is a big job, but with your background and commitment to education, we're convinced you can do it. In fact, you were our unanimous choice."

I smiled. Me? The unanimous choice? I thought. Is this what you want, Father?

Not long ago, I asked God to show me the next ministry assignment He wanted me to take. I promised Him I would give the assignment 100 percent and make it a priority to use the opportunity to uplift His kingdom. I prayed later that day. "Father, if this is what you want me to do then I'm willing. Just show me what to do and I'll gladly proceed."

The following week I learned all about the work of this ministry. We were to serve as the first point of contact for every student in our congregation, right from grade school up to university and college.

During our first meeting, my pastor made a request. "As your first assignment, we'd like for you to hold an education honors day. This will be an opportunity for the congregation to acknowledge the accomplishments of our grade school and high school students, especially those who made the honor roll last semester." I agreed and my team went to work on the project.

Joyce and Brenda were in charge of identifying the students selected for the principal's list or honor roll. Joan, John, and Robin were to organize a special ceremony to be held during the main worship service. My job as leader was to pull it all together, and then work with our church's hospitality committee to provide a brief reception of punch and cookies after the service.

At our second team meeting, the members proudly reported on their progress. "Joyce and I have discovered that of the more than two hundred students in our congregation, eighty have made the principal's list or honor roll," Brenda said. "Parents were eager to share their children's accomplishments with us. Some were selected as best science or math student, others had won art awards, and one student will be attending an exchange program this summer in France."

On the morning of our special day, all of the team members were present, with the exception of Joan. "Has anyone seen her?" I asked and checked my watch.

"Joan is here," Brenda replied, "but right now, she's in Sabbath School." Sabbath School was the part of our worship service dedicated to the teaching of the word of God. "She said to tell you not to worry," Brenda continued. "She promised to be out in plenty of time to help."

I usually attended Sabbath School, but I had decided to skip it due to my numerous responsibilities for that day. I turned to Brenda, my irritation growing with each passing minute. "Doesn't she know that we need her help? Doesn't she. . ."

"I'm sure she'll be here," another member of the team said, "Everything will be fine. The children will be arriving in the next few minutes, and we can proceed with the program."

I returned to my checklist and decided to review the preparations and plans for the reception. When I returned to the church lobby, I saw Joan arranging the certificates according to grade and aligning them with the carefully selected red ribbons. No words passed between us, but I allowed my body language to convey my displeasure with her earlier absence.

Moments later, Pastor Lewis tapped me on the shoulder. "It's time to start preparing for the service," he said. I acknowledged his comment and joined him and the elders in the lineup to proceed to the rostrum. As we stood waiting, Pastor Lewis said, "We missed you at Sabbath School."

With my mind on the events about to take place, I was able to momentarily dismiss the somber tone of his comment, but within seconds, his voice resonated once more in my mind. "We missed you at Sabbath School."

Earlier in the week, I'd been studying women in the New Testament and had become involved in a lengthy discussion with a friend about the faults I saw in Martha, sister of Mary and Lazarus. "How could she have been so busy that she missed spending time with Jesus?" I said.

Later that evening, in the quiet of my room, I thought about my day. While everything had gone well, I still had a nagging sense of inner disappointment. Pastor Lewis's remarks returned. I thought about Joan's absence. Rather than stressing over the preparations of the day, Joan had chosen to spend time with the Lord in study and prayer.

Sometimes, I allow life's priorities, even good priorities, to cloud my real mission and, like Martha, I miss "the good part." But God is merciful, and He helped me see that while doing things for Him is important, it is far more critical to build and sustain a lasting relationship with Him.

Now that is truly choosing the good part!

—YVONNE CURRY SMALLWOOD

A Good and Faithful Servant

*Give my greetings to Tryphena and Tryphosa,
the Lord's workers, and to dear Persis, who has
worked so hard for the Lord.*
ROMANS 16:12

Paul's mention of Persis stands apart from his comments about other women of faith in the early church. No stranger to trials and suffering, Paul acknowledges Persis's committed efforts on the Lord's behalf. Amazing praise, indeed!

Persis provides an admirable example of dedicated Christian service in times of persecution. The fact that Paul noticed and commended her service, as well as referencing her in a letter that has influenced Christians for thousands of years, is a celebration of her diligence for the cause of Christ.

In my own small way, I strive to advance God's kingdom. Although I may feel unnoticed and unappreciated at times, I wait for the day when Jesus greets me with the words, "Well done, good and faithful servant." Patience and perseverance are the bywords for faith in action.

*Send an encouraging note to someone
who quietly labors in the Lord's service.*

—ALEXANDRA ROSE

No Point in Hiding

Many Samaritans from the village believed in Jesus because the woman had said, "He told me everything I ever did!"
JOHN 4:39

At the well of Sychar, Jesus met a woman who challenged his identity. He reversed the situation to expose her as the wife of five husbands and current companion of another man. Her initial skepticism turned into recognition of the Messiah.

Amazed, the Samaritan woman told people in her village, and they came to hear Jesus for themselves. Her sharing of His mercy brought salvation to those who had been seeking it.

Sometimes I feel like concealing my sins by pretending they don't exist or aren't important. I should know by now that, just as with the Samaritan woman, Jesus knows everything about me, and there's no point in hiding anything. In fact, it's only by completely revealing myself to Christ that I find true freedom.

Are you keeping a part of your life from the Lord?

—ALEXANDRA ROSE

Your God Is My God

*But Ruth replied, "Don't ask me to leave you
and turn back. Wherever you go, I will go;
wherever you live, I will live. Your people will
be my people, and your God will be my God."*
RUTH 1:16

My husband had come to believe in Jesus while away at college, but his mother, sixty-four-year-old Sylvia, was still very resistant to Christ. Newly married and on vacation with my mother-in-law, I attempted to share my faith.

When I opened the Bible, Sylvia became defensive and our conversation ended with both of us frustrated over our religious differences.

Over the next few years, God demonstrated to me that His word is active, alive, and "sharper than a two-edged sword." Prayer, patience, and love would be the keys to soften my mother-in-law's heart.

As I spent time in God's word and faithfully prayed for Sylvia's salvation, I learned to love her deeply. Fourteen years later, at the age of seventy-eight, Sylvia accepted Christ as her Savior.

Do you have someone in your life who needs Jesus?

—LAURA BROADWATER

The Opportunity of a Lifetime

She talked about the child to everyone who had been waiting expectantly for God to rescue Jerusalem.
LUKE 2:38

Anna's reward for a lifetime of devotion to God came when she recognized the infant Jesus at the temple—but her work was far from over. Her happiness knew no bounds, and she wasted no time in sharing the miraculous news.

She was an eighty-four-year-old widow, dependent on the charity of others, but she didn't let anything deter her from telling anyone who would listen about the redeemer sent from God to save mankind.

God has rewarded me in countless ways, and even my trials have contained hidden blessings. His attention to every detail of my life never ceases to amaze me, but I confess that, unlike Anna, my eagerness for sharing my joy in the Lord is not always what it should be. Plagued by shyness or worried by what someone might think of me, I let another opportunity slip by—one I might never have again.

Don't allow anything to keep you from sharing salvation.

—SBT

Words of Great Importance

When she recognized Peter's voice, she was so overjoyed that, instead of opening the door, she ran back inside and told everyone, "Peter is standing at the door!"
ACTS 12:14

Poor Rhoda! It was undoubtedly the most exciting moment of her young life, but the adults refused to believe what she was trying to tell them. They dismissed her claim as a childish fantasy and returned to what they considered matters of "adult" importance. Eventually, they opened the door and discovered Rhoda had been telling the truth.

As soon as my youngest son, Owen, opens his eyes in the morning, he begins to talk and, often, silence doesn't return until bedtime. Sometimes, when I'm tired or distracted, I don't give his lengthy and convoluted conversations my full attention.

I might even find myself becoming impatient and ill-tempered, and that's when I utter a quick prayer and ask God to help me listen. I don't want Owen to ever feel like Rhoda must have felt that night—rejected and unimportant.

If no one listens, your child may stop talking.

—SBT

Plenty of Everything

*So she did as Elijah said, and she and Elijah and her son
continued to eat for many days.*
1 KINGS 17:15

The widow in Zarephath discovered the reward of selfless giving. She had enough food for one last meal. She was an unlikely candidate to provide a charitable donation, but Elijah asked her anyway. She explained her plight to him just as we might a week before payday.

"Look at these bills," we might say. "After paying for groceries, utilities, and the mortgage, I have nothing left to give." Yet the widow trusted God's prophet. She gave what she had and found more than she ever imagined.

Many years ago, I made a similar commitment, and I determined what percentage of my income would go into the offering plate each week. After each payday, I wrote my first check to God, no matter how high the stack of bills on my desk might be, or how tempted I was to route the money elsewhere. To this day, I am content with what I have. Things have a way of working out, just as God has promised.

Trust in God for all your needs.

—PATRICIA MITCHELL

Facing Forward

Remember what happened to Lot's wife!
LUKE 17:32

Who could forget Lot's wife? She turned to look back at Sodom as the Lord rained down brimstone on the city, and she became a pillar of salt. I've always felt sympathy for her because I know I would have done the same thing.

I would have glanced back, perhaps to see a spectacular fireworks show, but mostly to mourn my friends, my house, my belongings, and the life I had known. But God was very specific. "Don't do it," He said.

Commitment to a Christian life can make us feel like Lot's wife. At times, we must leave behind friends who live in deliberate sin. The Lord commands us to run from familiar routines, comfortable habits, or long-time addictions that keep us from a wholesome relationship with Christ.

Step forward to a life in Christ.

—PATRICIA MITCHELL

Silent Intercession

Once after a sacrificial meal at Shiloh, Hannah got up and went to pray. Eli the priest was sitting at his customary place beside the entrance of the Tabernacle.

1 SAMUEL 1:9

Near the beginning of my spiritual walk, my Christian friends impressed upon me that I must pray, pray, pray in order to maintain a close relationship with God. At that time, I happened to be bogged down in the incessant chores of motherhood—mopping up spills, settling spats, changing diapers, and making snacks—so, my quiet times were few and far between. Undermined by exhaustion, I also felt guilty about my unstructured prayer life.

Not that I didn't pray! Time and again the myriad details of raising our four children drove me to my knees—figuratively, if not literally. When I saw how God answered those unspoken pleas, I began to see how it is possible to "pray without ceasing." I discovered that prayer could be as simple as the continual uplifting of the soul to God, and thus began a quiet communion with Him that has lasted over fifty years.

Prayer is an ongoing conversation with God.

—ALMA BARKMAN

Special, Not Superior

Why am I so honored, that the mother
of my Lord should visit me?
LUKE 1:43

I am drawn to Elizabeth. She possesses many of the qualities I would like to emulate; the character traits I look for in a friend such as spiritual maturity, a kind heart, and a generous spirit. I see her as just the sort of genuine and likeable person who led me to dedicate my life to the Lord.

Our values as Christians make us special. However, I have met believers who have not only set themselves apart from others, but who have also placed themselves above everyone else. These were the people who made me question whether or not I should follow the Lord. I had no desire to be better than anyone else. I only wanted the peace and fulfillment I knew real faith could bring me.

I now strive to be a woman like Elizabeth—someone who can stay true to the Lord without judging those who have yet to believe.

We are special, not superior.

—SBT

Sewing for the Lord

*There was a believer in Joppa named Tabitha
(which in Greek is Dorcas). She was always doing
kind things for others and helping the poor.*
ACTS 9:36

Dorcas had the distinction of being the first woman raised from the dead by the apostle Peter. However, she was also a charitable woman who not only gave money to numerous causes, but also invested herself in doing a multitude of good works.

One of her many acts of love was making clothes for widows, young children, and the other needy members of her church community. She was content to serve God by helping those less fortunate with her wealth and her skill as a seamstress.

My aunt Helen is eighty-seven and has spent her life raising six children and running a business. She may not be as busy as she once was, but her love for God shines as brightly as it ever did. She spends her time making baby clothes and blankets for impoverished mothers overseas. Like Dorcas, she knows she can glorify God with her simple acts of kindness and generosity.

*God doesn't need leaders. He needs servants
to reach out to those in need.*

—SBT

The Masquerade of Rage

So Herodias bore a grudge against John and wanted to kill him. But without Herod's approval she was powerless.
MARK 6:19

I've learned that anger can often have an underlying cause. My own agitation and annoyance can stem from anxiety and sometimes unhappiness with a particular circumstance. Consequently, when someone close to me becomes angry, I try not to react to their irritation. Rather, I attempt to discover the source of their resentment. I've watched anger flare into fury and result in serious problems, but I've also come to understand that when anger is understood, it can be unmasked and recognized for what it really is.

When John the Baptist confronted Herodias for her sinful liaison with Herod, like many people, she refused to acknowledge any wrongdoing. Instead, her anger flourished into a passion for vengeance. Unrestrained, her wrath and obsessive desire for revenge resulted in the death of the man who had dared to criticize her lifestyle. Perhaps if her rage had been recognized as guilt and nurtured into repentance, John's life would have been spared.

Ask God to help you discover the true source of your discontent.

—SBT

Fear or Faith?

But when Sisera fell asleep from exhaustion, Jael quietly crept up to him with a hammer and tent peg in her hand. Then she drove the tent peg through his temple and into the ground, and so he died.

JUDGES 4:21

What I admire most about Jael is her bravery. This mighty woman of God used courage and cunning to help her people, despite the many risks to herself.

I'm not sure I could be so bold. When put to the test, I fall short for one reason—fear. I fear for the safety of my family or myself. I fear disappointing my husband, and I fear failure.

While God gave us a healthy dose of fear as a means of defense and protection, He doesn't want it to prevent us from going forward in faith and getting the job done. When we are open to Him, God shows us how He wants to use us and we can proceed with confidence.

When we push fear aside, we make room for faith.

—DIANNE DANIELS

Jesus Is Everyone's Business

*One of them was Lydia from Thyatira, a merchant of
expensive purple cloth, who worshiped God. As she listened
to us, the Lord opened her heart, and she accepted what
Paul was saying.*

ACTS 16:14

A dear friend of mine desperately wanted to find
employment, but her life was filled with duties inside the
home. What kind of work could she do? How could she
contribute financially to the household?

She met with a successful work-from-home company
and decided to join their team. Her biggest squeal for joy
was not over the new position, but because the company
was Christian based.

She earned much-needed money while working with
other believers. Every show she hosted included a short
presentation of the gospel. She was able to share her faith
openly, honestly, and in conjunction with every event in
her life. Her profits were lifted to the Lord in praise.

Like Lydia, my friend discovered she could live her
faith even during her work hours. Both women provide
examples of Christians combining work and faith in order
to give glory to God in all things.

Include Jesus in everything you do.

—JENNIFER DEVLIN

Ways of Worship

But as the Ark of the Lord entered the City of David,
Michal, the daughter of Saul, looked down from her window.
When she saw King David leaping and dancing before the
Lord, she was filled with contempt for him.
2 SAMUEL 6:16

King Saul's daughter Michal fell in love with the hero David, and even though Saul hated the young man, he reluctantly gave David his daughter in marriage. Jealous over David's popularity, Saul plotted to have him murdered, but Michal helped David escape.

Later, when David sent troops to bring home the Ark of the Lord, he celebrated the Ark's return by dancing before the Lord. Michal did not share her husband's deep devotion, and when she saw his joyful worship, she despised him. She considered his behavior undignified, especially for a king.

I was raised in a church where worship was done without displaying much emotion. Then, I visited a church where the congregation waved their hands and cried out to the Lord. Their exuberance embarrassed me, and I was tempted to judge them. Eventually, God helped me realize that we capture His heart when we are able to shed sophistication and worship Him freely and wholeheartedly.

God longs for us to come to Him as children who worship
Him in spirit and in truth.

—SUSAN E. RAMSDEN

Watch Your Step

*Here is Rebekah; take her and go. Yes, let her be the wife of
your master's son, as the Lord has directed.*
GENESIS 24:51

When Eliezer explained his mission to her family,
young and beautiful Rebekah realized that leaving her
home to marry Abraham's son, Isaac, was God's will for
her and she immediately agreed to go. Her humility and
trust resulted in her celebrated marriage to Isaac and her
inclusion in the direct lineage of the Messiah.

Years later, this same woman deceived her husband
and turned her two sons against each other. At first, I
found it difficult to believe that a young woman so deeply
devoted to her God could sink to such depths, but then
I realized it didn't happen overnight. When I stray from
my path of prayer and fellowship with the Lord, I give
my doubts and fears an opportunity to thrive. Before long,
I'm lost in a maze of negative thinking. Rebekah's story
serves as a warning that I am never safe from sin, and in
order to protect my faith, I must stay close to God.

God may raise you up, but you can still fall!

—SBT

Your Best Is Good Enough

Meanwhile, Jesus was in Bethany at the home of Simon, a man who had previously had leprosy. While he was eating, a woman came in with a beautiful alabaster jar of expensive perfume made from essence of nard. She broke open the jar and poured the perfume over his head.

MARK 14:3

Some Bible scholars have estimated the worth of the perfume used by the woman in Simon's home to anoint Jesus at approximately 300 pence, or one year's wages. There were other things she could have done to demonstrate her love and devotion, but she chose to give the very best she had.

This is what we must do as Christians. Our aim is not to impress our Christian friends or convince our conscience that we've done everything by the rules. Our objective must be to do our best in all things. Only you and God know the answer to the questions we must all ask ourselves—"Did I give my all? Did I do what I could?"

Jesus knew this woman had done her best. He praised her actions and defended her from those who ridiculed her extravagance and waste. This was His way of saying her best was good enough.

Your best will always be good enough!

—SBT

The Most Perfect Plan

*Just then, as Pilate was sitting on the judgment seat, his wife
sent him this message: "Leave that innocent man alone. I
suffered through a terrible nightmare about him last night."*
MATTHEW 27:19

Even if Pilate had wanted to heed his wife's warning, it
would have been difficult, if not impossible, for him to do
so. The religious authorities wanted Jesus dead, and they
had already incited the mob to call for His crucifixion.

God's plan is always perfect, and He never makes mistakes. Any influence Pilate's wife may have had on her
husband was no match for the will of God on that day
when Jesus suffered and died. Jesus Himself knew that
God's plan was in motion, and He had confirmed His vow
to stay in His Father's will the night before in the Garden
of Gethsemane.

I strive to stay in God's will and to accept His plan
for me even though I may not understand or agree at the
time. Just as with Christ's trial and death, what appears to
be a tragedy may in fact turn out to be a miracle.

*God's plan was perfect 2,000 years ago,
and it's still perfect today!*

—SBT

No Crystal Balls

*So Saul disguised himself by wearing ordinary clothing
instead of his royal robes. Then he went to the
woman's home at night, accompanied by two of his
men. "I have to talk to a man who has died," he said.
"Will you call up his spirit for me?"*
1 SAMUEL 28:8

Some of my most difficult moments as a mother hen have come when my chicks have left the nest. Whether it's my youngest heading off to school, my middle son leaving for summer camp, or my oldest boy moving out on his own, I can't help but worry. A long time ago, a friend treated me to a session with a so-called psychic. She said my future held only happiness and promise. I was very young, but even I knew that sorrow and setbacks were a part of everyone's life.

Years later, when I dedicated my life to the Lord, I learned that the Bible condemns occult practices. Saul's experience with the medium of Endor is a perfect example of why the future should remain a mystery.

I will probably always worry a little when my children are away, but I've learned he will be with me every step of the way—no matter what the future brings.

*You can handle anything that comes your way if you trust
God to lead you through it.*

—SBT

Pouring Out Her Love

When a certain immoral woman from that city heard he was eating there, she brought a beautiful alabaster jar filled with expensive perfume.

LUKE 7:37

I'm learning how to knit, and I make a lot of mistakes. I can correct them if I rip out the bad section and redo it correctly. Since I hate to do this, sometimes I just continue knitting and try to hide the mistakes later.

When we sin, there's no way we can go back and remove our mistake and make it right. Covering up doesn't work either. The woman who anointed Jesus' feet with her tears and oil knew she couldn't change what she had done or hide her sin.

However, she had faith in the one who would ultimately carry her sin and offered forgiveness. She poured out her love for Him in the only way she could. There is only one Savior who offers us forgiveness, and we should do no less than pour out our love to Him in gratitude.

Love flows from a grateful heart.

—LAURIE A. PERKINS

We Remember Her Name

Even before he made the world, God loved us and chose us in Christ to be holy and without fault in his eyes.

EPHESIANS 1:4

When Abraham Lincoln delivered the Gettysburg Address in 1863, he was unaware that his words, "The world will little note nor long remember what we say here," would reverberate throughout history. Sometimes, I think about Lincoln's words and wonder if the world will remember me after I'm gone.

Gomer never imagined her name would be remembered, but her personal story in the Old Testament book of Hosea is an object lesson to the Israelites—and to us. We may not know why God chose her sordid story of adultery in His attempt to communicate with the rebellious nation of Israel, but we do know it was all part of His perfect plan.

Hosea's devotion to his wayward wife dramatically demonstrates God's love and commitment to His people. Like Gomer, we may lose our way, but God will always provide a way home to forgiveness and redemption.

The world may forget us, but God never will.

—AUDREY HEBBERT

Poor Me or Pour Me

*So she did as she was told. Her sons kept bringing jars to her,
and she filled one after another.*
2 KINGS 4:5

Moving from France to America with no home, minimal finances, and a son struggling with a teenage crisis was stressful. Although friends housed us temporarily while we sought lodging, panicky thoughts often kept me awake during the night. Where will we live? How will we cope? What about our son?

The widow knew this kind of anxiety. If she didn't pay her husband's debts expediently, her sons would be taken as slaves. In desperation, she cried out to Elijah. He asked her to find empty vessels and to fill them with the only thing she possessed—oil. The oil speaks of God's unconditional love.

The prophet's advice certainly applied to my situation. Even in my bleakest moment, I still have God. As I pour Him into others who are needy, even by simply lifting them up in prayer and interceding—I find the answers to my own troubling questions.

*As I shift focus from "poor me" to pouring out for others,
God takes care of my needs.*

—JANEY L. DeMEO

Victors, Not Victims

Amram's wife was named Jochebed. She also was a
descendant of Levi, born among the Levites in the land of
Egypt. Amram and Jochebed became the parents of Aaron,
Moses, and their sister, Miriam.
NUMBERS 26:59

When Jochebed heard that every male born to the slaves would be killed, she didn't allow fear to stop her from concealing her infant son Moses. When hiding him no longer worked, she placed her trust in God to protect her child and set him adrift on the Nile in a papyrus basket.

What is a flimsy basket against the pharaoh of Egypt? I experienced that same feeling of helplessness when our son called to tell me that he and his wife were getting a divorce. Immediately, I thought of our two grandchildren, aged two and four. "What about the children?" I asked.

"Oh, they'll be all right!" our son replied.

I knew better. I pictured a bleak fate for those kids unless someone came up with a plan. I placed their picture in a prominent place in our home and prayed every day for them. God honored that plan.

Prayer is a powerful and effective weapon in any battle.

—JEWELL JOHNSON

He Makes All My Paths Straight

The two sons married Moabite women. One married a woman named Orpah, and the other a woman named Ruth.
RUTH 1:4

On a glorious summer day in the North Georgia Mountains, we drove from Dahlonega to Blue Ridge on thirty-five miles of narrow, curving roads. It was an unfamiliar route and, suddenly, I noticed that the compass over our dashboard showed we were traveling southeast. Blue Ridge was northwest of Dahlonega—we were going the wrong way!

Before I could even react, the dial changed to south, then southwest, and then north. "This thing's broken," I said to my husband. He laughed and explained that because the road has to follow the mountains, it often doubled back, but it would ultimately take us to Blue Ridge, just as the map said.

Naomi's life seemed to be filled with one wrong turn after another, but it ultimately led her to a place full of joy. As we follow the Lord, we must trust that no matter how things may look, He knows exactly where we're going and He will be faithful to take us there.

Even when nothing makes sense, God is watching over you.

—LINDA DARBY HUGHES

Investing in the Future

Caleb said, "I will give my daughter Acsah in marriage to the one who attacks and captures Kiriath-sepher."
JOSHUA 15:16

It's obvious that Caleb thought highly of his daughter, Acsah. The fact that Othniel risked his life in battle to win her hand suggests that he, too, regarded her as a very special woman. I wonder if the favorable opinions of these two men encouraged Acsah to establish an identity of her own and realize her full potential.

When I attended university to obtain my teaching degree, I learned that children who feel valued achieve more success at school than the ones who see themselves as worthless and insignificant.

God has given all of us the gift of encouragement. When we take the time to let someone know that we care and, more importantly that God cares, we are investing in his or her future.

Encourage someone today.

—SBT

An Open Heart

Then the woman told Elijah, "Now I know for
sure that you are a man of God, and that the
Lord truly speaks through you."
KINGS 17:24

Right in the middle of the account of the struggle between Elijah and Jezebel, the Bible relates the story of Elijah's escape from Jezebel's wrath and his stay with a poor widow who, like Jezebel, is a follower of Baal.

Elijah performs a miracle to ensure the widow and her son won't go hungry, but when the boy becomes deathly ill, Elijah pleads with God for the child's life and the boy is revived. As a result of witnessing God's power, the widow's heart is opened and she praises the power of God.

Jezebel's exposure to the power of God did nothing to alter her obsession to destroy all religions save the worship of Baal. Her heart remained closed, resulting in her ignoble death and a reputation for evil that remains even today.

I experience God's presence every day in countless ways. When I acknowledge His power and keep my heart open to the belief that He makes all things possible, He blesses me beyond anything I dreamed possible.

Keep your heart open to God's power.

—SBT

God's Gracious, Giving Girls

Joanna, the wife of Chuza, Herod's business manager;
Susanna; and many others who were contributing their own
resources to support Jesus and his disciples.
LUKE 8:3

This year in a California Sunday school, fourth-, fifth-, and sixth-grade girls studied the lives of Susanna and other remarkable women of the Bible. Through discussions, the preteens, who call themselves "God's Girls," discovered how the lessons could be applied to their own lives and reflected to others.

After each study, the girls made crafts, such as ladybug earrings, and attached notes sharing the truths they had gleaned. They gave their creations to classmates and friends who needed reminders of Jesus' love and compassion. Some crafts were sold at church, and the girls raised more than $1,000, which they then donated to support an orphan in China for a full year.

Like Susanna, God's Girls have already learned to demonstrate in tangible ways the kind of love that Jesus asks of all His followers.

No matter how old we are, we can use our talents and
resources to mirror God's goodness to those around us.

—SUSAN E. RAMSDEN

317

911, Keeping Your Cool

Thank God for your good sense! Bless you for keeping me from murder and from carrying out vengeance with my own hands.
1 SAMUEL 25:33

In an emergency, it's always best if at least one person keeps her cool. Abigail was such a woman. She was gifted with the ability to communicate, negotiate, and apply wisdom.

Life is peppered with crises: a medical emergency, a work situation, a family disagreement. Over the years, I've discovered which people in my life are most likely to keep their cool. I can reach out to that friend or family member and know that her prayers and presence will result in peace, not chaos.

Sometimes I need to be that person. Whether it's the second-floor bathtub pipe that's sprung a leak, or my four-year-old "Superman" who's taken a gouge out of his side while flying off his bed, I try to be an agent of peace in my home.

The key is to remember that while I may be the agent of peace, Christ is the source of peace. Regardless of my circumstances, He is always available.

God keeps His cool in a crisis.

—VICKI TIEDE

Facing the Enemy

Then Deborah said to Barak, "Get ready! This is the day the Lord will give you victory over Sisera, for the Lord is marching ahead of you." So Barak led his 10,000 warriors down the slopes of Mount Tabor into battle.

JUDGES 4:14

What an amazing woman! In a time when female leadership was rare, Deborah was asked to be a judge in Israel and to lead her people into battle. She showed no fear, but pushed forward to face her enemy. But look again and see the real star of the story—not a flesh-and-blood woman, but God Almighty.

The secret of Deborah's success was her remarkable relationship with God. He was the source of her strength, the strategist for her plan of attack, and the inspiration for her courage. She listened to God, depended upon Him, and in turn, He equipped her for success against the Philistines.

He can accomplish great things through women who stay tuned to His voice. It doesn't matter if she is giving commands or carrying out orders. He will guide and protect her.

You can face your enemy knowing God has gone before you.

—VIRGINIA DAWKINS

Stage Fright

This is what the Lord says: "I am going to bring disaster on this city and its people. All the words written in the scroll that the king of Judah has read will come true."
2 KINGS 22:16

When the high priest Hilkiah went to the prophetess Huldah to hear the word of God, she told him exactly what God wanted her to say. She wasn't concerned with the opinion of others or the consequences of her actions. God honored her with the gift of prophecy and, in return, she honored Him with devotion to His will.

The other day, I had the opportunity to visit with a friend with whom I lost touch about twelve years ago. In the course of our conversation, I mentioned my writing, and my friend made a lighthearted remark about my faith.

After we spoke, I realized that I had been reluctant to discuss my beliefs. I'm not sure why—perhaps I felt shy or maybe I was worried what she would think of me.

Later, I asked God for His forgiveness and vowed to use future opportunities to offer my most powerful testimony. After all, He has given me everything and deserves everything I can give in return.

Are you reluctant to discuss your faith?

—SBT

Stepping Back

The wine supply ran out during the festivities, so Jesus'
mother told him, "They have no more wine."
JOHN 2:3

It's no surprise that God picked Mary to be the mother of Jesus. He knew that whomever He chose would be the most important person in Jesus' life until His earthly ministry began. Mary had the faith and devotion to guide and teach the young Christ but, most importantly, she had the insight to know when her son's time had come.

When the wine ran out at a local wedding celebration, Mary seized the moment and directed everyone's attention to Jesus. She told them to listen and obey His instructions. Jesus had the solution at the wedding, and as people would shortly discover, he also had the answer to man's greatest need—salvation.

I have difficulty knowing when it's time to step out of the spotlight and give my children a chance to shine. It's not a decision I can make on my own, so I turn to God for the same wisdom and guidance He gave Mary. He hasn't failed me yet!

Mary knew that being a good mother was a gift from God.

—SBT

OCTOBER

He Knows My Name

After Jesus rose from the dead early on Sunday morning, the first person who saw him was Mary Magdalene, the woman from whom he had cast out seven demons.

MARK 16:9

*M*ary Magdalene, healed from the insanity of demon possession. Mary Magdalene, who offered financial support to Jesus' ministry. Mary Magdalene, who saw Him die and made plans to minister in His death. Mary Magdalene, the first to see the Risen Christ.

Mary Magdalene, who could almost be me. . . .

We don't know much about Mary, who came from the town of Magdala. Mark and Luke mention, almost in passing, that Jesus had once driven seven demons from her. The gospel writers point out that a group of women, Mary the Magdalene among them, watched the crucifixion, observed the burial (entombment), and were ready to anoint the body with spices after the Sabbath.

John alone paints the poignant picture of a weeping Mary trying to convince the gardener to tell where her Lord's body had been taken. Only when He called her by name and spoke intimately and directly to her as a beloved person, did she realize who He was—who He is. We know little else about her.

We know more about me. Elsi, who was healed from decades of depression and panic attacks by a loving word from the living Lord; Elsi, who in spite of such tangible proof of His love and care, continued to feel alone and afraid much of the time. Elsi, who heard the Lord call her by name.

Abused as a small child, I grew up feeling unloved and abandoned. The Christians I met in college seemed to truly care for each other. I wanted and needed to be part of that, so I accepted Christ into my heart.

Despite this decision, I continued my desperate search for love and acceptance. Two ill-advised marriages and the normal ebb and flow of life served to confirm my perception that I would never be good enough, could never be valued. My depression deepened. I tried different combinations of therapy and medication. Panic attacks forced me further away from other people. Decades passed.

Then, in a worship service, the Holy Spirit touched my heart, giving me compassion for the people involved in my childhood situation. That night, I entered the room resentful and angry, and I walked out with a new sense of empathy and acceptance.

Within a year, He touched me again. He told me clearly that if I loved Him, I needed to let go of my pain and fear. I had to let go and take His hand. I made the choice and reached for Him. As a result, my heart and my will were healed of both the pain and its terrifying effect on me.

Healed, functional, and growing in the Lord and in life, I left my familiar church to attend a new one. I joined an adult Sunday school class and began to make friends. A special service was announced for Maundy Thursday, the Thursday before Easter, in honor of Jesus' commands to His disciples at the Last Supper. I decided to go.

We learned about the Passover supper, shared communion, and participated in foot washing. When a neighbor poured water over my bare feet and patted them dry with a towel, I found myself in an extremely helpless place emotionally.

This vulnerability threw me into old feelings, and I started to weep. The tears frightened me even more, and I sat, hands covering my face, tears trickling between my fingers, unable to figure out what to do to help myself.

Our associate pastor, Cathy, came over and sat next to me. She put a hand on my shoulder and sat with me, praying silently. Everyone else had left, and we were alone in the church. After a while she said quietly, "Oh, Elsi, Elsi, Elsi."

We sat together in silence until I was able to think again, to talk, and to thank her.

The psalmist reminds us that God "determines the number of the stars and calls them each by name" (Psalm 147:4). Jesus told His disciples that the Good Shepherd "calls his own sheep by name and leads them out" (John 10:3). There's power in our name being spoken in love by someone we trust. Jesus spoke Mary's name, and she recognized Him at once. Cathy spoke my name, and I felt loved.

We may know little about Mary Magdalene, but I see myself in her story. I have felt hopeless, lived with overwhelming oppression bred by abuse and depression, and experienced spiritual emancipation. I believe Mary felt the same liberation when Jesus drove the seven evil spirits from her. The freedom and bright hope opened doors to an indescribable new life—akin to Dorothy's awaking in Oz, where her dreary, black-and-white life changed to vibrant color.

Jesus called Mary by name, and she responded by clinging to Him in gratitude and peace. God called me by name, and in His love sent people who knew my name. Now, I turn to Him for comfort and strength.

—ELSI DODGE

Get Past Your Past

Many Samaritans from the village believed in Jesus because the woman had said, "He told me everything I ever did!"
JOHN 4:39

Most of us know Christians who can't seem to forgive themselves, who can't let go of their past. They think they are unworthy of being completely forgiven, and they are spiritually stuck. Maybe that "someone" is you.

When Jesus befriended the woman at the well, He made it clear that He knew all about her past and that He could and would forgive her. All she had to do was ask. It's obvious she believed Jesus because she ran back to her village. When she arrived there, she told everyone she encountered about this man who knew everything she had ever done.

The townspeople were well aware of her past, yet they listened because she spoke from her heart. She was filled with the joy of divine forgiveness, and she couldn't stop talking about her miraculous encounter with Him. If you have sincerely asked for forgiveness, don't offend God by dwelling on your past.

Accept and cherish God's forgiveness.

—CONNIE STURM CAMERON

Minor Players with Major Influence

When you help the Hebrew women as they give birth, watch as they deliver. If the baby is a boy, kill him; if it is a girl, let her live.

EXODUS 1:16

Shiphran and Puah defied the pharaoh's edict to kill all Hebrew male babies. Their names may be difficult to remember, but Moses, one of the many children for whom they were willing to risk their lives, will be remembered and revered for all time. These courageous midwives are only two of the Bible's deceptively minor characters. It's a profound message repeated throughout God's word; there is no one too insignificant or unimportant for His great plan.

Shiphran and Puah have inspired me to obey God's will, to assist Him in the spiritual birthing of my fellow human beings, and to step out in obedience, courage, and faith from my tiny corner of the world. Their story is proof that I can make a difference.

As part of God's grand plan, we can help change the world.

—SANDI BANKS

When Things Appear Hopeless

*Hannah was in deep anguish,
crying bitterly as she prayed to the Lord.*
1 SAMUEL 1:10

It was our first year to have a Christmas tree with the roots attached. We planted it after the holidays, and then we waited and watched. The next spring we searched for signs of growth, but it had begun to turn brown. One day my neighbor asked, "Do you think your tree will survive?"

Wanting to remain positive, I replied, "Hopefully it'll bounce back soon."

She stared at me incredulously. Her look inspired me to increase my prayers for that pathetic little tree. Miraculously, the following spring, bright green needles replaced the brown ones. By summer, there wasn't a trace of dead needles anywhere. Today it stands a vibrant eighteen feet tall.

When Hannah prayed for God to open her womb and bless her with a son, her prayers came from the depth of her soul. She believed before she saw any evidence. What man sees as hopeless, God sees as hopeful. Our part is to ask Him, and then to believe.

God is honored with prayers from the heart.

—CONNIE STURM CAMERON

Fuel for the Fire

Please forgive me if I have offended you in any way. The Lord will surely reward you with a lasting dynasty, for you are fighting the Lord's battles. And you have not done wrong throughout your entire life.

1 SAMUEL 25:28

Abigail was beautiful, smart, and courageous but, more important, she tried to honor God in everything she did. She knew of David's rage, and she realized it would be futile to assuage his anger in a confrontational manner. Instead, she used persuasion, common sense, and kindness to subdue her powerful adversary and win her battle. God would later bless Abigail for preventing bloodshed and David's vengeance.

When my daughter, Emily, wanted to attend a rock concert last year, I found myself in the unenviable position of saying no to a teenager. Her anger was swift and dramatic, and as I felt my own outrage beginning to stir, I opened my mouth to react.

Abruptly, I realized that in a moment, there would be two angry people with no resolution. That's when I swallowed my harsh reply and tried some gentle words of reason. Emily was still annoyed and disappointed, but God had shown us how to resolve conflict with the love and respect we both deserved.

Responding with anger only fuels the fire.

—SBT

Deadly Dishonesty

*The property was yours to sell or not sell, as you
wished. And after selling it, the money was also yours
to give away. How could you do a thing like this? You
weren't lying to us but to God!*

Acts 5:4

When Ananias and Sapphira conspired to lie about
the money they received from selling a piece of land, they
underestimated Peter, but, more important, they underestimated God. With help from God, Peter exposed them
as liars, and God struck them dead. A harsh punishment,
indeed, but God needed His early church to know how
He felt about honesty.

As soon as my children were old enough to understand,
I told them how much God valued the truth. I explained
that no matter what they had done, lying about it would
always be the greater sin. I reminded them that even if
no one on Earth ever found out about their deceit, God
would always know.

Then it occurred to me I would do well to take heed
of my own words. What good was it to impress upon my
children the importance of honesty if I didn't give it the
significance it deserved?

Don't let dishonesty destroy the relationships you cherish.

—SBT

Broken Branches

This is a record of the ancestors of Jesus the Messiah, a descendant of David and of Abraham: Judah was the father of Perez and Zerah (whose mother was Tamar).
MATTHEW 1:1–3

One of my aunts is the self-appointed historian for our family. The last time I paid her a visit, she opened a large scrapbook, and there in front of me was the typical family tree—the mighty oak with a multitude of strong, straight limbs.

She introduced me to some of the more famous and important members of the family, and then she pointed to my name. I noticed my branch was rather crowded with a few names trickling off into space. "Hmmm," she said. "I should have used two branches for you." Suddenly I felt guilty for having five children because it made my aunt's family tree look lopsided.

I wondered what my aunt might think of Jesus' ancestors. What would she think of Tamar, who resorted to incest and prostitution to achieve her goal? Perhaps God constructed Jesus' family tree from imperfect and broken branches to prove that He can use anyone and everyone to create a miraculous result.

*Only God can take the flawed and failing
and create perfection.*

—SBT

God Knows Best

So Peninnah would taunt Hannah and make fun of her because the Lord had kept her from having children.
1 SAMUEL 1:6

Both of Elkanah's wives knew the misery of wanting something they couldn't have. His first wife, Hannah, had Elkanah's love, but couldn't bear him a child. His second wife, Peninnah, bore him many children, but knew that his heart belonged to Hannah. While Hannah turned to God for answers and comfort, Peninnah became bitter and mean-spirited.

After the birth of my first child, I had a great deal of trouble conceiving again. Like Peninnah, I isolated myself with envy and self-pity and rejected well-meaning friends and loving family members. I was so sure of what was best for me.

Now, when I feel the emptiness of loss or the ache of wanting, I console myself with God's promise not to harm me, but to help me prosper. He hears all my prayers and often grants my heart's desire, but only if it fits into the plan He has for me.

Only God knows what is best for you.

—SBT

Power of Agreement

His wife said to him, "Are you still trying to maintain your integrity? Curse God and die."

JOB 2:9

After suffering two back-to-back layoffs in the dot-com bust of the 1990s, my husband prayed for guidance in his career. Based on what he believed was clear direction from God, he traded in his director-level salary for the very unpredictable earnings of an entrepreneur.

On more than one occasion, when times were tough, I sounded a lot like Job's wife. "Are you still determined to stay this course? Haven't you had enough? Just get a real job!" My husband wouldn't budge. He was willing to take the good with the bad, as long as it was God's will.

Eventually, our finances improved, but not until I stopped undermining my husband's decision with my words and attitude. I've since learned the power and importance of staying in agreement with my husband, especially when he's striving to stay in God's will. Like Job, my husband chose to ignore my criticisms and stay true to God. I'm glad he did.

The people close to us need our support—not our criticism.

—RENEE GRAY-WILBURN

Divine Appointment

*If you keep quiet at a time like this, deliverance and relief
for the Jews will arise from some other place, but you and
your relatives will die. Who knows if perhaps you were made
queen for just such a time as this?*
ESTHER 4:14

Mordecai issued Esther a challenge. "Who knows but
that you have come to royal position for such a time as this?"
His words settled a heavy burden upon her shoulders. As
she considered her uncle's words, perhaps she remembered
the old stories Mordecai had taught her—stories of God's
power to deliver His people. Even so, Esther could see no
guarantee that God would part this Red Sea for her.

Nevertheless, she did know what her first move must
be; she would ask for fervent prayer. Prayer prepared her
to step into dangerous waters and, as a result, to save her
people.

As God's children, we know that He has placed us in
a particular city, neighborhood, or workplace as part of
His great plan. Where we are is never an accident; we are
there to help someone or to share our faith in some way.
Our first step must always be prayer.

*Earnest, heartfelt prayer has the power
to bring forth miracles.*

—VIRGINIA DAWKINS

Whispers of Guilt

During the fight, this son of an Israelite woman blasphemed the Name of the Lord with a curse.
LEVITICUS 24:11

The unfortunate fellow who blasphemed the Lord was executed for his sin. He left his mother, Shelomith, to endure the excruciating grief known to women who have lost a child. She was an Israelite in the company of Moses, and I doubt her son learned his sacrilege from her. She may have been an extraordinary mother, but if she were anything like I am, there would have been whispers of guilt to accompany the outcries of grief.

My children have made their share of both trivial and serious mistakes, and almost without exception, I find myself wondering how I failed them as a mother. I forget that they have wills of their own, and they will falter and sometimes fall on their journey. I've done my best to teach them, but life has lessons planned for them, as well. My guilt accomplishes nothing, but my prayers can put my children back on the right track—a path that leads straight to God.

Even the child of a perfect mother will stumble.

—SBT

The Heavenly Bodyguard

But I will confirm my covenant with you. So enter the boat—you and your wife and your sons and their wives.
GENESIS 6:18

Noah's wife was faced with a mind-boggling assortment of tasks. In her role as a loving mother, she had to help her three sons live in a world wicked enough to warrant divine destruction. At the same time, she needed to prepare them for the day when they would be the only people left on Earth.

As mothers, we face different circumstances, but similar challenges. A great deal of maternal energy goes into our efforts to help our children deal with an uncertain and often hostile world. When they step out into that world on their own, we lose sleep and wring our hands, hoping that we've done everything to ready them.

We need to take a deep breath and remind ourselves that if we've raised our children to love the Lord, He is with them every step of the way.

Your children are never alone with Jesus in their heart.

—SBT

Everlasting Triumph

When the period of mourning was over, David sent for
her and brought her to the palace, and she became one of
his wives. Then she gave birth to a son. But the Lord was
displeased with what David had done.

2 SAMUEL 11:27

Bathsheba's life began to spiral out of control the moment King David stepped into her life. Most of us know what happened when he spotted her bathing on the roof, but we don't know how she felt about being ordered into his presence, sleeping with him, or discovering she had become pregnant as a result of their liaison.

Knocked off balance with the news that her husband had been killed, she steadied herself for a brief period of mourning, and then found herself living in David's palace as one of his wives. When the infant son she conceived with David sickened and died, I'm sure there was little joy left in Bathsheba's life.

God took Bathsheba to the bottom, only to raise her up to become the mother of Solomon. When my heart is heavy and my smiles are forced, I try to remember that God uses periods of trials and tribulations to strengthen and prepare me for part of His great plan. God has a purpose for me.

My difficulties are momentary—my triumph is everlasting.

—SBT

Just Like Any Mother

*After the celebration was over, they started home to
Nazareth, but Jesus stayed behind in Jerusalem. His parents
didn't miss him at first.*

LUKE 2:43

When my son Dylan was a little boy, he was a master
of the disappearing act. One minute he was there; the next
minute he had vanished. I recall several rather embarrass-
ing incidents in which I found myself going door-to-door
searching for my slippery son. Needless to say, this did
little to enhance my self-esteem as a mother.

When Jesus was twelve, he traveled with his parents
to the Passover Festival in Jerusalem. It wasn't until they
returned home that Joseph and Mary realized Jesus was
missing. There are a number of reasonable explanations
as to why this occurred, but it made me feel better just to
know that it did happen. Keeping track of an inquisitive,
active boy isn't easy—even for the best of mothers.

*Mary may have been the perfect mother for Jesus,
but she wasn't a perfect mother.*

—SBT

Common Ground

Now I appeal to Euodia and Syntyche. Please, because you belong to the Lord, settle your disagreement.
PHILIPPIANS 4:2

In our rural community, we have vacation Bible school each summer, sponsored jointly by several small churches, each of which would not have the money or personnel to do it alone. For many years, one of the churches was the driving force, providing the director and most of the teachers. Then, another church decided to get more actively involved and sent a group of willing helpers to the organizational meeting.

Many of those who had been involved with the school for a long time gave up the classes they had traditionally taught so the newcomers could serve as they wished.

The first day, we had fifty-one children, including an active teen class. It wasn't long before all fears and differences were set aside. Even the adults made new friends in the Lord as we all worked through our differences to share our common ground—the message of the gospel.

When you share the yoke, the burden is lighter.

—JEAN CAMPION

We Have a Job to Do

So I will not send the promised disaster until after you have died and been buried in peace. You will not see the disaster I am going to bring on this city.

2 KINGS 22:20

I find the Lord's message to Huldah the prophetess both comforting and troubling. Sometimes, it seems like our world is headed for a major catastrophe. Every day, the news is full of disasters, both manmade and natural. These problems often leave me feeling powerless, and I have to watch that I don't become overwhelmed or apathetic.

My father used to tell me that there was nothing new under the sun. "There have always been wars and disasters," he said, "but you still have an important role to play. You need to be an informed citizen so that you can vote appropriately, support our leaders, and do what you can to make this world a better place."

My father is gone now, but his words remind me that I can do something after all. I can give to worthy causes, and I can lobby and vote for responsible government. Most importantly, I can pray. Until I join my father in peace, my job is to make the world a better place.

You have the power to make a difference.

—JEAN CAMPION

Essential Forgiveness

Then the Lord God asked the woman, "What have you done?" "The serpent deceived me," she replied. "That's why I ate it."
GENESIS 3:13

In the beginning, God walked in the Garden of Eden. Adam and Eve had a perfect relationship, and violence, hardship, and pain were unknown. Eve's sin changed all these things. When she succumbed to the serpent's wiles, she changed it all. Even though she accused the serpent of deceiving her, she assumed responsibility for what she had done.

The rest of her life would be one long reminder of her sin. When she found herself missing the intimacy she and Adam had once enjoyed with God, she would remember that terrible day. When troubles occurred in her marriage, she would know why. And when her son killed his brother, she didn't have to wonder what happened.

God forgave her, but did she ever forgive herself? I believe she did. Only forgiveness could provide the strength she would she need to shoulder and carry the burdens that continued to come her way.

If Eve can forgive herself, I can forgive myself.

—SBT

Don't Waste a Second

*Some women were there, watching from a distance,
including Mary Magdalene, Mary (the mother of James the
younger and of Joseph), and Salome.*
MARK 15:40

Mary Magdalene knew the true value of time. The moment Jesus brought light into her world of darkness, she dedicated her life to serving Him. Perhaps the years she spent in torment made her cherish every moment of every day. Later, when she became aware that time for her Lord was growing short, she intensified her efforts to make every second count.

Most people would agree that time becomes more precious as they grow older. I flinch when my children wish the hours away, but I did the same thing when I was their age. Not only do I now see the value of time more clearly, but I also recognize it as a priceless gift from God.

Despite this insight, I still spend hours pursuing pointless activities. Just as we want to see a gift we've given put to good use, I would like to demonstrate to God that I treasure the miraculous gift He's bestowed upon me.

Take a minute to thank God for the gift of another day.

—SBT

A Change of Heart

Once again Leah became pregnant and gave birth to another son. She named him Judah, for she said, "Now I will praise the Lord!" And then she stopped having children.

GENESIS 29:35

With the birth of each of her sons, Leah hoped to finally win her husband's love. Sadly, her efforts accomplished nothing, and she remained disappointed.

Perhaps she became aware of God's constant presence in her life, or maybe she recognized the futility of trying to please others, but eventually Leah underwent a change of heart. It's obvious from the name she chose for her fourth son that her focus had shifted to God.

The desire to be loved is part of being human. Leah's mistake didn't lie in her desperate need to find a place in Jacob's heart; it came from her dependence on Jacob to make her happy.

I've fallen into the trap of believing that my joy rested in the hands of another person. I've come to realize, however, that human beings are fallible and dependence can only lead to disappointment. God is the only unfailing source of true fulfillment.

God will never let you down.

—SBT

Tough Love

One day Dinah, the daughter of Jacob and Leah, went to visit some of the young women who lived in the area.
GENESIS 34:1

Dinah was the baby of the family, born to Jacob and Leah after six sons. The Bible doesn't tell us why she left the safety of her family's encampment, but it's quite possible she longed to visit with girls her own age. She may have taken advantage of an opportunity to escape the protective confines of her family. It's doubtful that her family would allow her to wander around unaccompanied.

When I was a teenager, I thought my parents' rules were completely unreasonable. Now that I'm a mother, I realize they made and enforced their rules because they loved me and wanted to save me from making serious, possibly catastrophic, mistakes.

I may be a grown woman, but God still knows what's best for me. He created His commandments because He loves me, and He expects me to follow them because He wants to protect me—emotionally, physically, and spiritually. Just like my parents, He wants me to be happy.

Obey the Lord and experience His love.

—SBT

A Mother in Mourning

Then Rizpah daughter of Aiah, the mother of two of the men, spread burlap on a rock and stayed there the entire harvest season. She prevented the scavenger birds from tearing at their bodies during the day and stopped wild animals from eating them at night.

2 SAMUEL 21:10

The stony site of Rizpah's lonely vigil protecting her loved ones' bodies from desecration was in sharp contrast to the shady trees of the manicured cemetery in which I stood.

"Dis way," said the elderly caretaker in broken English after consulting his map. He plodded along ahead of me in floppy black overshoes, using his shovel as a walking stick.

In search of my grandmother's grave, I tried to remember what I had been told about this woman I never knew. "She was short, just like you, with dark hair. She went to church. Died in 1928. Buried at site 991."

The old caretaker stabbed the sod with his shovel. When it scraped against stone, he brushed away the dirt and pointed to the embedded marker. "Dat's it, no?" He doffed his cap and gestured toward the gravesite. "Your grandmudder." For just a moment he stood in respectful silence, then turned and shuffled off between the tombstones.

The respect we pay the dead reflects the value we place on life.

—ALMA BARKMAN

No Contest

When Rachel saw that she wasn't having any children for Jacob, she became jealous of her sister. She pleaded with Jacob, "Give me children, or I'll die!"

GENESIS 30:1

Ever tried to achieve the impossible? Rachel did. Frustrated by her infertility and desperate to compete with her sister for Jacob's affection, she failed to realize that Jacob's devotion wasn't dependent on her ability to have children.

Her attempts to earn Jacob's love mirror the error we sometimes make. We may find ourselves trying to earn God's love. If we don't fully understand grace, we might end up believing we're good enough on our own to deserve His love. Perhaps we despair, believing our sins are so black that we're beyond redemption.

When I am tempted to compare myself unfavorably to someone I deeply admire—a more devout Christian, a missionary, a performer, or a writer—I try to remember that being a believer isn't about accomplishments or competitions. It's about God's love and sacrifice for us. It's all about Jesus!

We're all winners in the eyes of God.

—SUSAN E. RAMSDEN

More Than Meets the Eye

Then Joshua secretly sent out two spies from the Israelite camp at Acacia Grove. He instructed them, "Scout out the land on the other side of the Jordan River, especially around Jericho." So the two men set out and came to the house of a prostitute named Rahab and stayed there that night.

JOSHUA 2:1

Few people would associate the attributes of intelligence, faith, and courage with someone in Rahab's line of work. However, she proved that she possessed those qualities and more. She was probably judged based solely on her lifestyle. Preconceived notions and stereotypes prevented others from discovering the potential and blessings she still had deep inside.

Things haven't changed much. Our society often uses a set of worldly criteria to determine a person's worth. I've been guilty of subscribing to these faulty and prejudiced standards, but I try to remember that God alone has the right to judge a person.

Instead of jumping to conclusions about someone, I need to see them through God's eyes—a fallible human in need of love and understanding, just like me.

There is often more to someone than meets the eye.

—SBT

349

Waiting on a Promise

*Now Sarai, Abram's wife, had not been able to bear children
for him. But she had an Egyptian servant named Hagar.*
GENESIS 16:1

Sarah knew God had promised He would make Abraham into a great nation. When she believed her child-bearing years were over, she gave her maid Hagar to Abraham as a surrogate. She thought she was doing the right thing and believed she was helping God make good on His promise. As it turned out, all she did was make matters worse.

As the years passed with no child, Sarah might have had trouble sustaining her belief that God would indeed fulfill His promise. I have never been very good at waiting. I was the child who perfected the art of searching for presents in the weeks before Christmas. When I pray for something, I want it now.

Sometimes, I fall into the trap of thinking it would be easier—and quicker—to take things into my own hands. Like Sarah, I often complicate things and achieve less-than-satisfactory results.

God always keeps His promises.

—SBT

Positive Persistence

*Even he rendered a just decision in the end. So don't you
think God will surely give justice to his chosen people who
cry out to him day and night? Will he keep putting them off?*
LUKE 18:7

Jesus told the story of the persistent widow to illustrate
the importance of continuing to pray and never giving up.
The judge would have remained unmoved in his decision
if the woman had become discouraged and withdrawn her
plea for justice.

At first, I found it difficult to be persistent in my
prayers. I was a tenacious child, and when I wanted something, I went after it with singleminded zeal. I can clearly
recall my exasperated mother ordering me to quit nagging
her, so when I got older, I decided that dogged determination was not a very attractive quality.

I've discovered, however, that God admires persistence.
He is not going to become frustrated or annoyed with me.
On the contrary, my relentless petitions are proof of both
my sincerity and my belief in the importance of my prayer.
My devotion just might be the thing that convinces God
to look favorably upon my request.

*Don't give up—you might be one prayer
away from a blessing.*

—SBT

Disheartening Delays

And she made this vow: "O Lord of Heaven's Armies, if you will look upon my sorrow and answer my prayer and give me a son, then I will give him back to you. He will be yours for his entire lifetime, and as a sign that he has been dedicated to the Lord, his hair will never be cut."

1 Samuel 1:11

Hannah had been praying for God to bless her with a child for a very long time. As the years went by and she remained barren, perhaps she decided that God had chosen to deny her petition. This may be why she encouraged her husband, Abraham, to take a second wife, one who could provide him with the son he so desperately wanted.

Why did God take so long to answer her prayer? Maybe He was waiting for her to turn the matter over to Him completely, trusting Him to fulfill the promise He had made to Abraham.

I can remember countless times when God answered my prayers with a resounding "Yes!"—at the last minute. However, because I'm human, I sometimes still see God's delay as His rejection of my request. Instead of allowing myself to become discouraged, I should determine whether or not I am truly trusting God and placing the matter in His capable hands.

Don't let God's delay dishearten you.

—SBT

Just Worship!

But as the Ark of the Lord entered the City of David,
Michal, the daughter of Saul, looked down from her window.
When she saw King David leaping and dancing before the
Lord, she was filled with contempt for him.
2 SAMUEL 6:16

Embarrassed by my husband's long arms lifted in worship, I wilted. How could he? Slowly, surely, I inched away. People would call us fanatics. When he started to sway, I nearly bolted. Then memory brought poor Michal to mind, and her long-ago actions sounded a warning.

With exultant abandon, David had worshiped God. He danced and took his praise to the streets—in a loincloth. His wife, Michal, was disgusted. Her scathing rebuke afterward demonstrated her disdain for her husband's true intention.

I thought about Michal's subsequent barrenness and her status as a wife in name only. I rethought my original impression and, then, silently blessed my mate. I may be tempted to judge physical expressions of worship, but God is concerned with the heart. I should do no less.

Genuine worship is a matter of the heart.

—LAURIE KLEIN

Pointing Out a Problem

*When the Lord has done all he promised and has made you
leader of Israel, don't let this be a blemish on your record.*

1 SAMUEL 25:30-31

It's easy to give our Christian brothers and sisters a pat
on the back or a high-five and congratulate them on a job
well done. It's usually a pleasure to compliment them on
their admirable qualities. However, when it comes to telling someone that their actions may cause them harm, the
situation becomes difficult. It's a circumstance that most
of us would like to avoid.

Abigail was not only smart and beautiful, she cared
deeply about the spiritual welfare of her fellow Christians.
When David became enraged and threatened to kill Abigail's husband, Nabal, and all of Nabal's men, Abigail did
everything she could to calm David's fury.

Finally, she challenged him with the consequences of
his intended murder and vengeance. It was only then he
stopped and fully realized what he had been about to do.
He praised God for Abigail's words of caution and blessed
her for preventing him from committing a terrible act.

*Caring for one another may sometimes
mean confronting a problem.*

—SBT

Fanning the Flame

*Jesus turned around, and when he saw her he said,
"Daughter, be encouraged! Your faith has made you well."
And the woman was healed at that moment.*
MATTHEW 9:22

Afflicted with uncontrollable bleeding for twelve years, the woman was considered unclean and treated as an outcast. She risked the crowd's wrath and, perhaps, that of Jesus, by attempting to touch him.

I am always moved when I read His response to her. I can only imagine how she felt when he called her "Daughter"—perhaps the first kind words she had heard in twelve long years. Her faith accomplished what no person had been able to do, and I have no doubt that the spark of faith that helped her risk everything that day was fanned into a flame of devoted belief.

My faith in God started with a tiny spark, and when I asked God to help my faith grow, He worked in my life to increase and strengthen my beliefs. It's been a gradual process, much like a child growing into an adult; sometimes, my faith falters. When that happens, I am quick to ask for help again.

*Nurture your faith with prayer and
feed it with the word of God.*

—SBT

Hostages to Faith

But when she could no longer hide him, she got a basket made of papyrus reeds and waterproofed it with tar and pitch. She put the baby in the basket and laid it among the reeds along the bank of the Nile River.

EXODUS 2:3

The first day of school is always a bittersweet event. Still reeling from the speed with which the summer flies by, I watch my children trudge out to the bus stop. Although my thoughts and prayers go with them, once they are out of my sight, I have to put my faith in God to work and trust that He will watch over them until they return.

As difficult as it might be to relinquish my children's safety to God's will, I can only imagine how hard it was for Jochebed to put her precious baby in a basket and set it adrift on the Nile. It took courage, and it took a mother's passionate desire to keep her child from harm but, most of all, it took a deep-seated belief in God's perfect plan.

Trust the ones you love to God's tender care.

—SBT

Put Me First

*But Elijah said to her, "Don't be afraid! Go ahead
and do just what you've said, but make a little bread
for me first. Then use what's left to prepare a meal for
yourself and your son."*

1 KINGS 17:13

I studied the balance in my checking account and mentally added the bills that needed to be paid before the next payday. There were at least two large bills, a few small ones, and groceries to buy. Then there was my tithe. Surely, I can borrow from it this one time, I thought. God will understand my dilemma. If I make my usual gift to the church, I won't be able to buy food.

The more I wrestled with my decision, the more I realized that God was not buying my logic. "Put God first," said the still small voice within me. "Make Him your priority. He will always take care of you." So, with a leap of faith, I wrote the check, and reordered my obligations.

But that's not the end of the story. Just like the widow of Zarephath, God kept His word. Our cupboards have never been empty, and our obligations have always been met.

Putting God first makes all the difference.

—YVONNE CURRY SMALLWOOD

Entertaining Angels

When the princess opened it, she saw the baby. The little boy was crying, and she felt sorry for him. "This must be one of the Hebrew children," she said.

EXODUS 2:6

"We always have ketchup sandwiches for lunch," the grubby child whispered. Her hair was matted and lice-infested. The plastic grocery bag containing her belongings lay at her feet. Though she tried to project a confident air, her tiny hands shook.

This was my friend Barb's eighteenth foster child, and Barb's heart ached for her just as it had ached for the first one. She realized this would be a challenge, and I knew she wondered if she was up to the task.

There was no chance that she would turn the little girl away. Just as Pharaoh's daughter was caring enough to take action when she found Moses, Barb has always been compelled to do what her Christlike compassion dictates. She was obviously listening and taking notes when Jesus said, "Let the little children come unto me."

Do you know a child who needs Jesus?

—ROXANNE PUGA

NOVEMBER

Dreams Deferred but Not Forgotten

"How kind the Lord is!" she exclaimed.
'He has taken away my disgrace of having no children."
LUKE 1:25

*H*ave you ever longed for something that would completely revolutionize your life and the way people look at you? Perhaps you feel insignificant without a spouse and long to be married. Maybe you're tired of apartment living and want to buy a house. Possibly you're waiting for a job promotion that will bring higher status and more income. But we must remember that delayed blessings may be multiplied. Such was the case of Elizabeth in Luke's gospel of the New Testament.

Elizabeth and her husband, Zechariah, were both descendants of the priestly line of Abijah. Since priests were commanded to wed women of good character who had not been previously married or divorced, Elizabeth must have maintained a godly reputation and spiritual purity before marriage. The Bible tells us that Elizabeth and Zechariah were righteous people, committed to serving their God. Despite this devotion, Elizabeth remained barren into old age, and their prayers for a child remained unanswered.

Without children, a couple's inheritance might be passed to a distant relative or given to a family servant. Childless couples were made to feel as though they had failed, not only in their duty to each other, but also in their responsibility to the community to build up the population and continue the family line.

Elizabeth and Zechariah were finally rewarded for their steadfast faith when God chose them to become the parents of the man destined to prepare the world for the coming of the Messiah. The angel Gabriel delivered this news to Zechariah as he burned incense and performed his duties in the temple. Because the stunned father-to-be questioned the truth of Gabriel's words, he lost the ability to speak until the child's birth. Completing his week of temple service, he and Elizabeth returned home. She soon became pregnant.

God's blessings to long-suffering Elizabeth were only beginning. Her distant relative Mary of Nazareth was engaged and preparing to marry. When Elizabeth was in her sixth month of pregnancy, young Mary arrived for a visit. She had just received her own angelic message from Gabriel. God had picked her to give birth to the Messiah.

At the sound of Mary's greeting, Elizabeth's child leaped within her, and Elizabeth was filled with the Holy Spirit. Elizabeth gave a glad cry and exclaimed to Mary, "God has blessed you above all women, and your child is blessed. Why am I so honored, that the mother of my Lord should visit me? When I heard your greeting, the baby in my womb jumped for joy. You are blessed because you believed that the Lord would do what he said" (Luke 1:41–45).

Elizabeth was overwhelmed by the honor of Mary's visit, but when her unborn child leaped for joy upon hearing Mary's greeting, her happiness knew no bounds. She cried out to her cousin with great excitement, and she realized without being told how the young woman's life had changed. Most importantly, she praised Mary for trusting God's word.

Mary stayed with Elizabeth for three months, undoubtedly encouraged and supported during those early days of pregnancy by her now-experienced cousin. Just as amazement and perhaps criticism had probably swirled around Zechariah's loss of speech, Mary may have enjoyed refuge from the gossip generated by her situation. The greatest tie between the two pregnant women, though, was their faith in God and their willingness to obey Him in the middle of tough circumstances.

When Elizabeth's baby was born, neighbors and friends believed the boy should be named for his father, Zechariah, but Elizabeth insisted the child's name was John. When those attending the infant's circumcision ceremony didn't believe her, they turned to Zechariah for clarification. Surprisingly, he confirmed his wife's announcement. This restored his speech and prompted his prophecy of John's divine ministry.

Like Elizabeth, I have faced disappointment in giving birth after losing several babies to preterm birth. Despite seven miscarriages, God blessed me with four healthy children. The ob-gyn specialist who evaluated my miscarriages could find no reason for my repeated losses. I could not comprehend why God would take my little ones before I could hold them in my arms and raise them to love Him. Although I did not understand His reasons, I knew that my heart would heal only when I regained my trust in His purpose.

Have you discovered the joy of serving God and waiting on His mercies? Your hope may be deferred for a season, but fulfillment will come. If you trust and obey, God will take care of all relevant matters in His own time.

—ALEXANDRA ROSE

Tunnel Vision

This is all your fault! I put my servant into your arms, but now that she's pregnant she treats me with contempt. The Lord will show who's wrong—you or me!
GENESIS 16:5

When I find myself weary of waiting for God's response to my prayers, my imagination flies into overtime, and I come up with all sorts of wonderful ideas. Unfortunately, most of my schemes suffer from tunnel vision. Unlike God, who sees the whole picture with every detail intact, I am only human. I see what I want to see.

When Sarah lost faith in God's promise and gave her handmaid Hagar to Abraham, the only thing she saw was the son Abraham needed—the one Hagar could supply. She didn't take into account the potential problems caused by a major shift in the family dynamic. She didn't consider how she might feel with a pregnant woman and, eventually, a brand-new baby living in her home.

God knows the future. He also knows what's best for me. When I get ready to jump into a pool with no clue as to the depth of the water, I remember Sarah.

God has the whole photo album—not just one picture.

—SBT

Faithful Listening

*No wonder our hearts have melted in fear! No one
has the courage to fight after hearing such things. For
the Lord your God is the supreme God of the heavens
above and the earth below.*

JOSHUA 2:11

Rahab told the spies that everyone in Jericho lived
in fear of the Israelite's God. They had all listened to the
amazing stories of what the Lord had done for His people,
but with the exception of Rahab, the people of Jericho
heard the miraculous tales with their ears alone. Only
Rahab listened with her heart.

Someone may appear to be listening and, yet, not hear
a word. My children are particularly good at this form of
deception. It's also quite possible to listen and hear the
words without retaining a thing. I confess I've practiced
both these forms of listening when it comes to God's word,
but I know if I want to grow spiritually and stay close to
Him, I need to pay attention with my ears and my heart.

The heart hears the love in God's voice.

—SBT

Wisdom for Worried Parents

Deborah, the wife of Lappidoth, was a prophet who was judging Israel at that time.
Judges 4:4

My son has been married for just a few years and, as in any marriage, he and his wife have their differences. As a new mother-in-law I try not to meddle. Instinctively, I want to defend my child, even though I know he is not without fault.

In the Old Testament, Deborah was known as a prophetess. When asked for advice, she yielded to God and made herself available to Him. As knowledgeable as she was, she knew her real wisdom lay in seeking God for the answer.

We need to seek God for wisdom, especially on behalf of our children, no matter how old they are. We shouldn't interfere in their marriages but, sometimes, they turn to us for guidance. In order for us to give judicious counsel, we need to have a close relationship with our wise God.

When we put God first, our entire family will benefit.

—Connie Sturm Cameron

Mutual Benefits

*As the cloud moved from above the Tabernacle, there stood
Miriam, her skin as white as snow from leprosy.*
NUMBERS 12:10

Along with her brothers Aaron and Moses, Miriam
was a leader of the Israelites. When she discovered that
Moses was going to appoint seventy elders and prophets
to assist in leadership, she was not happy. She did not
want to share her role, and instead of trusting that Moses
was acting on God's behalf, she became jealous of the others. Her envy spilled over into resentment of Moses' wife.
The Lord heard her speak negatively about Moses, and He
punished her with leprosy.

When God brings about a change in our life, it may
be so others can benefit along with us. The introduction
of seventy elders would obviously make a difference in the
life of Miriam and her brothers, but it would have a profound effect on the elders and, perhaps, others, as well.
Sometimes we forget that it's not all about us.

*When God asks us to "let go,"
it may be so that others can grow.*

—CONNIE STURM CAMERON

You Are My People

*But Ruth replied, "Don't ask me to leave you and
turn back. Wherever you go, I will go; wherever
you live, I will live. Your people will be my people,
and your God will be my God."*
RUTH 1:16

Barbara and I didn't always get along. My mother-in-law had to learn that I would be good to her son, and I had to learn to love her despite her loud ways. We grew to love each other deeply. We shared lots of great family get-togethers and some very sad trials. I held her when her younger son killed himself. Later, she held me when her other son, my husband, died after a traumatic illness.

For eighteen years of marriage to her son we made meals, attended births and funerals, went camping, watched movies, cleaned house, celebrated holidays, went fishing, traded secrets, and prayed together. When my young husband died, she didn't stop being my mom, and I didn't stop being her daughter. We shared our grief.

Three years later, when I thought of marrying again, I had to ask Barbara's blessing because she was my mom, my family—my people! We are bound together by the same Heavenly Father.

*When you serve the same God, you share eternal love and a
bond that cannot be broken.*

—EVA JULIUSON

Providing Backup

*Give my greetings to Priscilla and Aquila, my coworkers in
the ministry of Christ Jesus.*
ROMANS 16:3

Priscilla didn't just talk a good game when it came to
being a Christian. She backed up her words with plenty of
action. Her commitment led her to take on a multitude of
tasks in the early church, and she appeared totally dedicated to furthering the gospel. When she called herself a
Christian, I doubt anyone questioned her identity.

Sometimes, I wonder if my lifestyle speaks for my
beliefs. If someone didn't know I was a Christian, could
he tell by my behaviors and attitudes? I'm not sure I always
give God the time He deserves. This is not something
anyone else can do for me.

I need to renew my commitment to the Lord, redirect
my focus toward Him, and work on making my actions
match my words. I heard once that it's not how long you
live; it's how you live while you're here.

Are you who you say you are?

—SBT

The God of Details

"Take this baby and nurse him for me," the princess
told the baby's mother. "I will pay you for your help."
So the woman took her baby home and nursed him.
EXODUS 2:9

Unable to hide her infant son any longer from those who wished to kill him, Jochebed set him adrift in a basket on the Nile. There, he was discovered by the pharaoh's daughter who rescued the child and, in an amazing set of circumstances, hired Jochebed to be a wet nurse to her own baby.

Sometimes, when we pray for God to work in our lives, we expect one significant, miraculous occurrence to answer our petition. This may well happen but, most likely, God will set into motion a sequence of small, deceptively unremarkable incidents. He is, after all, the God of details, and much of His work is accomplished through minor events.

I have to spend time in prayer to center my attention on God, and I must believe He cares enough about me to answer my requests. Only then will I see that the things I once thought of as unimportant or mere coincidence are, in reality, part of God's work in my life.

Ask God to open your eyes to His work in your life.

—SBT

A Footnote to Greatness

He was twenty-five years old when he became king, and he reigned in Jerusalem twenty-nine years. His mother was Abijah, the daughter of Zechariah.
2 KINGS 18:2

Mentioned only briefly in scripture, Abijah would be easy to overlook, but she must have had a tremendous testimony, one that deeply impacted her son, the good king Hezekiah. Ahaz, Hezekiah's father, had sold out, and thrown his lot in with Assyria. To assure his new allies of his sincerity, he adopted their religion, and the Bible contains a chilling description of Ahaz's sacrifice of Hezekiah's brother to those pagan gods. Despite this horrific example, Hezekiah turned out to be one of the greatest kings Judah had ever known, second only to David. Apparently, his mother was a profound influence in his young son's life and she endowed him with her steadfast faith.

There may be a young Hezekiah in your world, soaking up your example and learning from your life. Be diligent in sharing your faith, then watch and see what God does with the investment.

There are far more people behind the scenes than in the spotlight.

—PAULA WISEMAN

What Is Enough?

Then God blessed them and said, "Be fruitful and multiply. Fill the earth and govern it. Reign over the fish in the sea, the birds in the sky, and all the animals that scurry along the ground."
GENESIS 1:28

"From this home you can see three states," the ad boasted. The expansive mountain house was magnificent. It was far beyond our price range, but that didn't stop me from wanting it. I had been blessed with a nice home that sat on three acres of majestic woods. So why did I want more? When would I have enough?

Eve's lustful eye and greedy heart have retained their powerful message through time. She, too, appeared to have it all—she lived in paradise with her loving husband—but she still longed for more. She didn't understand that she already possessed the best of everything. She didn't realize that God had blessed her with more than enough because He never withholds good things from his children.

Have you thanked God for all your blessings?

—MARY CATHERINE ROGERS

A Biblical Matchmaker

One day Naomi said to Ruth, "My daughter, it's time that I found a permanent home for you, so that you will be provided for."

RUTH 3:1

Years ago, I introduced some Christian women to Christian men. These couples later married, and I became known as a matchmaker. A few people questioned the value of my efforts. "Shouldn't a woman leave marriage in God's hands?" they asked.

Perhaps the Lord used me to help these women build Christian unions rather than marriages where they might be unequally yoked to unbelievers. Twelve years have passed, and the marriages are still intact.

I'm certainly not the first person God has used as a matchmaker. Naomi quickly spotted the advantages of a husband for her daughter-in-law Ruth. She planted the seed for the relationship between Ruth and Boaz, and the blessings of that union included the grandfather of King David and eventually, the Messiah.

The selection of a spouse can have a huge impact on a person's faith. When we help Christian brothers and sisters find marriages and friendships that fortify their beliefs, we help them draw closer to God.

Faith needs to be the cornerstone of every marriage.

—RONICA STROMBERG

Life in the Light

Among them were Mary Magdalene,
from whom he had cast out seven demons.
LUKE 8:2

When Jesus met Mary, she was trapped in a dark world of endless nightmares. Shunned by the townspeople, she wandered alone and afraid, unable to enjoy even the simplest pleasures in life. Then Jesus healed her and made it possible for her to enter a world of light and laughter. No wonder she became one of His most devoted followers. I'm sure those who had known her before her miraculous change found it difficult, if not impossible, to recognize her.

When some of the people at church share their stories with me, I find it very hard to believe that they were once the people they describe. Many people have been completely transformed.

Only God can accomplish such a miraculous makeover. He can turn sorrow into joy, hideous into beautiful, and mistakes into moments of opportunity. All I have to do is believe.

Ask Jesus into your heart and get ready for a change.

—SBT

Disabling Disappointment

*So Jacob slept with Rachel, too, and he loved her much
more than Leah. He then stayed and worked for Laban the
additional seven years.*
GENESIS 29:30

For years, Leah lived with the misery of loving her
husband, Jacob, while knowing his heart belonged to her
sister, Rachel. God tried to make her feel loved by blessing her with children, but she became obsessed with winning Jacob's affections. Chronic disappointment affected
her judgment, and she took out her unhappiness on those
closest to her.

Eventually, she came to realize that God was the
source of her true happiness, but not until she caused
irreparable damage to her relationship with Rachel.

Disillusionment is part of being human, but a string
of disappointments can leave me feeling discouraged and
even depressed. Before I let my feelings affect my attitude
and relationships, I need to turn to God and ask for help.
He will send people and situations to lift my spirits and
give me the strength and courage to move forward.

Don't let disappointment keep you down.

—SBT

Faith Relays

I remember your genuine faith, for you share the faith that first filled your grandmother Lois and your mother, Eunice. And I know that same faith continues strong in you.

2 TIMOTHY 1:5

I can't remember a time when I didn't understand and believe the Good News about Jesus Christ. Like Timothy, I was blessed to have women in my family who raised me with a faith in God.

My upbringing may have resulted in a rather dull testimony. I had no addictions or jaw-dropping sins to report, but I also had few regrets. Now, as I raise my sons, I try to follow the example of women like Lois and Eunice. They conducted their lives in a manner that encouraged Timothy to not only live his own life for the Lord, but to become a missionary and pass that faith on to others. Their devoted teachings bore fruit.

Mothers and grandmothers can rest assured that it is possible to raise children in the faith. Their loving instruction is never in vain.

You can make a difference in a child's life.

—RONICA STROMBERG

The God Who Sees

Thereafter, Hagar used another name to refer to the Lord, who had spoken to her. She said, "You are the God who sees me."

GENESIS 16:13

People often rely on everything but God for their foundation. God promised Abraham that his seed would be as numerous as the stars in the sky. His wife, Sarah, became impatient and, in an act of self-reliance, she gave her handmaiden Hagar to Abraham so that he could have children by her.

Invariably, self-reliance causes its own problems. After Sarah achieved her goal, she mistreated Hagar so badly that Hagar ran away. An angel appeared to Hagar and told her to return to her master. God knew she needed a home, food, and support to carry the baby to term. Hagar returned to Abraham and Sarah and, as a result of her experience, she referred to God as El Roi or "the God who sees."

There have been times in my own life when I took matters into my own hands and other instances when I ran away from my problems. However, God has always been gracious to redeem my mistakes and set my feet upon the right paths.

Submission brings us closer to God.

—LAROSE KARR

Tied to God

*But Job replied, "You talk like a foolish woman.
Should we accept only good things from the hand
of God and never anything bad?"*
JOB 2:10

My house was literally falling apart at the seams. In a short period of time, the water heater broke, the old windows refused to open and alleviate the summer heat, the finished basement flooded from a power outage, and rain was falling on my face at night due to the leaky roof.

That was just the house. My child was having serious behavior problems, and I was at a career crisis, which meant our finances were at a standstill. Every part of me wanted to close up shop and die inside.

Fortunately, I did not take Job's wife's approach and voice my dark thoughts. If I had, I would have missed an opportunity for spiritual growth and the blessing of watching how God can repair the parts of my life that have come unraveled.

*When the seams of your life begin to come undone,
remember that you are still tied to God.*

—LESLIE J. SHERROD

Immediate Availability

Mary responded, "I am the Lord's servant.
May everything you have said about me come true."
And then the angel left her.
LUKE 1:38

God chose Mary to be the mother of His son for a multitude of reasons. Just like an employer looking for the perfect job candidate, God has specific qualities in mind when He selects someone to be a part of His perfect plan.

One of the most significant characteristics He looks for is availability. Mary no doubt had plans for her life, but when the angel Gabriel appeared and announced God's intentions, Mary didn't think twice before placing herself in His hands.

When an opportunity for me to serve God presents itself, I need to be available. It doesn't matter how hard-working, trustworthy, or reliable I am if can't spare the time to serve my Lord. My life may be brimming over with busyness, but if I make myself accessible to God, He will simplify my life and free up the time I need.

Make yourself available for God's work and God's blessings.

—SBT

You Just Have to Ask

She said, "Let me have another gift. You have already given
me land in the Negev; now please give me springs of water,
too." So Caleb gave her the upper and lower springs.
JUDGES 1:15

In the years following our daughter's birth, we prayed
for God to prepare a godly husband for her future. That
time had finally come, and when my daughter announced
her engagement, I was overjoyed.

As we discussed wedding plans together, we were
faced with the challenge of where to hold the wedding
and reception so that it would be beautiful—and afford-
able. Did we dare ask our friends to use their property on
the beach? We dared. It was a stunning wedding, and the
beautiful setting was a gift. It reminded me of another
woman who asked for an extra gift.

When Acsah got married, she was fearless enough to
ask her father for more blessings, even though he'd already
given her land. So, she asked him for springs. After all,
who can live without water? She asked boldly and her
desire was accomplished.

If we don't ask, we just might miss that
extra something God wants to give us.

—JANEY L. DEMEO

The Source of Our Strength

*She tormented him with her nagging day
after day until he was sick to death of it.*
Judges 16:16

Delilah badgered Samson until he finally caved in and revealed the source of his great strength. His admission came at a huge cost, and the entire village paid the price when it was destroyed. We are all tempted to nag in order to get our way, but as Christians, we shouldn't be berating anyone. We should be praying.

Only with God's intervention can we effect the changes we desire. It's vital to include ourselves in our prayers and ask God to show us how we might need to change. Occasionally, I ask God to show me what it's like to live with me. I don't always like what I see.

*Sometimes the only way to transform an unhappy situation
is to alter our own attitude about it.*

—Connie Sturm Cameron

A Process of Refinement

Then David comforted Bathsheba, his wife, and slept with her. She became pregnant and gave birth to a son, and they named him Solomon.

2 SAMUEL 12:24

When the infant son conceived by David and Bath-sheba during their adulterous affair died, no doubt she was devastated. Losing a child may be the worst thing a woman can endure.

As it turned out, though, the death of their baby brought David back to the Lord and made it possible for him to rebuild his marriage to Bathsheba. It wasn't long before the couple welcomed another son, the child who would become the mighty King Solomon.

Trials and sufferings enter a person's life for a variety of reasons. God often will allow problems in people's lives to bring them closer to Him. We don't learn much when everything is going well.

We may never know why God allows tragedy to touch our lives but, sometimes, we can look back over our lives and see that God was, indeed, in control and acting in our best interests.

Hardship and adversity help us become the people God wants us to be.

—SBT

Lost and Found

She fell at his feet and bowed before him,
overwhelmed with gratitude. Then she took her son in
her arms and carried him downstairs.

2 KINGS 4:37

Her son had died in her arms at noon, but she remained calm. She knew the prophet Elisha would help her, so she hurried to find him. Then, facing the man of God who had foretold the boy's miracle birth, she found herself overcome with emotion, and her faith faltered. After years of barrenness, why had God raised her hopes only to destroy them?

Years after my father left us, after I'd finally forgiven him, he told me something I had only dreamed of hearing. "You turned out all right," he said. I could have flown home without the plane; my joy was so great. Weeks later, death stole him from me. I had lost him twice. Did he love God at the end? Not knowing haunted me.

Then one day, I thought I heard my father's trumpet playing a praise song I had written called, "I Love You, Lord." What lives in me now is certainty. I'll see my father in heaven, and we'll have all the time we need.

God resurrects our hopes—even in loss.

—LAURIE KLEIN

One Way Out

At dawn the next morning the angels became insistent.
"Hurry," they said to Lot. "Take your wife and your two
daughters who are here. Get out right now, or you will be
swept away in the destruction of the city!"
GENESIS 19:15

In the wee hours of the morning, Lot's wife found herself running for her life. God was about to destroy the wicked cities of Sodom and Gomorrah by fire. What was she thinking in her haste to flee? What made her look back? Her curiosity turned her into a pillar of salt.

I can relate to her story. Even though God tells me to forget the past, I look back and relive it. I recall my early twenties, when I had a difficult time extracting myself from an abusive relationship. God wanted me to burn my bridges, and I spent years trying to put out the fire.

Now, I'm slowly learning every step forward is a leap of faith, and faith leads us to straight to God, our refuge and strength.

The only way out is forward.

—JAMIE BIRR

A Loving Parent

There is only one thing worth being concerned about. Mary has discovered it, and it will not be taken away from her.
LUKE 10:42

When Jesus reprimanded Martha for being worried and upset with her sister, He spoke to her not just as a friend, but also as God. As a close friend, he had the benefit of knowing her well, but as God, he knew everything about her. In chastising her, He knew exactly what to say and how to say it.

In our home, we have rules that everyone is expected to follow, but the method of enforcing these rules varies from child to child. All Connor needs is a gentle reproof and a stern look, while his younger brother, Owen, hardheaded and determined, usually requires something more emphatic.

We may not have the honor of entertaining Jesus in the flesh as Martha and her siblings did, but He still knows everything about us. When we make mistakes, He understands precisely how to react. It's a great source of comfort to realize that God is a loving and discerning parent who sees us all as individuals with different needs.

God knows what's best for each and every one of us.

—SBT

Sweet Revenge

So Herod put John in prison,
adding this sin to his many others.
LUKE 3:20

For Herodias, it started off as boredom, turned into discontent, was followed by outrage, and then erupted into a full-fledged need for revenge. Every time we feel the need to get our own back, or react in the manner of tit for tat, we take the first step into an area forbidden by God. Revenge is strictly His territory.

It's hard not to hit back verbally at a perceived, or even real, insult, but it will never give a believer any joy. Revenge may seem sweet at first, but it will soon turn sour and leave a long-lasting, bitter taste. If we trust God and practice patience, we will soon discover that the Lord has His own way of chastising the wrongdoer.

No believer is a victim in the Lord's scheme of things.

—RITA STELLA GALIEH

True Beauty

Who can find a virtuous and capable wife?
She is more precious than rubies.
PROVERBS 31:10

As our family settled around the dinner table on Mother's Day, my husband stood and read from the Bible. I listened from under the thick blanket of guilt imposed by the attributes of perfect womanhood in Proverbs 31. Her glowing description rubbed salt into my already wounded spirit.

An article I read later wisely suggested looking at these verses as spiritual principles instead of literal physical action. From this perspective, I discovered the woman of Proverbs 31 was trustworthy, watched carefully over her household, and reached out generously to others with compassion and kindness. She also created ways to use God's provisions, depended on strength from God, worked with a willing spirit, and spoke with God's wisdom.

I recognized these attributes as part of my own goal to develop inner beauty. Maybe this remarkable woman had something in common with me after all! I shrugged off my blanket of guilt, grateful that with God's help I can become a virtuous woman with a servant's heart.

Real beauty is not captured in the reflection of a mirror.

—MARION GORMAN

Toxic Envy

When Rachel saw that she wasn't having any children for Jacob, she became jealous of her sister. She pleaded with Jacob, "Give me children, or I'll die!"

GENESIS 30:1

When I was growing up, a family with two daughters lived down the street. The girls were inseparable, but everything changed when they entered high school. The younger of the two sisters was clearly the family beauty, and she became very popular.

The close and loving relationship shared by the sisters vanished when the older sister could no longer restrain her jealousy. She became increasingly bitter and angry and, as time went by, chances for a resolution grew more and more unlikely.

Leah envied Rachel because she was beautiful and because she was the recipient of Jacob's love. Rachel was jealous of Leah's ability to bear sons for Jacob. Left unchecked, these dark feelings poisoned everyone involved.

The world may have changed, but human emotions remain constant. Feelings of envy still damage our fellowship with God and with the people around us. We need to focus on our blessings rather than behave as though we disapprove of the blessings He's bestowed on others.

Restore your fellowship with God and He will give you the desires of your heart.

—SBT

Desperate Devotion

There was a famine during David's reign that lasted for three years, so David asked the Lord about it. And the Lord said, "The famine has come because Saul and his family are guilty of murdering the Gibeonites."

2 SAMUEL 21:1

David consulted God as to why the famine was occurring, but he didn't ask Him how to go about ending it. Instead, he went straight to the Gibeonites to find out what he could do to avenge Saul's actions. As a result, seven men, including Rizpah's two sons, died. Still the famine continued.

For the next six months, Rizpah guarded the unburied bodies of her sons. Moved by her plight, David gave all seven victims a proper burial.

Rizpah's devoted love for her sons reminded him of the close friendship he once had with Saul's son, Jonathan. He retrieved the unburied bodies of Saul and Jonathan and ordered that they, too, be given the honor of a dignified burial. Only when David began acting out of love did God end the famine.

Rizpah's tragic story is a tribute to a mother's love, but it also reminds me of the dangers—and futility—of bypassing God. Forgiveness and healing always starts with Him.

When we are motivated by love,
our actions are never insignificant.

—SBT

Brave New World

Release all the animals—the birds, the livestock, and the small animals that scurry along the ground—so they can be fruitful and multiply throughout the earth.
GENESIS 8:17

Hardship often reveals our hidden abilities, and Noah's wife was no exception. She was a remarkable woman long before she entered the ark, but her list of admirable capabilities grew significantly longer during her ordeal aboard the ark. After the flood, it took great courage to watch her sons go off to establish themselves. Something tells me Noah's wife truly understood the empty nest.

It's not exactly Dr. Doolittle around here, but I cherish family togetherness and our goofy pets. When we had to euthanize our elderly dog, and then our daughter left home, I ached. A grim diagnosis that same month shook me even further. Head in hands, I just sat.

It must have been God who sent the fawn. It frisked on the lawn, three feet from my window, as if to say, "Silly, the young are always with you." I couldn't help but laugh at such endearing awkwardness. With God's help, I can brave my foreign new world.

God encourages us in delightful ways.

—LAURIE KLEIN

The True Gift

While Jesus was in the Temple, he watched the rich people dropping their gifts in the collection box. Then a poor widow came by and dropped in two small coins.

LUKE 21:2

A heap of donations surrounded me: outgrown clothing, discarded stuffed animals, a baby doll with disheveled and torn hair, shoes thin from wear. These items had been packed in old suitcases and dragged to Honduras to be presented as gifts for people living in huts with dirt floors that would become mudslides during the rainy season. They were people who lived miles from running water and the nearest schools or health clinics.

We had come to provide health care and gifts, offering a week of time generously set aside from our business. As we saw the last person at our makeshift clinic, we were presented with a gift. Perhaps she was the family matriarch, her face etched with wrinkles, yet with gentleness in her eyes. She extended her hands and presented us with a bag of sugar and a chick. At that moment, I couldn't help but wonder if our gifts had represented a true sacrifice.

Do you understand what it means to truly give?

—KATHY PRIDE

A Tiny Gesture with a Mighty Message

But because the midwives feared God, they refused to obey the king's orders. They allowed the boys to live, too.
EXODUS 1:17

When the pharaoh gave the order to the Hebrew midwives Shiphrah and Puah to kill all newborn Hebrew boys, I'm sure they wondered how much difference two lowly midwives could possibly make.

Even if they saved the babies, the pharaoh would come up with another plan to destroy Hebrew lives. However, they knew in their hearts what God wanted them to do, so they did everything they could to protect the new infants.

When I see all the homeless and destitute people, I despair of ever making a difference. One day, a woman asked my husband and me for some money to buy something to eat. Instead, I invited her to eat lunch with us at a nearby McDonald's.

Later, I felt guilty because it had only been one meal. Then I remembered that no matter how little I had been able to do, I had done it in God's name. I had made a difference in that woman's day—and, perhaps, in her life.

No gesture is trivial in God's eyes.

—SBT

Did You Say Thank-You?

Then Hannah prayed: "My heart rejoices in the Lord! The Lord has made me strong. Now I have an answer for my enemies; I rejoice because you rescued me."

1 SAMUEL 2:1

When God finally answered Hannah's prayers for a son, she may have felt some remorse for being self-centered, for forgetting to thank and praise the One who made everything possible.

When her son, Samuel, was weaned, she turned him over to the priest in Shiloh, just as she had promised God. Instead of lapsing into sorrow and self-pity, she praised God for making her dream come true. In doing this, she kept her focus on God, which undoubtedly alleviated some of her heartbreak over leaving her son.

Occasionally, I feel as though the only times my children seek me out is when they want something. If this happens too frequently, I began to feel used, rather than loved and appreciated.

Sometimes I'm guilty of doing the same thing to God. I recite a litany of requests and forget to praise or thank Him. If I start off my prayers with a tribute to His greatness and gratitude for His countless blessings, I will probably find that some of my "needs" have disappeared from my list.

Take some time to make God feel loved and appreciated.

—SBT

DECEMBER

Let's Get Dressed

At that moment their eyes were opened, and they suddenly felt shame at their nakedness. So they sewed fig leaves together to cover themselves.

GENESIS 3:7

$\mathcal{I}$n my fourth-grade religion class last week, the operative word was *naked*. It started when Rachel, a very capable oral reader, stopped short halfway through the seventh verse of Genesis 3. With a panic-stricken look on her face, she whispered to me, "Will you please say this next word?"

"Naked," I said. "Adam and Eve realized they were naked." Snickers rippled across the room. The next reader, Mark, raced to verse 10, where Adam explains to God, "I was afraid because I was naked; so I hid." A fresh flurry of giggles broke out, most conspicuously among the boys.

During the rest of the lesson, I heard snippets of whispers, most of them involving the word *naked*. How could the main point—God's promise of a Savior—compete with the tantalizing concept of nakedness and the newfound permission to say the word out loud? Theology definitely took a back seat on this one, at least among my students.

At the end of class, Michael raised his hand. He had a gleam in his eye and the bearing of someone entertaining a fabulous thought. "Before sin happened," he began, "Adam and Eve were naked in the Garden of Eden?" I smiled and nodded. "So if sin hadn't have happened," he continued, "we'd all be sitting here naked, right now!"

Once again, I had to agree, but I felt a little uncomfortable with the idea. So did the girls, who responded with a chorus of *Ewww*, accompanied by looks of complete disgust.

"Well, there's one good thing about Eve's eating the fruit from the tree in the middle of the garden," I said in a futile attempt to get the conversation away from nudity. "After she did that, she needed clothes. Since I like to shop, I'd really miss not being able to wear clothes." I paused for a moment, unable to believe what I had just said, but I wasn't about to confess my complete lack of desire to run about naked. Give me those fig leaves, and plenty of them!

The kids, of course, had been thinking about being literally naked, but it's the other kind of nakedness that gives me cause for concern. The God-given purity Adam and Eve once wore in the Garden of Eden was lost forever with their knowledge of good and evil. With the promise of a Savior, however, God provided our first parents with additional clothing, poetically described by the prophet Isaiah this way:

> I am overwhelmed with joy in the Lord my God!
> For he has dressed me with the clothing of salvation
> and draped me in a robe of righteousness.
> I am like a bridegroom in his wedding suit
> or a bride with her jewels.
> ISAIAH 61:10

Salvation! Righteousness! Now those are clothes worth talking about. Fourth-graders don't know that yet, because they're only nine years old. I remember what it was like to hear the words *salvation* and *righteousness* at their age. Those were church words having nothing to do with my day-to-day life.

My best friend in high school, Chris, called herself an agnostic. When I responded to her questions about Christianity, she met my answers with a bemused patience, not unlike the reaction to the ramblings of a befuddled eccentric. She found it unnecessary to think about salvation at her age—death seemed very far away in those days—and righteousness meant being a good person.

Chris didn't lie, steal, or kill. She knew the difference between right and wrong and tried to do the right thing. So, she didn't need the garment of salvation, and she was already wearing the robe of righteousness. A lot of people I've met since then feel that way, and it's a sad thing.

I strive to make the concepts of salvation and righteousness concrete for the kids. I try to demonstrate what these pieces of clothing look like when they're worn in real life. For children, the garment of salvation often suggests something they might wear in heaven, and perhaps that's enough for nine-year-olds. It might take a while for them to understand that they're wearing the garment right here on Earth.

Some people may not be able to apply this concept to themselves right away, but they can clearly spot the spiritual nakedness of someone else. Then one day, they experience the heartache of watching a friend or loved one streak through life with no relationship to Jesus Christ. Suddenly, they feel God's garment of salvation wrapped around them for the first time.

God's robe of righteousness is a different matter. We all know decent, hard-working people who aren't committed Christians. They wear a robe of righteousness, but the trouble is, they've created it themselves. I'm not against homemade clothes, particularly because I sew many of my own outfits—too many, if you hearken back to the plural closets. I favor them over the ones I buy, but when it comes to righteousness, I let God do the sewing.

His robe of righteousness, given to Eve with the promise of a Savior, and to us by faith in Jesus Christ, is the genuine article. No one clothed in God's righteousness needs to worry about feeling naked in front of Him or anyone else. He sees us dressed in His own perfection—the garment guaranteed to last forever.

For my fourth-graders, the robe of Jesus' righteousness might seem abstract, but perhaps some of them have already found comfort on a creepy night when their conscience prodded them to guilty wakefulness. I hope they know, by now, that a sincere apology will always bring forgiveness. Then I hope they imagined themselves cradled in the Lord's loving hands and went to sleep with sweet dreams.

Now you know the level of conversation in my class. Eve ate a piece of fruit, and that's why we're not sitting here right now naked. To my knowledge, no parent has called Pastor's office to report the teacher who said she's glad Eve took that first big bite.

—PATRICIA MITCHELL

Jesus Rides the School Bus

"Take this baby and nurse him for me," the princess told the baby's mother. "I will pay you for your help." So the woman took her baby home and nursed him.

EXODUS 2:9

Quick-thinking Miriam made it possible for Moses' real mother, Jochebed, to be reunited with her son as a wet nurse. Even as a young girl, Miriam shared her mother's faith that God would protect the infant Moses on the river Nile. Perhaps it was this belief in God that helped Miriam find the courage and wisdom she would need to help her baby brother.

Unfortunately, children are sometimes dismissed as being incapable of deep faith because adults mistakenly believe this quality is a function of maturity and life experience.

When my youngest son, Owen, started kindergarten, I even worried about him riding the school bus. "Don't worry, Mom," he said. "Jesus will be on the bus with me every day, and He won't let anything bad happen."

I recalled teaching my son that Jesus would never leave him, but Owen had applied that knowledge to his own life with absolutely no help from me. Maybe kindergarten wouldn't be so bad after all, I thought, and I squeezed Owen's hand.

Never underestimate the faith of a child.

—SBT

Searching for Something

Among them were Mary Magdalene, from whom
he had cast out seven demons; Joanna, the wife
of Chuza, Herod's business manager; Susanna;
and many others who were contributing their own
resources to support Jesus and his disciples.
LUKE 8:2–3

Joanna's encounter with Jesus and His healing introduced her to a new life full of meaning and purpose. She brought her resources and respectability to a community full of people from diverse backgrounds.

However, she wasn't just a wealthy woman looking for a distraction. She knew where her allegiance belonged. She discarded a life of luxury and prestige and joined the ranks of fishermen and poor people in order to serve Jesus. God honored her devotion by placing her at the crucifixion and at the empty tomb on the morning of the resurrection.

It was very hard for me to leave a life where all my earthly needs and wants were met to embark on a search for something to fill the empty space in my heart. Like Joanna, when I found Jesus, there was no turning back. The more I discovered, the more I wanted to know, and as my faith grew, so did my conviction that there was nothing on Earth worth more than my salvation.

Do you know where your loyalties lie?

—SBT

Following Your Heart

I tell you the truth, wherever the Good News is preached throughout the world, this woman's deed will be remembered and discussed.
MATTHEW 26:13

A few years ago, I came to a serious crossroad in my life. One choice would make me popular, but it didn't feel like the right decision. In the end I followed my heart. I knew it was the right choice, and I've never regretted it.

There was once a lady who broke all protocol. Mary's deed didn't endear her to those who witnessed her act. In fact, she was rebuked for wasting money on a luxury item when so many people were going hungry. But she went from recrimination to renown as she took her place among the great supporters of Christ—simply because she followed her heart.

Are you following the crowd or following your heart?

—MARY CATHERINE ROGERS

Deserving Women

In those days a man named Manoah from the tribe of Dan lived in the town of Zorah. His wife was unable to become pregnant, and they had no children.

JUDGES 13:2

We don't even know her name, but her barren condition marked her as flawed and unable to fulfill her purpose. She probably had little or no self-esteem. God, however, had a vastly different view of this woman. He considered her deserving enough to receive a visit from an angel of the Lord and worthy enough to give birth to Samson, one of the last judges to appear in Israel.

It's hard to feel significant in a world that places such an inflated importance on appearances and accomplishments. If we allow the world to determine our value, we are bound to feel inconsequential.

I have been a stay-at-home mother since the birth of my first child. For me, it has been a dream come true, but there were times when I felt as though I should apologize for not doing more with my life. I fell into the trap of seeing myself through the eyes of the world and not the eyes of my Creator.

You are worthy in God's eyes!

—SBT

Doing Laundry for the Lord

God wiped out every living thing on the earth—people,
livestock, small animals that scurry along the ground, and
the birds of the sky. All were destroyed. The only people who
survived were Noah and those with him in the boat.

GENESIS 7:23

I imagine most nights found Noah's wife asleep as soon as she collapsed into bed. Where did she find the endurance to clean one more stall, prepare one more meal, and mediate one more family dispute?

Her strength came from following God's will. She understood that each and every task, no matter how mundane, brought glory to her Heavenly Father.

This morning, as my washing machine shuddered to a stop, I realized that it has cleaned just over 9,000 loads in less than nine years. Laundry's just one of the things I do while I'm trying to accomplish everything else.

Apart from the occasional day when I want to escape to some kind of resort, I love my life. Every load of wash, every meal, and every sink full of dishes can bring glory to God if I believe my actions have value. Every single thing I do, no matter how trivial or mundane, is part of God's plan for my life.

From endless days of endless chores,
God can create a beautiful life.

—SBT

The Know-It-All

Jesus said, "You're right! You don't have a husband—for you have had five husbands, and you aren't even married to the man you're living with now. You certainly spoke the truth!"
JOHN 4:17–18

When my six-year-old son's friend Greg threatened to chop my prized azalea with his toy hatchet, Vince told him, "You better not. My mom will be awful mad."

"She won't even know it was me," Greg replied.

"Yes, she will," Vince said. "She knows everything."

I chuckled as I listened through the open bedroom window while making the bed. In an eerie tone, I softly warned Greg that my flowers had better not be damaged. It was obvious Vince had no idea where my voice had come from. "See? I told you!" he said in a voice full of conviction.

Did you know that God is all-knowing, and that He has us in His sight at all times? Why, He even knows our thoughts and intentions. Still, He loves us. We are precious to Him. That's why He sent His Son to die for us.

God is the only "know-it-all."

—IMOGENE JOHNSON

Refreshing My Memory

"Now I am giving him to the Lord, and he will belong to the Lord his whole life." And they worshiped the Lord there.
1 SAMUEL 1:28

Like many Christians, I tend to give God more attention during troubled times. My prayers are passionate and heartfelt—and more frequent. Without exception, God either resolves my crisis or gives me the strength and encouragement to endure it. During the calm after the storm, my gratitude is deep and my praises sincere—but my memory is short, and sometimes I lose sight of what God has done for me.

Time didn't diminish Hannah's thankfulness. Long after God rewarded Hannah with the son she had desperately wanted, she continued to praise His name. In a gesture of profound gratitude, she relinquished Samuel to God. When he was only three years old, she took him to the temple at Shiloh and placed in him in the care of the priest there—no easy task for a loving mother.

Her devotion and faithfulness did not go unnoticed by God who continued to bless her with three more sons and two daughters. A woman, once thought barren, became the mother of six!

Have you forgotten God's blessings?

—SBT

Memorable Tuna Salad

*Jesus grew in wisdom and in stature
and in favor with God and all the people.*
LUKE 2:52

During His early years in Nazareth, Jesus learned countless things from Mary. No incident was insignificant; no detail was too small. Everything went into His storehouse of memories; everything would eventually impact His ministry to come.

Earlier today, my son Connor was making some tuna salad, and when he added a small amount of dressing, I said, "I don't think that's going to be enough."

He grinned. "It's a lot easier to add more than it is to take some out."

Several weeks before, he had listened and watched as I made tuna salad, and he remembered an inconsequential remark I made about salad dressing. I was reminded, once again, of the profound influence I had, not only on the boy standing beside me in the kitchen, but also on the man that boy would become. If I wanted him to know about God, then I needed to make sure God was in my words and actions.

*Everything I do and say can bring glory to God—
through me, and through those around me.*

—SBT

Jump Without a Reserve

Jesus sat down near the collection box in the Temple and watched as the crowds dropped in their money. Many rich people put in large amounts.

MARK 12:41

The more we give to God, the more He has to work with to accomplish His will. There are the obvious gifts like time, money, and other resources. But what about the intangibles like love, trust, or even our fear and hurts? What could Jesus do with that anxiety I have hidden deep within my heart?

Instead of putting my entire being in Jesus' hands, I tend to withhold some of myself, "just in case things don't work out." I've discovered that God doesn't want me to hold anything back, because my smallest problem is of the greatest importance to Him. It's only when I come to Him with my heart and soul wide open that He can truly help me.

When parachutists jump out of airplanes, they always carry a reserve, just in case the main chute fails. God wants us to jump without a reserve.

When you give everything to Jesus,
you will not go away empty-handed.

—CINDY BOOSE

Ezer Kenigdo

Then the Lord God said, "It is not good for the man to be alone. I will make a helper who is just right for him."
GENESIS 2:18

The first description of Eve in Genesis changed my perception of a woman's role in her relationship with her husband. I thought "helper" was equivalent to "assistant." In other words, women should stand ready to accommodate their husbands. They should shun the spotlight and stay in the background.

Nothing could be further from the true meaning of "helper." It comes from a Hebrew phrase (*ezer kenigdo*) that is used to describe God in Deuteronomy 33:26. I doubt anyone has ever used the word *assistant* in connection with our Lord—He is an assistant to no one, but a Savior to millions. He rescues us from sin and provides a haven of hope and peace.

Are you an assistant or a helper?

—SUSAN STANLEY

First Place for the Faithful

So Jacob slept with Rachel, too, and he loved her
much more than Leah. He then stayed and worked
for Laban the additional seven years.
GENESIS 29:30

Leah lived with the misery of knowing that Jacob's heart belonged to Rachel. Unfortunately, there are still women who try to cope with the heartbreak Leah knew so well. Equally tragic are the women who see themselves in second place behind their husband's job or hobby, and the children who don't think they count at all.

God knows how difficult it can be to approach someone directly to discuss a difficult situation. That's why He wants us to come to Him to talk about how we feel and to ask for His help. He wants us to find out firsthand that miracles can and do happen when we turn to God.

If we know someone paralyzed by emotional pain, God wants to hear about that, as well. When we pray on someone's behalf, we are seeking assistance that might very well change their life.

Your prayers can make the difference.

—SBT

Special Care for Special Needs

Why should the name of our father disappear from his clan just because he had no sons? Give us property along with the rest of our relatives.
NUMBERS 27:4

When Zelophehad died, he left no sons to inherit his allotted share of the Promised Land. In protest, his daughter Tirzah and her four sisters went to Moses with their request to inherit their father's land. He took the matter before God who granted the women's request, thus establishing a new inheritance law in Israel for men who died without sons.

In granting the petition of Zelophehad's daughters, God demonstrated His attention to the needs of all of His children. Far from unyielding and indifferent, He recognized the validity of the sisters' case and yielded to their request.

Situations like this give me the courage to approach God with all my cares and desires. Like a loving, attentive earthly Father, deeply concerned with my best interests, He is always ready and willing to listen.

Trust God to act in your best interest.

—SBT

The Grandmother from Hell

*When Athaliah, the mother of King Ahaziah of
Judah, learned that her son was dead, she began to
destroy the rest of the royal family.*

2 KINGS 11:1

A few months ago, I overheard an older woman make a disconcerting statement. With obvious pride in her voice, she told her companion that she had raised her own children and shouldn't have to take care of her grandchildren.

There are other women who scorn the privileges of being a grandparent and choose to do whatever pleases them. Even though my own grandchildren often wear me out and create additional expenses, I can't imagine not being involved in their lives.

Athaliah may be the most selfish and destructive grandmother in biblical history. When she killed her grandchildren so she could be the reigning monarch, she destroyed one of life's greatest blessings. Abdicating the responsibilities of nurturing your descendants can result in a shallow—and lonely—existence.

Grandchildren are God's gift of a second chance.

—ANN VARNUM

A Dynamic Duo

In fact, they once risked their lives for me. I am thankful to them, and so are all the Gentile churches.
ROMANS 16:4

Wherever Priscilla and Aquila lived, they opened their home and hearts to other Christians. Their gracious hospitality assisted many in furthering the work of the early church.

They met the apostle Paul in Corinth during his second missionary journey. They welcomed him into their home, and he joined them in their tent-making business while sharing his spiritual wisdom with them and the church.

Christians in the first century often faced life-threatening persecution, and that was especially true of Paul. This courageous couple risked their lives to keep him safe. I can only imagine the sacrifices that Priscilla and Aquila must have made to provide a welcoming home for the training and support of their fellow Christians.

I am humbled and challenged by the generosity and bravery of this dedicated couple. I want to discover more ways to be hospitable and to give support and encouragement to those who share the gospel in our world today.

When we are filled with Christ's love,
it will spill over to everyone we meet.

—SUSAN E. RAMSDEN

Conquering Conflict

*When the king heard what was written in the
Book of the Law, he tore his clothes in despair.*
2 KINGS 22:11

When the king discovered that his nation was in serious trouble and subject to God's wrath, he panicked. Then he realized that his only recourse lay in appeasing the Lord, so he sent his high priest to find Huldah, a prophetess. She lived a quiet life with her husband, Shallum, in a suburb of Jerusalem.

God used Huldah in this situation to serve Him in a very specific way. He chose her because she was a woman who stayed close to Him and followed His commandments. She maintained a consistently devoted and faithful relationship with Him and was rewarded with the inner peace that comes from living for the Lord.

She knew the satisfaction of pleasing God by doing her very best every day. The love and trust she shared with Him gave her freedom from fear and worry and allowed her to live at peace, not only with herself, but also with others.

Find freedom from conflict by growing closer to God.

—SBT

Someone Believes in You

Actually, she had taken them up to the roof and hidden them beneath bundles of flax she had laid out.
JOSHUA 2:6

God knew what was in Rahab's heart and what she was capable of doing in His name—and she didn't let Him down. She declared her faith to the two spies and then acted on that faith. I doubt she pictured herself as the sort of person who would ever play a significant role in the Lord's plan, but she wasn't aware of God's eagerness to use the unremarkable in remarkable ways.

I'm grateful that God can look past my insecurities and fears to see what's in my heart. I am also thankful that He is willing to use me despite my shortcomings. His belief in my abilities and His unconditional love has given me the self-confidence and courage to transform my dreams into realities.

God is looking for someone just like you.

—SBT

Aching Arms

*Zechariah and Elizabeth were righteous in
God's eyes, careful to obey all of the Lord's
commandments and regulations.*
LUKE 1:6

As the years passed, I wasn't sure if my aching arms would ever hold a baby. Every once in a while, I wondered if my prayers remained unanswered because God was unhappy with me or with something I had done. As it turned out, becoming a mother had nothing to do with me, but it had everything to do with God's will and God's timing.

I don't know if Elizabeth shared my fears. Perhaps there were moments when she worried that God had denied her desire because of her sin. If she did have any doubts, they were just a faint flicker compared to the searing flame of her devotion to God.

I can banish occasional fears and worries by drawing closer to God. If I follow His commandments, and if I'm quick to confess my sins and seek His forgiveness, He will pour out His blessings—not withhold them.

Trust in God to answer your prayers when the time is right.

—SBT

Fear's Greatest Foe

*First I should feed the children—my own
family, the Jews. It isn't right to take food from
the children and throw it to the dogs.*
MARK 7:27

Few of us have been spared the effects of fear's destructive power. Given the opportunity, it will take over our hearts, our minds, and our bodies, effectively paralyzing us. I have discovered that the only real antidote to fear comes from God. The Bible tells me that fear can't exist in the face of His unconditional, unending love.

The Syrophoenician woman was a gentile, but that didn't stop her from approaching Jesus. When He tried to rebuff her, she demonstrated a mother's daring and persisted in her request. Concern for my children has often equipped me with momentary bravery I didn't know I possessed.

However, my faith has blessed me with courage that is anything but fleeting. Staying close to God prevents me from feeding my fears and allowing them thrive and grow.

Fear doesn't stand a chance with God around.

—SBT

415

Standing By

Standing near the cross were Jesus' mother, and his mother's sister, Mary (the wife of Clopas), and Mary Magdalene.
JOHN 19:25

As I watched my niece and nephews relax on the boat with me, I couldn't help but recall a time when they were several feet shorter with gap-filled grins. Their mother—my sister—and I have shared the adventures of motherhood, from toddler tantrums to college choices. Even today, whether my day brings joy or sorrow, I know she is only a phone call or e-mail away.

Only the gospel of John tells us that Jesus' mother watched near the cross, but she wasn't alone. Her sister stood by her side. I wonder if their minds returned to the days when Jesus was a busy toddler, an inquisitive boy, and a teenager laughing with His cousins. No doubt they also remembered the young man moving steadfastly into His ministry, realizing His destiny as the teacher, the healer, and the Son of God. The Lord blesses us with sisters and friends who stand by us providing love in sunshine and shadow.

Fellowship strengthens faith.

—SUE LOWELL GALLION

Double-Check Your Answers

*So Sarai said to Abram, "The Lord has prevented me
from having children. Go and sleep with my servant.
Perhaps I can have children through her." And Abram
agreed with Sarai's proposal.*
GENESIS 16:2

It can very tempting to follow the suggestions of friends or loved ones, especially when they tell us what we want to hear. When Sarah encouraged Abraham to have a child with her servant, Hagar, I'm sure the idea appealed to him as a way to fulfill Sarah's passionate desire to be a mother and his need to have a son to carry on his name.

Unfortunately, he lost sight of God's promise that he would have a son with Sarah, and his decision to follow her suggestion resulted in nothing but more problems.

Friends and family may have great intentions, but sometimes their advice is not consistent with God's teachings. Recently, I came close to making a decision based on my reaction to a situation at church.

I had the support and encouragement of several close friends, but I knew in my heart that I was headed in the wrong direction. After spending time in God's word, I had my answer and understood the course I needed to take.

Listen to your friends, but double-check their answers with God.

—SBT

417

Water off a Duck's Back

But Job replied, "You talk like a foolish woman. Should we accept only good things from the hand of God and never anything bad?" So in all this, Job said nothing wrong.

JOB 2:10

Keeping our feelings in check requires effort; it's a lot easier to get angry, strike back, and respond in other negative ways to a situation we perceive as cruel or unfair. Experience has taught me that there is little or no lasting satisfaction in such a reaction.

Job's wife found herself in desperate circumstances, and she chose to lash out at both her husband and God. Perhaps her remarks provided some relief from her misery, but in the long run, they did nothing to alleviate her problems.

Recently, someone made a remark that angered me. I spent more time than I care to admit venting about it to my husband. He listened patiently and said, "Let it go, okay? Just like water off a duck's back, right?"

He was right, and his kind, practical advice helped me to relax almost immediately. Later, when I brought the matter to God in prayer, he blessed me with the forgiveness and peace I needed.

Don't waste precious time and energy on anger.

—SBT

Everything for the Lord

One day Ruth the Moabite said to Naomi, "Let me go out into the harvest fields to pick up the stalks of grain left behind by anyone who is kind enough to let me do it."
RUTH 2:2

When her husband died, Ruth chose to accompany her mother-in-law, Naomi, back to Naomi's homeland. Ruth made this decision based on her love for Naomi. Once they arrived in Bethlehem, it was this love that led Ruth to do everything she could to make sure Naomi had what she needed. In order to obtain food, she went out into the harvest fields to pick up the grain left behind. No task was too small or too menial for her to perform.

I feel this way about my love for God. He is the God of details and He takes care of everything in my life, big or small. Is there any reason why I shouldn't do the same for Him? Whether I'm cleaning the toilet or singing a hymn in church, I need to acknowledge that everything I do is for the Lord. No job is mundane or insignificant. God is not interested in the size of my task; He's far more concerned with the love that went into it.

Do all things with love in your heart.

—SBT

20/20 Vision

*There was no sparkle in Leah's eyes, but Rachel had a
beautiful figure and a lovely face.*
GENESIS 29:17

Like many women, Leah made the mistake of looking
at herself through her own eyes, or through the eyes of
others. Either way will result in a flawed view, and when
we can't see properly we run the risk of stumbling or falling.

Only God has 20/20 vision when it comes to His children. He tried to show Leah that He loved and valued her.
He blessed her with six sons, one of whom would be the
ancestor of Jesus Christ. Sadly, her jealousy of Rachel had
damaged her relationship with God and, for many years,
she couldn't see past the fact that the man she loved didn't
love her in return.

When I see myself with eyes clouded by emotions,
I remember that God values me and loves me with an
unconditional love. I turn to the Bible to restore my trust
in His word, and I ask Him to help me see myself as He
does.

Turn toward God and see yourself through His eyes.

—SBT

Prayer Threads

So Peter returned with them; and as soon as he arrived, they took him to the upstairs room. The room was filled with widows who were weeping and showing him the coats and other clothes Dorcas had made for them.

ACTS 9:39

Women have been giving handmade gifts for thousands of years. My creative presents didn't seem very special until I read about a woman named Dorcas, known and loved among the poor for her good works. When she died, a huge crowd gathered to grieve.

Many of the mourners wore clothing Dorcas had made for them, and I wondered if the items I had made over the years would carry any significance after my death. Then I realized that it wasn't about me; God helped me shift my focus to the people I had been trying to help.

I still enjoy making things and cooking for others, but now I pray for them as I work. The hours I spend sewing or baking are mingled with the thoughts and needs of others. I believe Dorcas did this as well, and God blessed her with a legacy that lives on to this day.

Bless others with your handiwork and your prayers.

—PAM HALTER

The Blessing of Being Different

Mary Magdalene found the disciples and told them, "I have seen the Lord!" Then she gave them his message.
JOHN 20:18

People who had known Mary prior to her miraculous encounter with Him must have been astounded by the changes in her. The religious authorities may have thought that once they killed Jesus, his religion would also die out.

Nothing could have been further from the truth. People like Mary remained as testimonies to the greatness of God. I'm sure others were drawn to her, curious about the changes Jesus had made in her life and wondering if having faith in Him could help them, too.

I can talk to someone about Christ, but it's my actions and lifestyle that provide the evidence to back up my words. Even if people don't know I'm a Christian, my behavior and attitude should indicate that there is something distinct about me. They may even ask me why I appear different. This is when the words become important and, like Mary, I can talk about the amazing changes Jesus has brought to my life.

Let your life speak volumes about the Lord.

—SBT

Loyalty unto Death

*They had been followers of Jesus and
had cared for him while he was in Galilee.*
MARK 15:41

Jesus had been denied by Peter and deserted by His other apostles, but several women, including Mary Magdalene, His mother, Mary, and Salome remained faithful. Later, these three women went to Jesus' tomb. They intended to anoint His body with spices, but they encountered an angel instead.

Salome is mentioned only briefly in the Bible, but those few words say a great deal about her character. While the men fled in fear for their lives, Salome stayed with her Lord. She showed great loyalty and a nurturing spirit, caring for Jesus even after his crucifixion.

I am challenged by Salome's determination to remain loyal unto death—and beyond. How dedicated would I be to God or another person if faced with the possibility of death? Salome may have played a small role in the Bible, but she raises a big question.

*Even minor characters in scripture can serve as examples
of loyalty, courage, and loving discipleship.*

—RONICA STROMBERG

Ready for the Truth?

*Don't let this be a blemish on your record. Then your
conscience won't have to bear the staggering burden of
needless bloodshed and vengeance.*

1 SAMUEL 25:31

Abigail knew how to speak the truth in love. She was
persuasive without sacrificing humility and respect. In
the midst of an unpleasant situation, she chose her words
with great care. She hurried to David before he could
unsheathe his sword to kill and reminded him of his position and his allegiance to God. The future king heard her
wise counsel, heeded her words, and blessed her for her
good sense.

In times of disagreements my voice can be sharp and
my words so cutting that they almost draw blood. I have
difficulty letting go of my anger, and it clouds my thinking.
Love can't be heard in my words of truth. I need to soften
my words and pray for God to temper my spirit. I want to
heal others with my words—not wound them.

Ask God to help you to speak wisely in love.

—VIOLA RUELKE GOMMER

When Jesus Opens the Door

*When they arrived at the house, Jesus wouldn't let
anyone go in with him except Peter, John, James,
and the little girl's father and mother.*

LUKE 8:51

Her daughter was dead, and her husband was off on a fool's errand. Outside the bedroom door, she could hear the mourners wailing. She smoothed her daughter's hair and wept. When her husband, Jairus, returned, he wasn't alone. Jesus, Peter, John, and James had come with him. While her husband searched for the Teacher, she had watched her daughter die. Acrid words of accusation filled her thoughts.

Jesus went to the bed. He took the little girl's hand and said, "My child, get up!" Immediately, the girl stood up, and recrimination was transformed into rejoicing. I've never had to watch a child die, but I've amassed countless prayers that appeared to remain unanswered and watched many dreams disintegrate to dust.

In times of despair, I find hope in the story of Jairus's unnamed wife. I continue to pray, and I continue to believe because Jesus has not forgotten me. He will open the door.

You never know when Jesus will step through the door.

—CINDY HVAL

Sharing the Spoils

She was baptized along with other members of her household, and she asked us to be her guests. "If you agree that I am a true believer in the Lord," she said, "come and stay at my home." And she urged us until we agreed.

ACTS 16:15

As a new Christian, Lydia discovered early the benefits of sharing her faith. After her conversion, she returned home with her miraculous news, and it wasn't long before her entire household became Christians. God blessed her further by inspiring her decision to invite Paul and his followers into her home—a choice that undoubtedly led to many remarkable dialogues about her new beliefs.

On numerous occasions, I have confided in a trusted friend. It gave me the chance to voice my thoughts and concerns and hear another person's perspective and opinion. Invariably, I felt better and, quite often, I had new insight into my problem or a possible solution.

The same thing happens when I share my faith. Whether I'm telling a friend about a blessing I've received, or talking to someone about what God has done for me, the results are amazing. My faith is rejuvenated and strengthened, my appreciation for God's goodness deepens, and I am filled with the urge to share even more.

Bring your faith to life by sharing it.

—SBT

Gifts for God

She arrived in Jerusalem with a large group of
attendants and a great caravan of camels loaded with
spices, large quantities of gold, and precious jewels.
When she met with Solomon, she talked with him
about everything she had on her mind.

2 CHRONICLES 9:1

The queen of Sheba wanted to acknowledge Solomon's greatness with the most expensive and beautiful gifts she could find. She went to a great deal of expense and effort to make the journey to see him, so it's quite obvious she held Solomon and his wisdom in very high esteem.

Sometimes, I feel inadequate when it comes to conveying my gratitude to God, and I experience frustration when I try to express how much He means to me. Even if I had the queen of Sheba's wealth, there would be no point in lavishing costly gifts on God—He has no need of possessions.

The things I should give Him, the things He values most, wouldn't cost me a dime. The greatest gift I can give Him is my love. Other gifts of significance include my time, my obedience, and my praise. There are so many ways to express my love and my thanks. It's easy to be generous with the One who makes everything possible.

Be generous with God.

—SBT

Palm Tree Pulpit

*She would sit under the Palm of Deborah, between
Ramah and Bethel in the hill country of Ephraim, and
the Israelites would go to her for judgment.*

JUDGES 4:5

Aware that the role of women in leadership roles could be a sensitive issue, I felt it wise to use discretion when I offered to conduct a Bible study as part of a course I was taking. As a result, I issued invitations only to the women of the Sunday school and received an enthusiastic response.

However, the night before the first class, a young man phoned. "Would you mind if I took the study along with my wife?" he asked.

"Not at all," I replied. "If you're comfortable with a woman teaching, that's fine." Before the sessions ended, men comprised a third of the class.

The princes trusted Deborah and she, in turn, supported their authority. This remarkable relationship allowed the individuals involved to set aside their pride and adopt a humble attitude in answer to the call of God. Gender is meaningless when it comes to accomplishing His purposes.

Mutual respect leads to mutual support.

—ALMA BARKMAN

CONTRIBUTORS

Sandi Banks is Mom/Gramma to nine special young ladies. She is the author of *Anchors of Hope*, and her stories have been published in *Reader's Digest*, *A Cup of Comfort® for Mothers*, and *A Cup of Comfort® Book of Prayer*. Visit her website at *www.anchorsofhope.com*.

Alma Barkman of Winnipeg, Manitoba, Canada, is a freelance writer and photographer. She has had numerous articles and poems published, and she is the author of seven books. She is also a regular contributor to *Daily Guideposts*.

Jamie Birr's publishing credits include *A Cup of Comfort® Devotional for Mothers* and *Centred on Love: Daily Devotions* (a South African women's devotional). She lives in northern Indiana with her husband, three children, and two very spoiled dogs.

Cindy Boose lives in South Carolina with her husband and four teenage daughters. She is looking forward to having more time for writing and discovering what other new works God has prepared for her to do.

Laura Broadwater has been married for twenty-four years and is the mother of two great boys. Her youngest son's graduation and the end of a job she thoroughly enjoyed has her looking forward to what God has in store.

Connie Sturm Cameron has been married to Chuck for twenty-nine years. They have two children, Chase and Chelsea, daughter-in-law Elizabeth, stepdaughter Lori, and three grandchildren. Connie is the author of *God's Gentle Nudges*. Visit her website at *www.conniecameron.com*.

Jean Campion is the author of *Minta Forever*, a historical novel, and *Return to Rockytop*, its sequel. A retired writing teacher, she and her husband of more than forty years have three grown children.

Dori Clark has been married to Duane for forty-six years. She is the mother of three and grandmother of eight. Dori has been published in *Live*, *Lifewise*, *Discipleship Journal*, and *A Cup of Comfort®* books.

Debora M. Coty is the author of *The Distant Shore*, *Smiles to Go: Hugs, Humor and Hope for Harried Moms*, and a contributor to *Heavenly Humor for the Woman's Heart*.

Katherine J. Crawford and her husband, Gary, live in Omaha, Nebraska. Her desire is to share hope, humor, and, above all else, to write well enough to share God's love with the next generation.

Dianne Daniels keeps busy mothering her two young daughters and writing to encourage Christian women. She has written for several compilation books, including *A Cup of Comfort® Devotional for Mothers*.

CONTRIBUTORS

Virginia Dawkins has been published in several *Christian Cup of Comfort®* volumes. She lives with her husband in Meridian, Mississippi, and is a member of the Mississippi Writers Guild.

Janey L. DeMeo is the founding director of Orphans First, a nonprofit ministry to suffering children worldwide: *www.orphansfirst.org.* She is a pastor's wife and speaker who has written hundreds of articles and several books. Visit her website at *www.carepointministry.com.*

Jennifer Devlin is the author of *Life Principles for Christ-like Living.* She is also the founder and director of Ministry for Life (*www.ministryforlife.com*) and lives in Huntsville, Alabama with her husband, Bob, and son, Owen.

Elsi Dodge is a single, retired teacher from Boulder, Colorado. Her articles have been published in a variety of devotional guides, books, and travel magazines. Her website is *www.RVTourist.com.*

Tracy Donegan is a freelance writer, childrens' book author, parish editor. Her children, Nate and Emily, constantly inspire her.

Beth Duewel is a freelance writer and speaker. She lives in Ashland, Ohio, with her husband of twenty-one years and three children: Brittany, Joshua, and Brooklyn. Catch more of her writing at *www.bethduewel.com.*

Liz Hoyt Eberle and her husband juggle retirement and their large blended family with her writing. Her work has appeared in numerous anthologies, devotional books, newsletters, and newspapers. She adores hearing from her readers—e-mail her at *eberle2@hotmail.com.*

Kriss Erickson has been a freelance writer for more than thirty years and has had more than 400 pieces published to date. She has her master's degree in counseling. She is currently studying Reflexology and Reiki.

Sandy Ewing lives with her husband, Tom, in Estes Park, Colorado. She is a writer and a speaker. At present she is making a quilt for her first great-grandchild.

Suzanne Woods Fisher lives in California. She is a contributing editor for *Christian Parenting Today.* Her first novel, *Copper Star*, was recently published. Find Suzanne online at *www.suzannewoodsfisher.com.*

Darlene Franklin is the author of two books (*Romanian Rhapsody* and *Gunfight at Grace Gulch*) as well as numerous magazine articles, personal experience stories, and devotionals. Visit her website at *www.darlenehfranklin.com.*

Rita Stella Galieh scripts and co-presents a weekly radio program broadcast Australia-wide and on missionary radio. She makes guest appearances with her evangelist husband on TV. She has contributed to *A Cup of Comfort® for Christians* and *His Forever.*

Sue Lowell Gallion is interested in inspirational writing and writing for children. She lives in the Kansas City area with her husband and two teenagers. She participates in a Bible study group for moms through her church, Colonial Presbyterian.

Evangeline Beals Gardner has written short stories, inspirational articles, newspaper interviews, and Sunday school curriculum. This is her third *Cup of Comfort*® volume. She lives with her husband, two daughters, a dog, and two cats.

Viola Ruelke Gommer has published many of her writings and photographs, including *Upper Room, The Secret Place*, a contribution to *A Cup of Comfort*®, *The Quiet Hour*, and a contribution to *Chicken Soup for the Nurse's Soul*. E-mail her at *vgommer@aol.com*.

Marion E. Gorman is married to Jim. She is retired except for writing, gardening, scrapbooking, and enjoying her large family. She has been published in *Mature Years, Seek, Alive*, newspapers, and anthologies.

Alicia Gossman-Ṣteeves is a wife, the mother of three boys, and works as a court clerk for the city of La Junta, Colorado. She enjoys her children, her new grandkids, reading, cooking, and cycling.

Renee Gray-Wilburn, a full-time mom of three, has published approximately fifty pieces, in both children's and adult markets. She lives in Colorado Springs, Colorado.

Pam Halter is a former home-schooling mom and children's author. She lives in New Jersey with her husband, Daryl, two daughters, and three cats. Her son and daughter-in-law have blessed her with a granddaughter, Kendall.

Audrey Hebbert lives in Omaha, Nebraska, where she is a freelance writer, a volunteer Bible teacher, and mentor for young Christians. She enjoys her two children and their families, including three grandchildren. Her website is *www.audreyhebbert.com*.

Linda Darby Hughes is a freelance writer and editor in Douglasville, Georgia. She began writing for publication at the advanced age of fifty-one, and her work has since appeared in numerous magazines, newspapers, and anthologies. E-mail her at *dathasgirl@comcast.net*.

Cindy Hval's work has appeared in *A Cup of Comfort*® *Devotional for Mothers*. She's a correspondent for the *Spokesman Review* newspaper in Spokane, Washington, where she lives with her husband and four sons. E-mail her at *dchval@juno.com*.

Sally Jadlow is wife to one, mom to four, and grandma to eleven. She serves as a chaplain to corporations in the Kansas City area. Her latest book is *The Late Sooner*.

Imogene Johnson's poetry, devotionals, fiction, and personal experience pieces have been published in many periodicals. She lives in rural Virginia, where she teaches an adult Bible class and participates in her church choir.

Jewell Johnson, a retired registered nurse, lives in Arizona with her husband, LeRoy. They have six children and eight grandchildren. Besides writing, Jewell spends her time reading, walking, and quilting.

CONTRIBUTORS

Eva Juliuson is a mother and grandmother who sends out regular short free e-mail prayers to help jump-start others into a deeper prayer life with God. E-mail her at *evajuliuson@hotmail.com*.

Charlotte Kardokus is a wife of thirty-three years, mother of two, grandmother of three, contributor to *A Cup of Comfort® Devotional for Mothers*, and a longtime member of Oregon Christian Writers.

LaRose Karr lives in Colorado with her husband and is the mother of four grown children. Her work has appeared in numerous compilation books, devotional guides, newsletters, and on websites. E-mail her at *larosekarr@bresnan.net*.

Betty King is the author of four books including *The Fragrance of Life* and *Safe and Secure in the Palm of His Hand*. She is a lifestyle and devotional columnist and speaker. Visit her website at *www.bettyking.net*.

Laurie Klein's award-winning work appears in *The Worship Bible*, *Soul Matters for Women*, *Grace Givers*, *Extraordinary Miracles in the Lives of Ordinary People*, and numerous other journals and anthologies.

Rebecca Lyles recently moved to Boise, Idaho, from Phoenix, Arizona. She has written numerous articles and stories and two books: *It's a God Thing* and *On a Wing and a Prayer*.

Patricia Mitchell, former editorial director with Hallmark Cards, is a freelance writer and editor specializing in Bible studies and methodology, inspirational articles, and Christian devotionals.

Karen Morerod lives in Kansas City, Kansas, with her family. Her passion is making God's word come alive through Bible study and drama.

Laurie A. Perkins lives with husband, Philip, in Needham, Massachusetts. Laurie has contributed to *A Cup of Comfort® for Christians* and has published a novel, *Blood Diamonds: A Cryptic Crime Suspense*.

Connie K. Pombo is an inspirational speaker, author, and founder of Women's Mentoring Ministries in Mt. Joy, Pennsylvania. She can be reached at *www.womensmentoringministries.com*.

Kathy Pride is a wife, mother, and passionate champion for those whose hope tanks are running low. Her first book, *Winning the Drug War at Home*, is a book of hope and healing for parents of teens seduced by drugs.

Roxanne Puga has been teaching and researching a Bible study on women in the Bible for the last year. Her work has appeared in *Design* magazine and *Lyrical Iowa*.

Susan E. Ramsden, an educator and writer, is a wife, mother of one daughter, and grandmother of two. She and her husband, Howard, have coauthored a book, *The Way Home*.

Colleen L. Reece learned to read by kerosene lamplight and dreamed of one day writing a book. God has expanded one book to *140 Books You Can Trust*, 5 million copies sold.

Susan J. Reinhardt's devotionals and short stories have appeared in *The RevWriter Resource, LIVE,* and *His Forever.* Current projects include a novel and a nonfiction book. She resides in Pennsylvania.

Mary Catherine Rogers is an award-winning freelance writer from Georgia. A recent widow, she is the mother of three adult children and one spoiled Yorkshire terrier.

Alexandra Rose, PhD, is the author of *Behind the Veil* and *Shakespeare's World,* in addition to several articles and short stories. She is a member of Mogadore Baptist Church and teaches college English.

Lori Z. Scott has published devotions, short stories, articles, poems, and puzzles for all ages. She is the author of *Meghan Rose on Stage* and *Meghan Rose Has Ants in Her Pants.* Visit her website at *www.MeghanRoseSeries.com.*

Kim Sheard's work has also appeared in *A Cup of Comfort® Devotional* and *A Cup of Comfort® Devotional for Mothers.* She lives in Fairfax, Virginia, with her husband, Henry.

Donna J. Shepherd is a columnist, and her devotionals appear in *Daily Grace for Women* and *Anytime Prayers for Everyday Moms.* She is the author of a children's book, *Topsy Turvy Land.* Visit her website at *www.donnajshepherd.com.*

Leslie J. Sherrod is the author of *Like Sheep Gone Astray* and a contributor to *A Cup of Comfort® Devotional for Mothers.* She lives in Baltimore, Maryland, with her husband and two children. Visit her website at *www.lesliejsherrod.com.*

Susan Kelly Skitt has contributed to several women's devotional books and is a speaker with Women's Mentoring Ministries. She lives in Bucks County, Pennsylvania, with her husband and two sons. Visit her at *www.livingtheadventurouslife.blogspot.com.*

Yvonne Curry Smallwood is a wife, mother, and grandmother. Her stories have appeared in several publications, and she credits God for each opportunity afforded her to share His word.

Maribeth Spangenberg and her husband, Steve, are the proud parents of nine children. She writes for home-schooling magazines and websites and loves to encourage other mothers to stay the course.

Susan Stanley, a wife and full-time mom by choice, is a former corporate consultant and current freelance writer. She writes during naptimes and at night.

Contributors

Cara Stock's background includes banking, running heavy equipment, and being a construction secretary. She is the mother of two and grandmother of two. She lives in the Cayman Islands with her husband and son.

Priscilla Blair Strapp is an educator, writer, and speaker who works with high school students and women from all strata of society. She lives in Philadelphia, Pennsylvania with her husband and three children.

Ronica Stromberg is the author of two children's books, *The Time-for-Bed Angel* and *The Glass Inheritance*. Her stories have appeared in fourteen anthologies. She writes internationally, mainly for Christian magazines and children's publications.

R. J. Thesman has self-published several books which were used to teach English to international students. R. J. operates an editorial service called Do It Write and also works full-time for a Christian ministry.

Vicki Tiede is a home-schooling wife and mother. She is the founder of Grace Lessons Ministries, a speaking and writing ministry designed to encourage and equip women.

Ann Varnum hosts *The Ann Varnum Show* on WTVY TV in Dothan, Alabama. She is the author of *Sunny Side Up*, and coauthor with her sister of two *Field O' Dreams* cookbooks.

Christine P. Wang is a freelance writer and assistant editor for two trade magazines. She has been published in *A Cup of Comfort® for Christians* and *A Cup of Comfort® Book of Prayer* and is currently writing her memoirs. Contact her at *cpw25@cornell.edu*.

Jennifer E. Whyman lives in St. Louis with her loving husband, Dan, and three great kids. Jenn loves reading, writing, and praying. Sharing her love for Jesus and serving Him is her passion!

Paula Wiseman lives in Robinson, Illinois, with her husband and three children. Her work appeared in *A Cup of Comfort® Devotional for Mothers*. She is currently working on a novel.

Elisa Yager is the mom of two great kids. When not writing, she is a full-time human resources manager for a manufacturing firm located in Hatfield, PA. She is a regular contributor to *Cup of Comfort®* series, and would love to hear from you; she can be reached at *Proud2blefty@yahoo.com*.

Subject Index

435

Subject Index

Scripture Index

Scripture Index

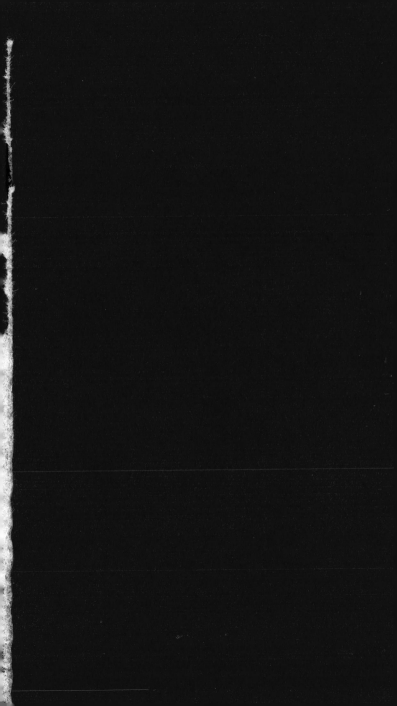